The Loss of
INNOCENTS

The Loss of
INNOCENTS
CHILD KILLERS AND THEIR VICTIMS

CARA E. RICHARDS

A Scholarly Resources Inc. Imprint
Wilmington, Delaware

First published 2000
Printed and bound in the United States of America

Scholarly Resources Inc.
104 Greenhill Avenue
Wilmington, DE 19805-1897
www.scholarly.com

Library of Congress Cataloging-in-Publication Data

Richards, Cara Elizabeth, 1927–
  The loss of innocents : child killers and their victims / Cara Richards.
      p.   cm.
  Includes bibliographical references and index.
  ISBN 0-8420-2602-9 (cl. : alk. paper). — ISBN 0-8420-2603-7 (pa. :
alk. paper)
    1. Infanticide — United States. 2. Infanticide — United States — Case
studies. 3. Child abuse — United States. 4. Child abuse — United States —
Case studies. I. Title.
HV6541.U6R53   2000
364.15′23′0973 — dc21   99-39723
                                                                CIP

To the memory of children

who have suffered untimely deaths

because of the actions of others

About the Author

CARA E. RICHARDS studied at Queens College before receiving her Ph.D. in anthropology at Cornell University. Her diverse field work topics have led her to the Onondaga and Navajo Indian Reservations, the city taverns of New York, and development and change projects in Lima, Peru. She has taught at Universidad de Servicio Social, Cornell University, Ithaca College, and most recently at Transylvania University where she is professor emerita of anthropology.

Acknowledgments

The research for this study began in 1983. Since that time, officials in state, national, and local organizations as well as students, colleagues, and friends have provided information or made suggestions. It would be impossible to name them all, but I do wish to express my thanks to everyone who has been helpful and encouraging. I also want to give my heartfelt appreciation to all my students and colleagues who have listened patiently to many preliminary papers and drafts. To those people whom I have inadvertently failed to mention, my apologies.

There are some individuals who made particularly significant contributions. I had invaluable assistance in this research from Dorothy Chandler Weaver, a former student of mine at Transylvania who is working on a doctorate in anthropology at Rutgers. She and I argued over the classification of cases, worked out problems with variables, discussed interpretations, and generally were collaborators on all but the actual final writing. She did the early data entry and computer analysis. Because of her high level of involvement, she is listed as coauthor of most of the early papers based on the research, and is the reason the term "we" is so often used in this book. The final data analysis was compiled by Spence Millard, a friend and a former student who works as a free-lance computer consultant. His knowledge of data analysis was sorely tested by my inconsistencies in data entry, but we persevered and finally had numbers with whose accuracy we were both satisfied.

At various stages of the research I had significant help from Jules Delambre, systems analyst for the

Cabinet for Families and Children, and from Robert Hurst III of Vital Statistics. Several members of the Lexington, Kentucky, Police Department were also helpful. Mary Horn provided information about the Child Protective Services in Gainesville, Florida, and Jane Hensen of the *Atlanta Constitution* sent me useful data on events in Georgia.

Transylvania University personnel were helpful during the research and the analysis periods. Charles Shearer, president, and James G. Moseley, the vice president and dean, were unfailingly supportive. Funding for some analysis was received from the David and Betty Jones Faculty Development Program at Transylvania. Dr. Margaret Upchurch gave me valuable information and suggestions about evolutionary psychology. Dr. Dorothy Neff provided suggestions about data collection and analysis, some of which I regretted not following earlier on in the process. Carolyn Tassie at the Transylvania University Library was most diligent in tracking down additional newspaper articles from a variety of sources around the country, and in finding references that were relevant to this study. The work would have been much more difficult without her help.

Jeanie Donahoe, librarian at the *Omaha World-Herald*; Connie Gallagher of the Children's Services Division, Oregon; and Sarah R. Kaplan of the Child Maltreatment Fatalities Project of the American Bar Association also provided important information.

Richard M. Hopper of Scholarly Resources Inc. was a most patient and helpful editor. He endured reading and rereading some of the grimmest material with no complaint. Michelle M. Slavin, the project editor, answered many questions promptly and efficiently. Ann M. Aydelotte was a diligent and thorough copyeditor. Sharon L. Beck, the desktop publisher, input all corrections and formatted this book. No one writes a book alone. Many of the best characteristics of this work are due to the contributions of all these individuals. The weaknesses and errors are my own.

Contents

Introduction

On February 19, 1983, a 2-month-old baby girl was
treated for a fractured skull in a Bowling Green,
Kentucky, hospital. It was her second visit of the new
year; in January, doctors had treated her for a broken
arm. On February 24 a judge removed her from her
parents' custody and placed her in a foster home,
where she made it through March with no hospitaliza-
tions. Then, on April 11, the same judge overruled a
Department for Human Resources recommendation
that she remain in foster care and returned the baby to
her parents, claiming that under state law he had no
choice. Six days later she was again taken to the
hospital, where brain scans on April 19 and April 21
showed no activity. She was pronounced dead after
doctors removed her from life-support systems. An
autopsy performed on that same day confirmed that
she had died of "shaken child syndrome." According to
the coroner, violent shaking made blood vessels burst
and the brain swell, causing respiratory failure
(Case 226).

Cases such as this one helped drive this study. Why
can we not tell when a child is at great risk? And what
clues can help judges, police, or social case workers
decide when parental rights should be terminated
immediately, when a brief separation is enough to
remedy an abusive situation, or when a child will be
safe despite problems? There obviously are some
guidelines, although they vary from one state to
another. For example, in Kentucky, in 1993, children
could be removed immediately only if a judge ruled
that they were in imminent danger of death or serious
injury, or if they were being sexually abused. However,

according to the executive director of the Governor's Office of Child Abuse and Domestic Violence Services, "Bruises and burns do not meet the definition of 'serious physical injury' " (*Lexington Herald-Leader*, March 17, 1998). Parental rights are terminated occasionally, but cases such as the 2-month-old above suggest that the indexes of risk need to be improved, that the existing indexes require better enforcement, and that better coordination is needed between the various official organizations that have the power to make decisions. The processes that place a child in a foster home or that terminate parental rights over that child are complex and involve state and local courts, law enforcement personnel, and various child protective agencies. When a child is killed, blame rarely can be allocated to one individual or even to one agency. The investigation is further complicated because confidentiality laws do not permit child protective agencies to reveal either names or information about any previous contact that family members may have had with social service agencies. In addition, most states have laws requiring that the integrity of the family be preserved. The ambivalence with which these safeguards are regarded, and the difficulties that they pose for agencies charged with protecting children, are discussed at greater length in the final chapters of this volume.

Sometimes in the process of protecting the child and preserving the family, the potential of danger to the child may not seem as real or as obvious as the clear risk to the rights of the parents. The decisions that must be made by people in all the agencies involved are extremely delicate and difficult. Consequently, a major purpose of this volume is not only to add to the information that decision-makers can use to render their judgments about child placement more accurately but also to provide substantive data to evaluate the limitations and utility of confidentiality laws. Indeed, how much information should be confidential when a child has been killed?

Another purpose of this volume is to provide the general public with information about the complexity and difficult nature of child killings. It is easy for the news media and an outraged public to expect simple solutions. For example, after one recent killing in Kentucky, a talk show host held a discussion of the case and said at the outset: "I don't want to hear about the need for more social workers, or more money for Social Services. That child should have been taken out of the home." When a special task force on which I served investigated the circumstances of that death as well as others, the cases turned out to be much more complex than the talk show host had suggested. The line between state interference with individual rights and state protection of innocent, helpless children is a narrow one, difficult to define through legislation. The more information available to the public and to lawmakers, the greater the possibility for rational action in this area.

Another impetus for the research came from *The Selfish Gene* (Dawkins, 1976). Experts in the growing field of sociobiology, now often called evolutionary psychology, suggest that human males might instinctively copy our biologically close relatives — monkeys and apes — and try (unconsciously) to increase their own reproductive success by killing a new partner's infants fathered by another male. A 1984 article by Martin Daly and Margo Wilson based on Canadian statistics supports this hypothesis (Hausfater and Hrdy, 1984:487–502). Newspaper accounts of children killed by their mother's lover seemed all too frequent, but I wanted to collect more evidence. A later book by Daly and Wilson (*Homicide*, 1988) gives additional statistical support to biological reasons for homicide. These authors specifically devote a chapter to the murder of children, with a number of hypotheses. Since their research offers some data for testing hypotheses based on evolutionary psychology, the Daly and Wilson hypotheses are discussed here in more detail in Chapter 8.

The original data base for the study came from the *New York Times* Index categories of murder, manslaughter, and fatal child abuse. Newspapers were chosen as a source of data because of the relative ease of access as well as the fact that a newspaper article gives names, dates, and pertinent information that cannot be obtained easily from other sources. An upper limit of age 12 was chosen for the victims because the *New York Times* Index usually gives the ages of victims that age and younger. Those over 12 but under 18 are referred to as "teen-agers," and the ages of older victims are not consistently given in the Index. Consequently, by choosing 12 as the upper limit, my students and I were able to avoid looking up irrelevant articles. In addition, in 1983, when I started the research, children 12 and under were less likely to be members of gangs, become involved in rows over lovers, attempt to prove their manhood, or otherwise engage in lethal fights. All cases of children 12 and under in the United States that appeared in the *New York Times* Index from 1977 through 1993 were examined.

A smaller sample using the same criteria but including fewer years was taken from the *Omaha World-Herald* for the purpose of testing for biases in the *New York Times*. Moreover, in the early 1990s, the *Chicago Tribune* ran a series in which it reported every death of children age 14 and under in the Chicago area in 1991 and 1992. These deaths were also incorporated into our sample when the victim was 12 or younger. A shorter series of cases from the *Louisville Courier-Journal* was also collected, and, during the course of the research, cases from the *Lexington Herald* (later the *Lexington Herald-Leader*) were added as they appeared. Neither paper was searched systematically for the entire sequence of years, however. Neither has an index as complete as that of the *New York Times*, and to use them more extensively would have added a disproportionate number of cases from Kentucky.

Occasional cases in our files were mentioned in articles from the *Reader's Digest*, and several have been discussed by various authors in books or articles. When these cases are used as examples, information from those books or articles has been incorporated for additional details. Material from those sources was also used when it provided details on specific variables that had not been mentioned in the newspaper articles. These works are listed in the Bibliography under the appropriate case number. And finally, when cases were cited as examples and when more information was needed, newspapers from the locale where the crime took place were sometimes used to provide details that were not present in the *New York Times* report. These are also cited under the appropriate case number in the Bibliography.

The research was originally begun to provide material for a class on research methodology at Transylvania University in Lexington, Kentucky. The purpose was to examine the feasibility of employing newspapers to study social problems. The topic of child fatalities appeared to be both narrow and specific enough to use as a focus. To test the validity as well as the amount and type of bias in newspaper articles, the original plan was to compare the statistics from the *New York Times* with a total official count of such incidents from one state (Kentucky was the obvious choice) together with local newspaper articles. The results of preliminary tests for bias and validity are reported in Cara Richards and Dorothy Weaver, "Newspapers as a Source of Data" (1993). Bias appeared to be primarily regional—that is, the *New York Times* reported extensively on killings in New York City and the northeastern states. Cases from other parts of the country were reported less often and with fewer details, and they also tended to be the more spectacular ones. Data such as age and gender of victims from the newspaper corresponded well with national statistics, however, so that later the idea of relying on newspaper sources for a more extensive study was not unreasonable (Richards and Weaver, 1993:7).

While collecting the newspaper accounts was simple, it was also slow and tedious. The first real problem surfaced in trying to collect the official statistics. The Kentucky Department for Human Resources (now the Cabinet for Families and Children) was unable to release any names because of confidentiality laws, although it could provide most of the other information: age and gender of the victim, and even the relationship of the presumed perpetrator to the victim. The inability to obtain names seemed to be only a minor inconvenience at first because Human Resources also provided information on when the death was reported and the county in which it occurred. If I collected death certificates of homicide victims ages 12 and under from Vital Statistics — which are public records, of course — I believed that I could match these certificates with the Human Resources records and have the names I wanted. With names, local newspapers, police blotters, or court records could be checked and any additional information gathered for the study. At no time did I plan to interview anyone other than police involved in the cases. The Lexington authorities were willing to cooperate, but everyone needed names.

This approach did not work. The requested death certificates came from Vital Statistics, but when I tried to match their ten to twelve child homicides per year with about the same number of fatal child abuse cases from Human Resources, there were only one or two matches per year. In other words, Human Resources staff were reporting eight to ten cases of child deaths from abuse or neglect each year that were not listed as homicides, and Vital Statistics records were reporting eight to ten cases of child homicides per year that were not in the child abuse records. What was going on?

To be blunt, I had assumed that a dead child was a dead child — that is, that records would be consistent from one governmental office to another. As the dimensions of my "little" research project grew, however, I learned that there were a number of problems with the whole issue of fatal child abuse and murdered children. The different definitions used by various branches of government obscure both the extent and the nature of the problem. The incomparability of both the definitions and the statistics obtained from them prevents any easy sharing of data between agencies, which increases the difficulty of effective understanding or cooperation. While various national agencies have attempted to clarify differences in definitions between states, these federal efforts have often added to the confusion. As late as 1991, most states did not include "death" as part of their definition of child abuse (Kaplan, 1991:6). Although this system may be changing now, records of dead children are usually stored in archives separate from child protective division files. Once the case is closed, the file in the child protective agency is no longer active. In Kentucky the part of the Cabinet for Families and Children that is concerned with child abuse does not have the death certificate identification number of a deceased child even if his or her record had previously been part of an active file—a natural consequence of the mission of the agency. It cannot provide any help for children who are deceased, so the records are removed from case loads and archived. Vital Statistics, which does have the information, may not always classify the death in the same way as does the Cabinet. Without a name, which the Cabinet is forbidden by law to release, lists of children who died from particular causes consequently vary when those lists come from different agencies.

State legislatures, however, have become more familiar with the complexity of the problem. For example, as mentioned, the 1998 Kentucky Legislature has just passed a new law (House Bill 142) that expands the circumstances under which children can be removed from abusive homes by allowing judges to issue emergency custody orders in cases of repeated physical injury or neglect of basic needs. It also specifies other factors that a judge should consider, such as whether another child in the family has been beaten or murdered. In addition, the law gives a sixty-day time limit for judges to act on a petition to terminate parents' rights. At present that process can take years, so a child is left in an indeterminate state where his or her adoption into a permanent home is impossible. (Currently, children average over two years in custody, and many wait much longer.) The law presently awaits the governor's signature, but he is known to support it (*Lexington Herald-Leader*, March 17, 1998).

Another result of the mission of child protective agencies is that newborns abandoned in trash baskets or incinerators have not always been classified as victims of child abuse. If the infant dies, such cases are always labeled as homicides, at least at the start of the investigation. A number of cases, particularly those before 1985 when national concern about child deaths greatly increased, were never reported to child protective agencies at all because the infant was already dead when officials of some sort were involved. As recently as 1990, in Kentucky, if such an abandoned child had no siblings, protective services were not usually informed of the death. In 1996 the Legislature passed an act empowering a review panel that is expected to close most of these information gaps.

Confidentiality laws that prevent the release of names of families involved with child protective agencies cause serious problems. Accountability, investigation, and research are all hampered when these laws continue to apply after a child dies. Yet many people working in the general area of child abuse believe that confidentiality laws are essential to keep families coming in for assistance. Consequently, the issue poses dilemmas for state or national legislatures.

The statistics on which most reports are based also vary in many details. The ages of the children included, the proportion of neglect cases involved, and the qualifications of individuals who signed the death certificate or determined the cause of death differ from one jurisdiction to another. Compared with this nightmare of definition and classification in published statistics, newspaper accounts seem to be models of consistency and clarity, although there are problems here, too. For instance, cases mentioned on one day may not be followed up on subsequent days unless the case attracts the attention of an editor. There was no lack of articles on the Atlanta child murders, for example, or on the case in New York City of Lisa Steinberg, who was beaten to death in 1987. Joel Steinberg, who was convicted of killing her, was a lawyer who had illegally adopted the child. His live-in lover, Hedda Nussbaum, a former Random House editor, was originally charged too, but the charges against her were later dropped when she was seen as a victim, also abused by Steinberg (Case 385). This killing attracted enormous attention in the *New York Times*, but the sordid little cases of newborns abandoned in trash baskets were usually given only a tiny paragraph and not mentioned again. Any incidents of this sort that occurred outside the city were ignored entirely by the *New York Times*.

Newspaper accounts have a number of other weaknesses and strengths for research of this nature. In 1966, Eugene Webb et al. pointed out in *Unobtrusive Measures* that "although there may be substantial errors in the material it is not usual to find masking or sensitivity because the producer of the data knows he is being studied by some social scientist" (1966:53) — that is, reporters want to please editors, and editors are concerned about selling newspapers, so they are not likely to suppress information just because they do not want some social scientist to read it. Of course, this vantage point can also be a disadvantage. Since the newspaper writers and editors are not concerned with the researcher's goals, bits of information that the social scientist is interested in may be left out of the article, or not even sought by the reporters. For example, whether an uncle is a mother's brother, a father's brother, a mother's or father's sister's husband is usually unimportant to a reporter or an editor. Consequently, it is rarely made specific, although the information is of major concern to a sociobiologist. Newspaper articles often include details that are interesting, even entertaining, but not directly relevant to the purposes of the researcher. The writers do not slant their reports because of the researcher, but neither do they necessarily include desired information.

The data in newspaper articles may be quite spotty, as Webb et al. indicate. They raise the question of whether it is possible to estimate the missing information or to determine whether the absent material is crucial to the research (1966:54). One solution is to gather enough material so that missing pieces may be supplied in other articles, while another solution is to compare information compiled from one set of data with material from other sources. Because of the enormous amount of material in the general fields of child abuse, homicide, and domestic violence, it is not difficult to compare newspaper-based statistics with data from other sources on a range of variables. We found that when data were truly comparable, the newspaper information agreed well with that from other sources (Richards and Weaver, 1993).

A major strength of newspaper articles is that they mention factors in the case in context and do not deal with single elements at a time, as statistics usually do. Thus, one may see how variables interact with each other and make patterns apparent that might otherwise be missed. One example is the high rate of suicide of perpetrators, which cannot be determined from statistics of either suicide or murder alone. (Because of problems of time and space, suicide is not discussed in detail in this book but must await a separate publication.) Moreover, another strength of newspaper articles is that although they are constrained by libel laws and the information given to reporters, they are not bound by the confidentiality restrictions that prevent social service agencies from providing information. And newspapers are easily accessible, unlike records in official documents. For recent years, electronic sources such as Newsbank and Dialog have provided coverage of the nation's newspapers wider than any single library can manage without these services.

On the other hand, a major weakness of using newspaper articles for a data base is due, in part, to a problem with the U.S. criminal justice system. Cases often drag on for years; unless they are extremely newsworthy, editors lose interest and do not publish information on the outcome. A new reporter on the case may be so unfamiliar with the reports of the past that he or she makes errors in details that may seem insignificant. For example, the age of victims or perpetrators may vary from one article to another, which can frustrate a researcher interested in that particular detail. Furthermore, information that has occupied a major position in most studies of social problems, such as race or ethnic group and socioeconomic status, is not always specified in newspaper articles. Indeed, race is often deliberately not mentioned, and socioeconomic status may be simply ignored. If a woman is the perpetrator and is unemployed, one cannot judge her economic status; the occupation or income of her partner, if she has one, makes a difference but is rarely mentioned, unless he is one of the perpetrators (or is rich or famous). Also often overlooked in the statistics is that people engaged in criminal behavior — particularly the drug trade — may be able to afford an affluent life-style despite having no legal employment. And while a reporter may add a qualifying adjective such as "well-to-do neighborhood" or "working-class community," a mere street address is only helpful when the reader is thoroughly familiar with the community.

Despite the shortcomings of newspaper articles, however, a case-by-case review and analysis appears to be a useful approach for identifying patterns, if enough examples are collected. A number of states have begun to use a case review method for all child abuse deaths, but this approach is so recent that a large data base has not yet been accumulated and tends to be confined to a single state or even to a small area within that state. The information and conclusions in this volume are based on 833 cases within the United States from 1977 to 1993. There are 1,098 victims and at least 992 perpetrators in the data base. There are 107 cases where no perpetrator was identified before 1993 when I stopped collecting data. (There had to have been at least one perpetrator for each of those 107 cases, but there may have been more, so the 992 figure is a minimum.) Since the last data were collected in 1993, the question of the timeliness of the material is a legitimate one. Although no new cases have been added to the data base since 1993, constant attention to newspapers has not produced any surprises or changes. Numbers would increase, of course, if the years since 1993 were added, but there would be little, if any, change in categories, patterns, or conclusions.

Cases were analyzed for over twenty variables. Not all of them have been used in the preparation of this volume. Because of differences in the amount of information supplied by the newspaper accounts, the total sample in the various tables presented in each chapter changes from one variable to another. For example, not all reports gave the gender of the victim, and some did not give the age. Tables reporting age and gender together, therefore, have different totals from tables based only on age or only on gender. There are also three separate categories used for tables: victims, perpetrators, and cases. The total in each category is different, and the results in variables also often differ from one category to another. For example, the percentage of victims killed by guns is different from the percentage of perpetrators who used guns. Thus, caution is advised when reading or comparing tables.

The circumstances of the crime turned out to be crucial; they cut across gender, age, household situation, and economic lines. Dorothy Weaver and I made our classifications independently by a year at a time; and, after each year was completed, we compared our results. When we differed on a classification, we discussed the reasons and refined our guidelines. After we finished the process, we went back over the whole list, year by year, and corrected any misclassifications to fit our final operational guidelines.

Much of the information that surfaced during the analysis deserves additional research. Although our data support current thinking in the field in many areas, some of the results of the analysis are surprising. The level of suicides of perpetrators, for example, is astonishingly high, but nevertheless only a small percentage of the known perpetrators killed themselves as well as the children. The percentage would almost certainly be lower if the unknown killers were included, but it would still be considerably higher than the rate for the general population. Some close attention needs to be given to the question of what the differences are between those who commit suicide after killing children and those who do not. It may be significant, for example, that those who systematically abuse a child over a number of years before the killing rarely, if ever, take their own lives.

The analysis revealed expected gender variation in the method used to kill the children. Men were more likely to shoot or beat their victims to death, whereas women were more likely to smother or drown them. But surprisingly, when more than one person was involved in killing a child, the methods used varied in frequency from the methods used by individual killers, regardless of their gender. Clearly the dynamics of interpersonal relations play a major role in the killing of the child. These dynamics cry out for additional investigation. Daly and Wilson have provided some excellent hypotheses in their book on homicide (1988), but not all of our data support the hypotheses of evolutionary psychology.

It was also interesting to learn that when there are several perpetrators who collaborate to kill a child, one of them is almost invariably male. In 150 cases in our files with known multiple perpetrators, only four involved women acting without a male collaborator. In two of those cases, the perpetrators were openly lesbian, meaning that there was at least one person playing a male role. (Homophobic people should note that all but a tiny fraction of the 1,098 children in our files were murdered by heterosexuals.) Women alone kill children. Men alone kill children. Women and men together kill children. But why do women together without males so seldom kill children? Daly and Wilson look for an answer through what they term "selection thinking" or evolutionary psychology, which is based on biological factors. Are other explanations equally possible? The question deserves more research.

By 1993 it became clear that very little new information was emerging. Additional cases were adding numbers to patterns that had already become apparent. The patterns themselves were determined as much or more by the circumstances of the killings than by the socioeconomic characteristics of either victims or perpetrators. Some demographic characteristics are useful, however, in assessing risk to children. Our figures confirmed that the first three years of life are the most dangerous and that caregivers are the predominant killers at that time. Beyond these bare statements, however, the picture grows increasingly complex. The categories of circumstances included numbers of people who are not found in the child abuse statistics: distant relatives, neighbors, friends, and strangers as well as the expected caregivers. Differences between sets of circumstances are profound regarding feasibility for possible successful intervention. They suggest possible directions for legislating changes, for child protective and law enforcement agencies as well as for future research.

The book chapters are organized around the patterns that emerged from the data analysis. In a general overview of the data, Chapter 1 covers demographic information about victims and perpetrators; the relationships between killer and victim; and the methods used to kill the child. The circumstances surrounding the crimes, including the way gender and age of the perpetrators relate to the methods used and the gender or age of the victim, are also tabulated. The second chapter examines a subcategory of perpetrators: multiple killers, including both serial killers and mass murderers. Since these types of crimes have attracted a great deal of attention — one author even talks about a "serial murder boom" (Jenkins, 1994:2-4) — it is useful to discuss them separately, although some cases could be included in more than one chapter. Killings by mass murderers were almost always the result of a sudden attack. Serial killers, especially males, often also abused their victims sexually. The decision to place multiple murderers in a separate chapter was based on the possibility that they might differ from individuals who kill only one victim, so that looking at their cases separately might reveal useful information.

Details of cases involving juvenile perpetrators occupy the third chapter. Violent juvenile crime has increased dramatically in the past few years even as adult crime has declined. It seemed worthwhile to look at juvenile killers in closer detail for many of the same reasons that multiple murderers were separated out. Focusing on juveniles might reveal how they differed, if at all, from adult killers. The fourth chapter gives examples of perpetrators who were in despair, whose marriages or lives were disintegrating, or who had serious fears for their children's future. These people, wrong though they might be, also had the welfare of the children at heart or believed that they did when they killed them. This same chapter also gives examples of perpetrators who were diagnosed at some point as having serious psychological problems. Some of these people who had a history of psychiatric care or treatment successfully used this defense at their trials. In addition, we included in this category a few people who seemed out of touch with reality as most of us know it — they were convinced that their children's bodies were occupied by demons, or dragons, or devils. We might have included them with the perpetrators who made bad decisions (Chapter 7), but their reasons seemed far enough removed from mainstream beliefs to put them in the psychologically disturbed category.

Chapter 5 gives examples of the most common form of child murder: violent abuse or physical mistreatment of some sort, usually in the home. The general category deals with cases where we do not have enough information to distinguish between perpetrators who killed in a sudden burst of fury, those who systematically abused the victim for months or even years, or those who were clearly mentally or emotionally disturbed. It is probable that most of the cases described in this category could be placed in another one if more information were available. In some cases it is also possible that the first instance of what might have become a pattern of sustained abuse resulted in a fatality. Along with the examples of these ambiguous cases, this chapter also offers examples of cases classified as sudden attacks, when the perpetrators succumbed to sudden rage either at the child or at the world in general. It includes a number of cases of newborn infants (less than 2 days old) who were savagely attacked by their mothers. Other newborn children who were neglected and died from lack of care are more appropriately included in other chapters. Moreover, Chapter 5 also has a few examples of mass murderers, thus demonstrating the role that sudden rage plays in cases of mass murder.

Examples of the sustained abuse murderers, probably the ones more people think of when they think of fatal child abuse, are found in Chapter 6. The children in these cases suffered from physical abuse for months or even years. These are the cases where lack of intervention by child protective agencies creates the most vehement outcry by the general public and where confidentiality laws arouse the most criticism. Sadly, they are also the cases that are most difficult to write about—details are frequently grim and often gory—and the ones where people have the least empathy with the perpetrators.

Chapter 7 presents examples of children who were in the wrong place at the wrong time. These children were killed as a result of random violence, quarrels directed at other people often not even known to them, and their presence during some other crime. The children themselves were not the targets; or, if they were the targets, they were killed because they were witnesses who could identify the culprit in some crime. This category includes bystanders at robberies, victims caught in gang war crossfire, and children murdered when hired killers struck at the wrong house. The chapter also cites cases where ignorance, stupidity, and poor decisions by the perpetrator are involved, including those cases where parents for religious reasons failed to obtain medical help for their sick children, who died as a result of this withholding of care. People who used drugs and forgot about their children, or shared their drugs with their children, are also described. In all these cases, it is unlikely that the killer intended such serious consequences.

Some of the problems of attempting to research this subject appear in Chapter 8. It places child killings in a historical context and discusses various theories that have been suggested by experts in the fields of homicide and child abuse to explain murders and child slayings. The final chapter presents some possible approaches that might alleviate the problem. Because so many factors are involved in what is a complex situation, there is no easy solution, and no single program or approach will eliminate the problem if, indeed, it can be eliminated. Many of the recommendations may help to decrease the number of child deaths, however, although it is obvious that more research is needed to determine the best and most effective directions in which to proceed.

It is crucial to keep in mind throughout the volume that most parents, and most adults, do not kill children and that most children do not die by violence. It is also essential to realize that no single factor or combination of factors will pinpoint a potential killer or victim all or even 90 percent of the time. Combinations of factors, and especially the context in which a particular constellation of variables occurs, may be more valuable for assessing risk.

In presenting all of these cases, socioeconomic status, ethnic group, and race have not been given major attention, although studies done so far indicate that poverty and low socioeconomic status are correlated with most social problems. Poor children are killed in disproportionate numbers; individuals who are unemployed are overrepresented among the perpetrators. But as the demographic figures in this study show, the socioeconomic gap is not nearly so great as the broken home disparity—that is, children from broken homes are overrepresented to a greater extent than children living in poverty or in poorly educated families. Since poverty is correlated with race and ethnic group, often people in particular minority groups commit a disproportionate number of crimes against children. But it is important to remember that just because a group is disproportionately represented, it does not mean that most of the killers or victims come from that group.

Numerically, a group underrepresented by percentage may actually have more of both victims and perpetrators.

A result of the fact that poor and minority groups may have proportionately more victims and killers is that the focus of attention has been on them, on people who use drugs, and on people who are not well educated. Neglecting the numerically larger but proportionately smaller group distorts our understanding. It can lead the public to believe that *only* the poor, minorities, or the uneducated abuse children. While that belief may be comforting for the better-off majority, it is incorrect: people who are well educated and financially well off also kill children. Why? Children in what could be called model families — that is, families with both parents present, in comfortable economic circumstances — die at the hands of family members or by the actions of friends, neighbors, employees, or strangers. Because these socioeconomic groups are usually overlooked in discussions of child fatalities, I have made a point of emphasizing them in the examples. Simply because some groups are underrepresented in the child-killing statistics, one cannot assume that they are either statistically insignificant or that the patterns of behavior exhibited by them cannot contribute anything to understanding the causes of the murder of children.

Another reason for not attempting to document ethnic group, race, or socioeconomic status is that when a case-by-case method is used, such categorization becomes more complex. How does one classify a case, for example, where there are multiple victims — Afro-American, Caucasian, and Hispanic — with a mixed-race killer? Or what is the socioeconomic status of a man with a law degree who practiced his profession successfully for a number of years, but who lost his job and then failed as a taxi driver shortly before the crime? His wife was supporting the family until he killed her and their children. Where does one classify the wife of a university professor, or the daughter of an important city official? Coping with such complications does not seem to promise new insights when so many studies have already shown correlations with socioeconomic and ethnic or racial variables.

The complexity of child killings as revealed in the case-by-case review demonstrates the weakness of a simplistic search through the statistics for monocausal solutions. No two killings are alike, nor can all of them be prevented in the same way. Some may not, for all practical purposes, be preventable. A closer look at each case is essential if we, as members of society, hope to reach more effective, equitable, humane, and just solutions to the various problems involved. This closer look requires better access to information available in Social Services files, police investigative reports, FBI files, medical and school records, or wherever else the relevant data are stored. Some types of child murders, however, may respond to actions not directed at the protection of children at all. For example, a reduction of violence in the society as a whole will cut down on the number of children caught in the crossfire of quarreling strangers. And if fewer people were involved in drug dealing, or if it were less lucrative, fewer children would be killed in drug-inspired crimes and wars.

It may not be possible to identify prospective victims or perpetrators with our present state of knowledge, or even in the foreseeable future, but just as knowledge about predisposing factors for illness has led to changes in our living habits and improvement in health care without necessarily targeting specific individuals, so the information here may make a more accurate risk-assessment profile possible and legislation more realistic. Those people who make decisions that can have life-or-death consequences for children deserve all the assistance possible.

This research has taken far longer than I anticipated, and the results are much grimmer than I expected. It has been difficult to study and difficult to write about. Any satisfaction comes from the fact that patterns have emerged, along with questions for further research that may lead to better understanding of this scourge. Again, I emphasize that it is essential to remember that most parents do not kill children; even most abusive parents do not kill. Nonetheless, for most of us, the description and tally of this sample of children who are murdered — a tally that goes on year after year — are horrifying and depressing. The same complaints and cries for change have been raised over and over again, with little result. But commitment to improving the lot of children needs money, dedication, and an understanding of the complexities involved. There is some indication now that things are changing for the better as more people focus attention on the problems. And as the population becomes better educated on the dimensions and complexity of these problems, we can look forward to improvement in both the treatment of perpetrators and the safety of children.

CHAPTER I

An Overview: Looking at the Numbers

Unlike all but a few varieties of creatures, the violent death of children is not caused by predators of another species, but by other humans, often the parents. However, human children, like the offspring of everything from aardvarks to zebras, are most likely to die by violence during the first year of life. Neither the victims nor the perpetrators are unusual in most demographic characteristics, except for the murder that unites them. This chapter begins with consideration of the victims and perpetrators, then the methods used, and, finally, the circumstances of the crimes. The main data base consists of all the articles in the *New York Times* indexed under murder, fatal child abuse, and manslaughter of children 12 years old and under in the United States between 1977 and 1993. These data have been supplemented by information from other newspapers, books, and magazines.

Who Are the Victims?

In our files we have 1,098 victims. That figure does not appear in all the tables because information on the variables that we looked at differed from one article to another. For example, there were 50 victims whose precise age we do not know, either because the newspaper article did not give it, or because the body was not identified by someone who knew the child's age and the forensic examination could not give an exact age. Similarly, there were 68 victims whose gender we do not know for the same reasons. Among these 68 are 46 victims where we know neither exact age nor gender; we have only enough information to know that they fall into the age range of our sample.

A few cases are unusual because of the lack of detail that is not due to the newspaper's failure to include material; rather, information is simply not available. For example, in 1983, in Miami, Florida, workers preparing a one-bedroom apartment for a new tenant found the body of a boy between 5 and 8 years of age encased in cinderblocks in a closet. Police questioned current and former tenants of the apartment house but no one "knew anything." There was no way of knowing how long the body had been walled up in the closet. The body did not match the description of any child reported missing in the area, and no solution was ever reported (Case 222). We have a few other cases in our files where the victim was never identified and no child was ever reported missing. These cases are always distressing. Often the victim is buried by sympathetic strangers, such as church members or the police from the area where the body was first discovered.

Although no one can point out a potential victim with any certainty just by looking at income, occupation, or residence, age alone is a strong factor. Our data agree with all other studies on child fatalities in this regard. Children under age 3 are most at risk. Out of the 1,048 victims of known age, 493 or 47 percent were 3 years old or younger (Table 1.1). Newborn babies — that is, infants less than twenty-four hours old — make up 8 percent of the victims 3 years old and under.

Each 3-year age group decreases in number. Thus, 4 to 6 year olds make up 18.5 percent of the victims; 7 to 9 year olds 17.8 percent, and 10 to 12 year olds 16.6 percent. Some of this difference is probably due to the increased strength and decreased physical vulnerability of children as they grow. Infants in their first year have weak neck muscles and poor coordination. A strong shaking, which an older child would survive, can kill them. Their vision, coordination, and general grasp on life are weaker than that of older children. They cannot escape a pillow held over their faces, for example. If someone fails to feed them, they die because they cannot search for their own food or water, as an older child might. They cannot survive being hurled to the floor, an act that would hurt but probably not kill a 10 or 12 year old. While older children can run into another room or even out of the house to escape dangerous situations, an infant or a child under 3 cannot easily do so.

A child old enough to talk well can complain, inform people about a problem, or scream, but a baby can only cry, and a child under 3 usually is not able to give details or does not know where to go for help when parents and household members become abusive.

Besides being more vulnerable, small children are also more demanding and therefore more apt to be the focus of resentment by older people who are unwilling to give up their own interests to tend to the needs of a small child. Babies cannot clean up their own messes, and many of those messes, such as excrement or vomit, are disgusting to adults or older children. All of these factors help to explain why children age 3 and under are more likely to be killed than older children.

If age is a significant factor, gender is less so. The gender of newborn babies is not a major determining factor in whether they become victims. (In this regard the United States differs from countries such as China or India in which female infants are killed more often than males.) For older children, gender is a factor but not a particularly important one in our records. Most studies of child fatalities indicate that boys are killed more often than girls, and our records bear out this finding to some extent. Male victims represent 52.6 percent of all victims, compared to 47.4 percent of females (Table 1.2). When both gender and age of victims are compared, however, the difference in gender mortality varies somewhat with age. For children 3 and under, boys are more likely to be killed than girls, 54.1 percent to 46.0 percent (Table 1.3), but the difference in the gender of victims between 4 and 9 is not significant. Between the ages of 10 and 12, boys again outnumber girls 53.8 percent to 46.2 percent. We do not know whether this variation in the gender-to-age relationship is significant; it needs more research to ensure that it is not a statistical artifact — that is, simply the result of having a sample rather than all victims of those ages.

Who Are the Perpetrators?

Is it possible to determine in advance who the potential perpetrators of child killings might be and therefore protect children? People who work in the fields of child abuse, child welfare, law enforcement, or in any of the professions where the health and safety of children are major concerns would welcome a positive answer to this question. There are strong American values that insist that people not be punished for what they *might* do but only for acts committed; therefore, the question of identifying potential killers of children is extremely sensitive and complex. And once identified, how should potential killers be treated? It is essential to pinpoint the factors that assist in assessing risk to a child, but equally essential to differentiate between those factors that are not associated with high risk.

Our cases have a minimum of 992 perpetrators. What are their ages and genders? In 107 cases, no perpetrator was identified, but there was at least one; since no perpetrator was identified, neither age nor gender is known. For the remaining 885, the gender was not given for one perpetrator under age 14. For thirteen perpetrators neither age nor gender was given (Table 1.4). Ages were not given for 155 perpetrators (Table 1.5), of whom 91 were males and 51 were females (Table 1.6).

The largest group of perpetrators (43.9 percent) are between 20 and 29 years old (Table 1.5). A fairly typical example is 28-year-old Ralph Cortez, of San Jose, California. In 1978 he shot his 6-year-old son Frank in the forehead at close range. Ralph had demanded money from his son, but Frank said that he had none. When Ralph searched the boy, he found a dollar bill in his pocket. The *New York Times* article does not specify whether Ralph shot the boy before or after he searched him (Case 41).

Six percent of the perpetrators are 14 or younger, all but six of them males (Table 1.6). Male killers outnumber females in every age group. Very few individuals — eleven (1.5 percent) — are 50 or older, and only three are female. Some 23.6 percent are between the ages of 20 and 24, the most numerous single group, and 70.9 percent of those are males. Another 20.3 percent are between the ages of 25 and 29, and 69.6 percent of them are males. The largest percentage of females appears in the 35-to-39-year-old group, where only 58.8 percent are males and 41.3 percent are females. The group with the lowest proportion of women is the one between the ages of 45 to 49, where our files record only one female. To some extent the preponderance of perpetrators in their 20s is to be expected since people of that age are most likely to have a significant amount of interaction with children age 12 and younger. The possible significance of the varying proportions is discussed in more detail in Chapter 8, but we do not have a definitive explanation at this time.

Our files list no female perpetrators under age 11 or over 61. The largest number of female perpetrators, like the largest number of male perpetrators, is in the 20-to-29-year-old age range. An example is Barbara James of Buffalo, New York. In 1989, when she was 28, Barbara stabbed to death her two daughters, Victoria, age 1 1/2, and Brittany, 6 months. Her 9-year-old son by a previous marriage was in critical condition in the hospital with ax wounds to his head and neck. A social worker whom police had sent to the home discovered the bodies. The *New York Times* article stated that the police had had the family "under investigation" for several months (Case 439).

The oldest killer recorded in our files is a male, age 66; the youngest are two males age 4, although there is one 3 year old who was reported as having accidentally shot himself. He is counted as an accident in Table 1.17 under "wrong place/time." His father was charged with negligence for leaving a gun where the child could get it.

Of 38 cases of killers 14 years old and younger, only seven killed more than one victim. The highest proportion of perpetrators who killed more than one child was in the 45-to-49-year-old group, where five of fourteen perpetrators (36 percent) killed two or more victims 12 or under (Table 1.7). In the age group with the most killers (20 to 24), twenty-one of 172 perpetrators (12 percent) killed more than one child. A certain amount of this difference may occur because younger parents have fewer children. Older parents have had time to complete their families, have more children, and thus have more potential victims at hand, but other factors such as frustration with their occupation, job stress, and depression associated with aging and being older parents of young children may also be involved. Age of victims and killers is discussed at greater length in Chapter 8.

One of the more alarming trends shows up at the young end of the age spectrum. There are a total of 161 perpetrators age 19 or younger — that is, killers who are teenaged or younger make up 22.1 percent of our sample of 730 perpetrators whose ages were given in the newspaper articles. Because of public concern about young killers, juveniles (under 18) are discussed in more detail in Chapter 3.

History and Economic Status

We wanted to learn whether the history of perpetrators could be of some help in identifying high-risk individuals. We looked for information on previous emotional or psychological problems, involvement with the legal system, and involvement with child protective agencies. We also examined employment history and socioeconomic status. For this analysis we did not use very short newspaper articles that gave only the names, addresses, and ages. We used articles long enough to mention earlier legal or emotional problems; if none was mentioned, it seemed probable that there was none. These longer articles also provided more information about employment and socioeconomic status. The results were somewhat surprising.

Some 58.8 percent of the perpetrators had no previous psychological problems mentioned in the articles and only 4.1 percent were specifically said to be under the influence of drugs or alcohol at the time of the crime. Of the remainder, 29.4 percent had some previous history of mental instability and 7.7 percent committed suicide without leaving a note (Table 1.8). According to the March 1998 *Federal Register* — a daily publication by the National Archives and Records Administration that includes, among other items, notices from federal agencies and organizations — 5.4 percent of the adult population in the United States have serious mental problems and almost 24 percent have some mental disorder (as defined by the *Diagnostic and Statistical Manual of Mental Health*). If we consider all people who kill children as having severe mental illness, then the figures in Table 1.8 are meaningless. But if we look at the 37.1 percent in our files with psychological problems (including the 7.7 percent who committed suicide but left no note), then the figure is clearly high compared with the nearly 24 percent of the general population who have some mental disorder. Our data on the involvement of drugs and alcohol are conservative in that they almost certainly underestimate the effects of those substances.

It is instructive to look at the proportion of victims killed by perpetrators in these categories. The 37.1 percent of the perpetrators with some previous history of emotional or psychological problems killed almost one-half (48.4 percent) of the victims (Table 1.9). The 4.1 percent in our files with a history of drug or alcohol abuse killed 8.5 percent of the victims. Between them, perpetrators who had a history of mental illness or who abused drugs and alcohol accounted for over one-half of the victims in our files. The largest category of perpetrators (58.8 percent), with no reported psychological or drug problems, killed only 43.2 percent of the victims — that is, although they were a smaller percentage of the perpetrators, those with drug, alcohol, or emotional problems killed the most victims.

Although studies too numerous to mention indicate that certain minorities and lower socioeconomic groups living in cities are overrepresented in the statistics relating to perpetrators, data from those same studies as well as cases from our files show that child killing is not confined to those groups. Examples that illustrate the difficulty of using such general factors as socioeconomic status, ethnic group, or urban residence to identify specific individuals at risk are found throughout this volume. As we know, no area of the country is immune and no socioeconomic class fully escapes these crimes. Poverty may be a contributing factor but is not an essential one. Since newspaper articles often do not mention the socioeconomic status of either victims or perpetrators, the sample size was smaller than normal when we did use it for analysis. The same is true for the employment data.

We do not know what effect unemployment has on encouraging violence against children. Tables 1.10, 1.11, and 1.12 indicate what our files show about the perpetrators' occupations. Only 308 of the cases (40 percent) with 360 perpetrators provided enough information regarding employment to be useful. After eliminating 113 perpetrators who were either under age 18 or were in college (on the assumption that if juveniles or college students were employed, their work was probably part-time), 247 perpetrators are left. Of these, 81 (33 percent) were living in poverty, 145 (59 percent) were employed in specific occupations or living with an employed partner, and 21 (8.5 percent) were reported only as "working" or were in illegal occupations (Table 1.10). The distribution of employment of couples is detailed in Table 1.11. The economic status of these cases was difficult to determine. Most often, the woman was charged as the perpetrator and her partner worked, but in a few cases (7) the male was the perpetrator and the woman worked. In a few other cases (2) both the male and the female were charged as perpetrators and both were employed. Occupations of all employed perpetrators (including those in illegal occupations) are classified in Table 1.12.

Only 36 (14.6 percent) of the 247 adult and noncollege perpetrators were specifically described as unemployed in the newspaper articles. This percentage is high and probably significant. During the years of our study (1977–1993), the national unemployment rate was never higher than 6.6 percent (in 1984) (*Statistical Abstracts* Table 662, p. 422). Unemployed people not only may lack funds but they also are often frustrated and have time on their hands, according to numerous studies of unemployment. The old saying that the devil finds mischief for idle hands may have a grain of truth in it. Police records indicate that crime rates tend to rise during holiday seasons when vacations often occur.

Using unemployment as an indication of poverty may be misleading. Drug dealers often have a great deal of money but no given employment, and other people in illegal activities may also have a comfortable life-style without being officially employed. All of the perpetrators listed as unemployed in newspapers therefore may not be poor. Some may be gainfully, though illegally, employed. Although Table 1.12 lists perpetrators under "other" who, according to the newspapers, were engaged in illegal activities, undoubtedly there were some whose illegal behavior was not known to reporters. In addition, illegal activities bring their own dangers that may put children at risk.

Another 33 perpetrators (13.4 percent) were on welfare and 12 (4.9 percent) were either homeless or lived in public housing. Since there are specific guidelines for welfare and public housing, these people could be presumed to be living in poverty. These persons plus the unemployed make a total of 33 percent of the perpetrators who were probably poor. The highest national percentage of both insured and uninsured unemployed between 1980 and 1993 was 7.2 percent in 1985 (*Statistical Abstracts* Table 664, p. 423). And the highest percentage of the total U.S. population, including adults without any children, living below the poverty level between 1977 and 1993 was 15.1 percent in 1993 (*Statistical Abstracts* Table 749, p. 482). Both figures are well below ours.

The figures for families with children are not as good. In 1993, 22 percent of families with children under 18 were poor (*Statistical Abstracts* Table 745, p. 480). This percentage is closer to but still well below ours of 33 percent of the adult perpetrators living in poverty. When all 360 perpetrators are counted, including juveniles and college students, however, there are only 22.5 percent who could be presumed to be poor, almost identical to the percentage of children under 18 living in families who are poor in the national statistics. Poor children are more at risk in every way, but the risk may not be quite so great as it has been depicted.

Of the 166 perpetrators employed, the largest number (42.2 percent) involved people in jobs requiring little education or special training such as stock clerk, construction laborer, and gypsy-cab driver (Table 1.12). Only

7.8 percent of the perpetrators were professionals (physician, lawyer, college professor). Another 9 percent of the perpetrators were in managerial positions, and 19.3 percent were employed in positions that required some technical education (electrician, carpenter, mechanic). There were fewer killers as the skill and education level rose, which fits the general research about both abuse and fatalities of children. Any recent U.S. Census as well as any economics or business textbook shows that the population of professional and managerial people is smaller than that of technically trained individuals, which in turn is smaller than the population in occupations requiring less education and training. Thus, the pool from which potential child killers might come is also smaller. The relative frequency of our cases from these different groups parallels the relative frequency of those groups in the population as a whole—again supporting the position that child killers are not limited to any particular socioeconomic category in the general population. Given the characteristics of our data, it would be premature to conclude that members of any one group are more or less likely to kill children than members of any other group. A much more detailed analysis is necessary before any such conclusion can be made with confidence. But in any case, no socioeconomic group is immune. As our files reveal, there are rich victims and perpetrators, just as there are poor victims and perpetrators.

Methods

The methods used by the perpetrators to kill their victims vary widely. Of 1,001 victims where the cause of death was given, 24.3 percent were shot, 23.2 percent were beaten to death; and 15.0 percent were stabbed or slashed. Another 14.5 percent were strangled or suffocated; 7.3 percent were burned (directly by scalding or in ovens, or indirectly through house fires); and 4.7 percent were drowned (Table 1.13). The rest of the victims (11.1 percent) were killed by a variety of methods including injection, poison, dog bites, being thrown out of windows or off roofs, and in other ways that were not used frequently enough to list separately in the analysis. Some of the bizarre means by which children died are hidden within the general cause of death. For example, one child was suffocated by a ten-foot python, another by being force-fed chocolate cake; the cause of death in both cases was listed as suffocation. The child who was given a tumbler full of whiskey by a party guest, however, is included in the 11.1 percent killed by "other" methods, as is the victim killed by a lethal intravenous injection administered by his physician father.

Methods differ in the proportion of victims killed compared to the proportion of perpetrators who used the method (compare Tables 1.13 and 1.14). Although 23.2 percent of the victims were killed by beating, 29.6 percent of the perpetrators beat their victims to death. That means that people who beat children to death did not kill as many children at a time as those who used other methods. For example, while 24.3 percent of the victims were shot, only 21.8 percent of the perpetrators used guns. Thus, beating was the method most often used by killers, but they had fewer victims than those who used guns.

The methods used also show a gender bias (Table 1.15). Some methods were used more often by females, although only in drowning did the number of female perpetrators exceed the number of male perpetrators. Males are much more likely than females to shoot their victims (91.1 percent versus 8.9 percent). In a case where the circumstances might have alerted careful observers, Nicholas DePrima Sr. (48) was charged with killing three children and his wife. In 1977 he lived with his wife Rosemary, his two children Nicholas Jr. (5) and Donna (8), and a stepdaughter Kim (10) in Bayonne, New Jersey. He allegedly shot them all, "apparently disturbed over marital problems," according to the *New York Times*. Further, this incident was not the first time that DePrima had used a gun; in 1961 he had been sentenced to seven years in prison for shooting a police officer. He had had "sporadic" employment, mostly odd jobs, including work as a longshoreman. Although he said that he had not worked for five years before the shooting, he had $247 in his pocket when he was arrested. The first news article reported that DePrima had an arsenal in the house. The second, more detailed, called him "obsessed with weapons" and said that nine guns as well as knives, blackjacks, and other similar implements were found in the home. The same article suggested that he may have been employed as a "hit man." DePrima kept newspaper clippings of mob leaders whom he "hero worshipped," including a well-known man in the numbers racket. Despite all this evidence he pleaded not guilty. He had called police to his home, he said. There was no additional information in the *Times* (Case 10).

Women and men both beat their victims to death in proportion to their frequency in the perpetrator population—that is, 69.1 percent of the killers were male, and 69.4 percent of the people who beat children to death were male; 30.9 percent of the perpetrators were female, and 30.6 percent of the people who beat children were female. Women were overrepresented among the killers who suffocated or burned their children but were still roughly equivalent to their proportion in the sample population, keeping in mind the size of the sample group. One notable exception is in drownings, where, as noted, women outnumbered men; and women were also overrepresented among the killers who used unusual methods.

It is informative to compare methods used by different types of perpetrators. The comparison of methods used by mothers, fathers, and mothers' lovers is particularly revealing. We had 323 individual perpetrators who fit into one of these categories (Table 1.16): 37 percent were mothers, 43 percent were fathers, and 20 percent were mothers' lovers (these figures are rounded off). Beating was the most frequent method used by 102 perpetrators—32 percent of the total 323. Mothers were underrepresented—that is, although 37 percent of the perpetrators were mothers, only 18 percent of the beating deaths were caused by mothers. Mothers' lovers, however, were overrepresented; although only 20 percent of the perpetrators were mothers' paramours, 39 percent of the beating deaths were caused by them. If the use of specific methods was strictly connected to the number of perpetrators in a particular category, then 37 percent of the mothers, 43 percent of the fathers, and 20 percent of the lovers should have used this method. When the expected number does not appear, the category is said to be over- or underrepresented and some unidentified factor is involved.

Shooting deaths show a different pattern from beating deaths. Shooting was the second highest cause of death, with 19 percent of the killers using guns. Fathers accounted for 71 percent of the gunshot deaths, far above their percentage (43 percent) in the perpetrator population. Mothers (16 percent) and mothers' lovers (13 percent) were both underrepresented, mothers even more than their lovers. Conversely, mothers were overrepresented in the deaths caused by drowning (68 percent), by smothering (56 percent), and by burning (58 percent). All are far above the mothers' 37 percent of the 323 individual perpetrators.

Gender may explain the difference between the frequency with which men rather than women use guns, but gender does not explain the difference between the rate of shooting by fathers and by mothers' lovers. Nor does gender explain why the lovers beat children to death at a higher rate than fathers, or why mothers acting alone were much less likely to beat children to death than the female child killers in general, who were almost as likely as males to use that method (Table 1.15). This topic needs much more research; clearly, more than simply the act of killing children is involved. One suggestion is that beating is a very personal method of killing. It is possible that the people less closely related to a child than a parent find it easier than mothers and fathers do to beat children to death, at least when acting alone.

Mothers were also more inventive in their use of ways to kill their children, as indicated by their overrepresentation in the category "other." An example of one of the women counted in the "other" category is 25-year-old Tanya Adams. In 1979 in Seattle, Washington, she was found guilty of throwing her two children, Ryan (2 1/2) and Christopher (1 1/2), off the Pasco-Kenwick bridge into the "icy" Columbia River in February. The defense argued that she was innocent by reason of insanity, but the jury did not agree and she was found guilty of two counts of murder. She faced up to two life terms, but there was no information in the *New York Times* as to the sentence (Case 63). The males counted in Table 1.16 were more traditional in their methods.

Circumstances Surrounding the Killing

If age, gender, and history of the victims or perpetrators only serve as broad general guides to potential risks, what about the circumstances of the crime? The circumstances as we defined them are a complex combination of factors including the relationship of the perpetrator to the victim, the household composition of the victim's home, the events surrounding the crime, and events leading up to the crime. Added to the age and gender of the victims and perpetrators, plus the history of the perpetrators, the combination of factors that we call circumstances surrounding the killing may offer the most hope for understanding and preventing child killing. We have classified circumstances surrounding the crime in several ways. Table 1.17 lists the number of victims according to the circumstances of the killing, with violent abuse as the largest category. It includes cases of sustained abuse, used when the newspaper article reported previous involvement with Social Services because of abuse, or described a victim with bruises in various stages of healing. Violent abuse also includes cases of sudden attack when the article specically stated that there was no indication of previous abuse, or made it clear that the murderous attack was unexpected, sudden, and without warning. Most of the cases in the category are those where there was not enough information in the newspaper article to distinguish a case of sustained abuse from one of sudden attack or to place the case in another listed category.

The next largest category contains cases where the victim was in the wrong place at the wrong time — the victim may have witnessed a crime, was killed because the family was a target, or was killed by a stray bullet during a conflict between individuals or groups not involved with the victim or the victim's family. Three-year-old David Manwarren Jr. was probably killed because his family was a target. In late November 1977 the *Battle Creek* (Michigan) *Enquirer and News* had interviewed Christmas tree dealers, among them David's father. David Manwarren Sr. asked the newspaper not to publish his home address because "there are people looking for us." He did not elaborate, but a week later David (22), his wife Gloria (also 22), and David Jr. were killed. The younger David died of a shotgun blast delivered at close range, but no perpetrator was identified (Case 23). In another case, in Harlem, New York City, in 1980, a family member was apparently the target. Ten-year-old Jesus Garcia was sleeping back to back with his 8-year-old brother Jose when a bullet that police suggested was meant for their 13-year-old brother killed Jesus and wounded Jose. Their brother got home just before the shooting, shortly before midnight. Again, no perpetrator was identified (Case 108).

The same category also includes a few victims who were killed "by accident." The words "by accident" are in quotation marks because police regarded the death as a negligent homicide or manslaughter. Examples include two children, one 3 and one 4, who apparently shot themselves. In one case no one was charged; in the other the father was charged with manslaughter. It is difficult to see what the difference was in the two cases, except for the time in which each occurred. The 3-year-old, Dwaine Willis, was playing in his parents' bedroom in Brooklyn in 1981. His mother was in another room and heard a shot. She found her son on the floor, hailed a passing car, and rushed him to the hospital, where he died forty-five minutes later. The boy's father, Lesmoire, had owned a jewelry store for seven years. He kept the gun for protection, but it was unlicensed although he had applied for a permit. The newspaper stated that the permit was denied because Lesmoire was a Jamaican immigrant. No charges were filed (Case 175). The 4-year-old, Ernest

Russell, shot himself in the abdomen in 1991, in the Bronx. His father's gun, also unlicensed, had been left on the couch overnight. Ernest found it and shot himself about 8:20 in the morning. He was rushed to the hospital where he died soon after 6:00 in the evening. His father was first charged with endangering a minor, then, when Ernest died, with first-degree manslaughter (Case 688). Public attitudes had changed considerably between 1981 and 1991, which could account for the difference in the treatment of the fathers.

The third highest category in Table 1.17 is "mental or emotional problems" — that is, problems of the perpetrator, not the victim, and it includes postpartum psychosis when the victim was not newborn. Cases were placed in this category when the killer was medically or legally diagnosed as mentally disturbed either at the time of the crime or previously. In some of the cases, the perpetrator had sought help from a mental health facility and been turned away. In other cases the perpetrator successfully used insanity as a defense during the trial. We also included people who were described as "severely depressed," or who indicated that they despaired of being able to take care of their children, or who believed that the future for the children was worse than death.

Almost 7 percent of the victims were killed after being sexually abused. Sexual abuse and sustained abuse are counted separately because sexual abusers who kill their victims are not usually family members. Moreover, family members who physically abuse their victims over a period of time before killing them do not always also abuse them sexually. Combining cases of sexual abuse with those of sustained abuse would obscure the insight that the perpetrators had very different relationships with their victims. Most sexual abusers are male, and most male sexual abuse killers are strangers to their victims. The case of Barbara Jo Brown, 11, is an example. In 1981, in Angola, Louisiana, two young men, one 17 and one 19, killed her with a brick after raping her. While she was being raped, she was also stabbed with broken bottles and jabbed with pointed sticks. Both attackers — strangers — were convicted. The 17 year old was sentenced to life in prison because the jury could not agree on a death sentence. The other killer attempted to avoid a death sentence on the grounds that he was mildly retarded and had been severely abused by his father. His numerous appeals were rejected, and he was executed on July 30, 1987. He said that he did it and did not deserve clemency but, the newspaper reported, he also said, "I would like to live" (Case 478).

A number of sexual abusers were also serial killers. Cases involving serial killers were classified separately and accounted for 5.7 percent of all victims. Despite a popular stereotype, not all serial killers are motivated to molest their victims; accordingly, the serial killers were separated from other sexual molesters who killed their victims.

Almost 6 percent of the victims were killed by what we called "bad decisions." The category includes cases usually classified in the child abuse statistics as "neglect." These neglect cases may make up 45 percent or more of the child abuse and neglect cases reported in national statistics. While neglect may harm children, it is rarely fatal, except in cases where parents for religious reasons fail to obtain medical help for a seriously ill child. Another 4.5 percent of the victims were killed in a variety of situations too infrequent to classify separately. Nine of these cases, less than 1 percent of the total victims, were considered mercy killings. The next category, almost 4 percent of the total victims, was "newborn" infants. These are discussed in more detail below, as is "escalating argument," the smallest category.

Although almost one-half of the victims fell into the 3-year-old or younger group, looking at the separate circumstances of the cases demonstrates that age is not the only factor that needs to be considered in assessing the risk to a child (Table 1.18). For example, the 7 to 9 year olds provide most victims who were sexually abused before being killed, with the 10 to 12 year olds next highest. The 0-to-3-year-old group, usually at highest risk, has only 11 deaths (18 percent) combined with sexual abuse, compared to 24 deaths (39 percent) in the 7-to-9-year-old group, and 18 deaths (29.5 percent) among the 10 to 12 year olds. The group with the lowest percentage is the 4-to-6-year-old children with only 8 deaths (13 percent of the total 61 sexually abused victims). Overall, although 47 percent of all the victims in our sample are 3 years old or younger, 69 percent of the victims who were sexually assaulted as well as killed were between age 7 and 12. Only 31 percent of our total sample group are in that age range.

"Escalating argument" — that is, the situation when an argument between individuals becomes increasingly intense until it erupts in violence — is another circumstance in which the pattern of age association is reversed. There the largest group of victims (15) are in the 10-to-12-year-old category. Younger children are probably not so likely to get into long and increasingly heated arguments either with each other or with adults. The information from these two categories indicates that children of different ages are facing different sorts of risks. Risk assessment instruments need to be adjusted accordingly.

Newborn babies — that is, infants less than forty-eight hours old — make up 8 percent of the victims 3 years old and under. Newborns whose mothers give birth unattended are especially vulnerable. There are legitimate reasons why a birth might happen away from a hospital or birthing center; perhaps the baby arrives too quickly, or transportation problems delay the mother's getting to help in time. Even under such circumstances, most women in our society are not alone during the birth process. Nevertheless, when a mother is unattended, the reasons for the lack of help may also be factors that put the baby at risk. Thirty-eight deaths in our files are newborn infants, and almost all were unattended births.

Abandonment is a passive way to kill a newborn. In our records, we have mothers who wrapped the baby in plastic, a sheet, or a blanket and put him (referring also, of course, to "her") out of sight in the house in a drawer or a closet; or outside in the trash, a dumpster, or a garbage can; or otherwise out of sight. For example, in 1993, 19-year-old Valerie Nethers of Letcher County, Kentucky, was alone when she had her baby at home in the bathroom. She wrapped the newborn little girl in a towel and stuffed her in a drawer (Case 898). In 1987, in Urbandale, Iowa, near Des Moines, a 14-year-old girl put her baby in a plastic garbage bag and hid it in a bedroom closet where the girl's mother found it three days later (Case 569). Perhaps the most unusual disposal method was practiced in 1991 by a 17-year-old girl on Long Island, New York, who had concealed her pregnancy from her family. When her baby boy was born, she wrapped him in plastic and later set him adrift in a picnic cooler on a lake near her home (Case 838). A number of newborn infants whose parents were never found were simply put in bags and dumped in trash bins or landfills.

All of these methods at least give the baby a chance of being found before he dies so the mother does not directly kill her child. Indeed, a young mother who acts in this manner may be continuing a state of total denial about her pregnancy. Sometimes she claims not to have known that she was pregnant and even may not have told anyone about the situation. Our records include babies born at home in a bathroom, on the hall steps outside a relative's apartment, in a bedroom, in a dorm room at college, and even in the bathroom adjoining the emergency room of a hospital where the girl went for treatment of "stomach pains." In a recent case that received national attention but occurred too late to be included in this study, a girl gave birth in the restroom at her high-school prom. After the birth, she returned to the dance floor. In many abandonment cases the mother tries to convince herself that the pregnancy never happened.

Other newborn infants do not even have the slight chance at life that abandonment gives them. Their mothers do not seem to be denying the fact of the birth so much as they are stunned or enraged by it. These babies die violently. For example, in Chicago in 1992 a newborn baby boy, whose 19-year-old mother had given birth to him unattended at home, was stabbed to death with scissors (Case 705). A year earlier in Old Bridge, New Jersey, a 20-year-old woman who gave birth unattended at home stabbed her newborn baby girl 175 times with fingernail scissors, then tossed the infant out the window (Case 690). These cases are described in more detail in Chapter 4.

Even children who are born in hospitals or birthing centers, however, may not be safe. In one unusual case in 1993, Urbelina Emiliano, 23, got pregnant in New York City. She returned to Mexico and resumed relations with Fortino Perez, 26, whom she had dated previously. They married, and a few weeks later she told him that she was pregnant by another man. They then began to conspire to kill the child, according to the newspaper account. Urbelina did not want the baby to come between them, and Fortino did not want to raise another man's child. The baby was born about a week after they came back to New York, where Fortino found work as a kitchen helper. When the mother and newborn girl were discharged from the hospital, the two buried her alive in the backyard with the help of Fortino's brother, who dug the hole. The crime was discovered when Urbelina got pregnant again and went to the same hospital. Employees there asked her about her first child; when she could not explain what happened, they notified police (Case 780). There was no additional information on the case, which is almost a classic fit for hypotheses of evolutionary psychology: the male kills because the child is not his, the female to maintain the new relationship. The hypotheses of evolutionary psychology are discussed at greater length in Chapter 8.

The Relationship between Victims and Perpetrators

Biological parents kill the majority of the victims (51 percent) (Table 1.20). Police and social workers are aware of this fact, although people interviewed by members of the media always seem to express surprise when a case is publicized. Parents, by definition, spend considerable time with their children, so their predominance among *abusers* is not surprising. But parents who kill their children are destroying any chance of passing along their own genetic and cultural heritage. One would assume, therefore, that it makes little biological sense for parents to kill their offspring. Mothers should be especially unwilling to destroy them since, unlike fathers, a mother rarely has any doubt that the child is hers. However, we have numerous examples discussed in the following chapters.

Statistics must always be read with care, particularly when samples are used. One needs to consider the characteristics of the population from which the sample is drawn. Since biological parents are present at some point in the life of all children, one would expect them to be in a majority in almost any sample drawn that includes the adults with relationships with the child. Of 275 parents in our data base who were acting alone, more killers were fathers (52 percent) than were mothers (48 percent) (Table 1.21). However, the difference is not great. Considering that male killers, regardless of the age of their victims, far outnumber female ones, mothers are overrepresented. One of the reasons is the presence of newborn babies in the sample. Newborn infants are most often killed by their mothers, although we have records of two fathers who were also charged along with the mothers, as well as one father who acted alone (see the McKay case in Chapter 4). Children even a few days older, however, are more apt to be killed by males.

In addition to the percentage of 831 victims killed by individual biological parents, 11 percent were killed by neighbors, friends, or in-laws (Table 1.20). These murderers are classified together because all had a relationship with the family of the victim but were not usually members of the household. Some in-laws are biological relatives of the victim, and some are not. For example, the spouse of a biological relative of the victim is an in-law but not a biological relative of the victim. A man who kills his wife's young brother is a brother-in-law of the victim but not his blood relative. In our data, these nonbiological relationships are counted as "in-laws" and not biological kin. Biological relatives of the victim are counted as such (say, grandparents, aunts, uncles, or cousins), not as in-laws.

A neighbor was charged with the death of Carolyn Sue Perry, age 11, in Louisville, Kentucky, in March 1978. The child had been missing two days when her body was found in a closet of a vacant apartment across from her home. Lyle Johnson, 18, who lived about a block away, was convicted and sentenced to life and twenty years, to run concurrently. While he confessed to the crime, the defense argued that the confession was coerced and that his brother was the killer. The jury obviously did not agree (Case 495).

Parents' lovers, who are not always counted in national fatal child abuse statistics (depending on whether they are caretakers of the child at the time of the crime), killed 10 percent of the victims. One of the more gruesome cases involving a mother's paramour was reported by the *Omaha World-Herald* in 1992. It occurred in November 1991 in Waterloo, Iowa. Darren Gerdeman, 3, lived with his mother and his mother's boyfriend, Gary Buck. One day when Darren misbehaved, Gary shot him in the head with a pellet gun and then slashed his neck to keep him from screaming and to "stop his suffering." According to the doctor, the knife was not particularly sharp; it took Darren "a few minutes" to bleed to death, and Gary held him over the edge of a bathtub while waiting for him to die. Gary later told police that he planned to dispose of the body and blame the murder on an unidentified relative. Darren's body was wrapped in a garbage bag and placed in a picnic cooler in the apartment where it was found on November 25. The newspaper articles did not explain how it came to be discovered. At his trial, Gary pleaded innocent by reason of insanity but was found guilty. A mandatory life sentence went with the conviction (Case 882).

Only 9 percent of the victims were killed by strangers. Some 8 percent were killed by biological kin other than parents, such as aunts, uncles, cousins, and grandparents, and 6 percent by people with some business connection with the family, such as baby-sitters, nurses, parents' co-workers. Another 3 percent were killed by step relatives, 2 percent by foster relatives, and less than 1 percent by an adoptive relative.

When several people take part in the killing, the pattern changes slightly. Parents still predominate, but only 48 percent of the victims were killed by a group involving at least one parent (Table 1.22). Another 20 percent were killed by groups of strangers. An interesting bit of information that does not show up in the table is that at least one male was present in virtually all cases when more than one individual was involved. We suspect that cultural rather than genetic factors may play a role in the reasons why women acting alone or with a man kill children, but all-female groups seldom do. We do not know what these factors are, but there are a number of possibilities, one being the cultural expectation that the women will follow and the man will lead when there is a male in the group. In the absence of a male, the presence of even one woman who is reluctant to kill a child may inhibit the others. The opinion of other people may be more important to women in our culture; hence, a woman acting alone has no disapproving other person present to act as a deterrent.

Sometimes an individual with little connection to the victim, a mere acquaintance, is responsible for a killing. Such was the case in Queens, New York City, in 1988. Sunday, June 19, was the last time that anyone saw Anthony Shawn Owens, age 12. On Monday, no one answered the phone or came to the door of his home. Anthony's grandmother, worried because she could not reach her daughter Sharon, Anthony's mother, called friends. Apparently nothing more was done at the time because it was not until six days later, on June 25, that police, called by neighbors who complained about a strong odor, found the badly decomposed bodies of both Anthony and Sharon. Just hours later, Gregory Hector, 26, a maintenance man at Belmont Raceway, confessed to the crimes. At that point, the police had not found any evidence linking him to the killings although he had a "casual relationship" with Sharon, according to the newspaper reports. Hector admitted that he had no motive — not sex, not drugs, just "an urge came over him to do it." Neighbors called him "unstable" and said that he had been despondent since his sister died in January, when he began using drugs and his attitude changed. His friends said that they had had to stop "hanging out" with him. Hector claimed several other killings, but his friends and neighbors were not sure whether that claim was true. He had no police record and maintained that he had not been on crack at the time of the crimes, although he did use crack. Without any later article in the *New York Times*, the outcome is not known (Case 418).

It is impossible to compare the percentage of killings by these other people to the percentage of the population at large in these same categories because the percentage of parental lovers, friends, acquaintances, in-laws, neighbors, and step kin are impossible to find in national statistics. Since every family has more relatives, friends, neighbors, and acquaintances than parents or parental lovers, one could expect these figures to be the highest of all if the rate of killing were the same for all categories. Since relatives, friends, neighbors, and acquaintances kill comparatively few children, however, the preponderance of parental killers is shown to be all the more serious. Indeed, the figures show that none of the relationships mentioned can safely be disregarded when assessing the danger to a child.

But what about that 9 percent of victims who were killed by strangers? Strangers who kill occupy the nightmares of conscientious parents. Many adults today remember being warned as children about going anywhere with strangers or even talking to them. Constant messages are given to parents by police, by schools, and in the mass media to caution their children about interacting with strangers. These warnings are valid, yet only a relatively small percentage of children (9 percent) in our files fell victim to strangers in those cases in which an individual perpetrator was identified (Tables 1.20 and 1.21). The figure was much larger for victims killed by groups of perpetrators. Thirty victims out of 150 (20 percent) were killed by groups of strangers. Undoubtedly, a number of children whose killer was not discovered during our sample period were also killed by strangers. Since some of the perpetrators who were identified years after the crime turned out to be parents, relatives, friends, or neighbors, however, we cannot assume that all of the unidentified perpetrators were strangers.

Living Arrangements

Living arrangements can help to identify potential victims. Of the total cases in our data base, 631 specified the household situation of the victim. In examining those cases, it became clear that a large percentage of victims killed by present or former household members or biological relatives were not living with both biological parents (Table 1.23). Such homes were classified as broken or blended. These broken or blended homes consequently consisted of those where biological parents were separated by estrangement, divorce, or death; those with a single parent; those where one parent had remarried or was living with another partner; and those where the children were in foster or adoptive homes. In only 26 percent of the cases were both biological parents present. In 1994, according to the 1995 *Statistical Abstract of the United States* (Bureau of the Census), 69 percent of all children under age 18 — excluding those with their own households — were living with both biological parents, 23 percent with their mothers only, 3 percent with their fathers only, and 4 percent with neither parent.

A racial breakdown shows a different picture. In 1994 only 33 percent of black children under 18 were living with both biological parents, 53 percent with their mothers only, 4 percent with their fathers only, and 10 percent with neither parent. Among whites, the percentage living with both parents was 76 percent. Among Hispanics who (according to the census) could be either black or white, 63 percent were living with both parents (Table 79, p. 65). Even the lowest figure — the 33 percent of black children living with both biological parents — is higher than the 26 percent in our records, however. In addition, that 33 percent refers to children under 18. The percentage of children under 12, the limit of our sample, living with both parents is undoubtedly higher. The low figure of children 12 and under living with both biological parents in our data compared to children under 18 in the general population emphasizes the importance of the broken home as a risk factor.

In Table 77 of the 1995 *Statistical Abstract of the United States*, counting children under 18 living with couples in 1990, 81.5 percent were living with both biological parents, 14.6 percent with their mother and a stepfather, 1.6 percent with their father and a stepmother, and 2.1 percent with adoptive parents; for 1.1 percent, the mothers or fathers were not known (Table 77, p. 64). Even in the case of black couples, the lowest figure in the table of children living in couple households, 63.6 of the children were in homes with their biological parents. Again, our figures emphasize the broken home (which in our data includes blended, foster, and adopted families) as a risk factor.

The broken home was a major risk factor only when the perpetrator was a relative, a lover, or a present or former household member. In a substantial number of cases (31 percent), the household composition was not relevant because the killer was someone from outside the household who was not a biological relative or former household member. These killers included friends, neighbors, acquaintances, or strangers. The killings often took place during some other crime, such as robbery. Whether the parents of the victim were both in the home or were separated, or whether the victim was adopted or a foster child did not seem to be factors in the crime. The significant variables were the relationships that neighbors had with the family members, or other circumstances of the killing, such as attempted robbery or rape. Descriptions of some cases of this last type, whose victims were in the wrong place at the wrong time, are given in Chapter 7. These children, as well as those killed for other reasons by people outside the household, excluding baby-sitters, are never represented in the fatal child abuse and neglect statistics because the killer was not a caretaker of the child. We believe, however, that to understand the full scope and factors involved in the problem of child murders, these uncounted victims should be included in any study of child killers and their victims.

Family Life-styles

Family life-styles that are not directly correlated with marital or economic status may have a profound effect on children's safety. Some patterns of living expose children to risks even when their parents (biological, step, or adopted) are caring, loving, and economically comfortable. For example, drug involvement of any sort increases the risk to children both in the family and in the general neighborhood. Those children who were killed by random bullets fired during drug conflicts were in the wrong place at the wrong time; the bullets that killed them were not directed at them. Drug involvement also made victims of children killed because a family member, or even the entire family, was engaged in the distribution or sale of drugs and became targets when deals soured. Although some of these children may have been accidental victims, others were targeted by people who killed them to intimidate or punish family members.

Children already are exposed to danger if members of the family are drug users, even when they have no conflict with angry dealers or law officers. They can be endangered by users in at least three ways: by household members who become violent while under the influence of drugs, by users who share their drugs with the children, and by users who simply forget that there are children around to care for while in a drug-induced other world. Any of these situations may be fatal to children in the home. The February 1994 *Reader's Digest* cited two brief examples of violence by drug users: a 4-year-old girl was battered and bitten by her parents (Case 854), and a 13-month-old infant was raped and murdered by her mother's lover (Case 855). Methamphetamine was the drug involved in both cases. The *Reader's Digest* accounts did not give the exact date of either crime.

Parents who share their drugs can be just as dangerous. In 1987 in Cedar Rapids, Iowa, John and Karen Richmond were charged with child endangerment when their 2-month-old son died of an overdose of morphine—eaten, not injected. Heroin is a source of morphine. It is highly unlikely that a

2-month-old infant could have taken the drug unaided. The newspaper article made no comment on whether one of the parents might have given the
drug accidentally, but the charge suggests that the police thought that the
administration was deliberate (Case 570). And finally, parents or caregivers
who use drugs may also forget the needs of a baby. In late 1990, 7-month-old
twin girls died of starvation and dehydration because their mother was high
on crack and lost all sense of time. Her five older children managed to survive
the neglect—another example of why older children are less likely to become
victims (Case 639). This case is described in more detail in Chapter 7.

Let me add that drug use or some type of drug involvement is not the only
family behavior that places children at risk. In Chapter 7, we discuss further
some cases in which a child's life was endangered by religious beliefs that led
to reluctance on the parents' part to call for medical assistance. These incidents were classified under "bad decisions." In other cases where religious
beliefs were a factor, the child was placed at risk because a parent or care
giver had exaggerated beliefs about demons and engaged in behavior that was
different from the usual practices of other members of his or her religious
affiliation. These cases are discussed in Chapter 4, which deals with mental
and emotional problems, because insanity was often used successfully by the
defense in the perpetrator's trial and because the beliefs of the perpetrator
seemed wholly out of touch with reality. Although religious convictions determine the life-style of millions of people, the behavior of the individuals in
these cases did not seem based on the mainstream beliefs with which most
Americans are familiar.

Family Conflicts

Children may become victims of conflicts between family members or between family members and neighbors or other outsiders. If one of the parties
in a domestic dispute is violent, not only his children (the perpetrator in this
type of case is most often a heterosexual male) but also his extended family
members are in danger. A recent example of a child endangered when the
father and mother separated was reported on April 23, 1998, on CBS television news. The father injected his son with HIV-tainted blood so that the
boy would die and he would not have to continue to pay child support. The
child now has AIDS. Estranged, separated, or divorced fathers who kill or
attempt to kill their children of the former marriage appear frequently in our

files. Had the boy mentioned died during our data-collecting period, the case would have been classified as follows: violent abuse (greed), broken home, perpetrator male, age not given, father of victim, employed (he worked at a low-skill job in a hospital where he had access to the tainted blood), method "other."

Even when a divorced or estranged spouse or lover is not violent, children may be at risk when a relationship ends. If they remain with their mother (the most common situation), they may be in danger from the mother herself or from someone with whom the mother begins a new relationship. If they are sent to relatives (another common solution), they may be endangered there. Indeed, relatives are involved more often than one would expect from reading the child abuse literature. When biological relatives, non-kin in-laws, neighbors, acquaintances, or strangers kill children, the deaths are not usually counted as child abuse fatalities unless the killer was the child's caretaker at the time of death. Among the murderous relatives mentioned in newspaper articles, one can find brothers, sisters, maternal and paternal cousins, uncles, aunts, grandparents, great-uncles, and great-aunts. Biological kin, other than parents, make up 8 percent in our perpetrator-victim relationship sample (Table 1.21). One example is the case of Danny Hillman, age 4. Theda Rice, from Davenport, Iowa, working as a waitress in Los Angeles, had custody of her grandsons, Daniel Hillman and his two brothers, whose ages were not given. No mention of why she had custody was made in the brief newspaper article. Neighbors, according to the *Omaha World-Herald*, reported that while Theda worked, the boys were "routinely" tied to chairs. In December 1989 a social worker investigating the report found Danny crammed under a table two feet by two feet by sixteen inches, tied "like a pretzel," with his ankles fastened behind his neck and his hands behind his back. He had also been severely beaten. This punishment was because he had not gone to sleep the night before. When the social worker found Danny, he was unconscious and later died from the beating. The article gave no additional details (Case 574).

Another case in 1986 involved an uncle. Whether he was the mother's or the father's brother was not indicated in the *New York Times* account. Blair Stratford, 23, threw his niece Jasmine Spencer, 8 years old, from an eighteenth-floor balcony in Manhattan, New York City, at eleven o'clock one morning. Blair fled the apartment and stole a bicycle to escape; police chased him along Lexington Avenue before he was caught. There were no additional articles on this case, and no report of the outcome was in the *Times* before 1993 (Case 350).

Foster Parents as Killers

If children are in danger from all parties in a disintegrating marriage, then where can they go, or where can child protective workers shelter them? Foster homes, group homes, orphanages, and relatives have all been suggested. However, in these facilities as well as in youth shelters for emergency use, there are not nearly enough spaces for children in crisis. Any person working with a child protective agency can relate horror stories of failed attempts to find a place to put a child taken out of a dangerous home in an emergency. More than one worker in such a situation has stayed in the office all night, watching over the child — a move that is preferable to keeping a hospital vigil over an injured child in intensive care.

There are several types of foster homes: 1) kin fosters — that is, relatives of the child who agree to take on the role of caregivers until the parents can reassume responsibility, or some other alternative is reached; 2) state-sponsored foster parents who are unrelated to the child; 3) private fosters, where some organization, often a religious group, arranges the fostering; and 4) parafosters, who are friends of the child's parent(s). The state or local government usually assumes at least some of the cost and provides support services for all but private and parafostering, which may be quite informal, but how much and how thorough the support is for the other foster parent types varies from state to state. Foster homes also are not immune to violence. Twenty-four of the victims recorded in our files were killed in foster homes, most by one or both of the foster parents but a few by other people in the household.

The amount of screening undergone by a foster family depends on the type of foster. State and private foster parents are scrutinized most carefully, and individuals chosen often receive special training. Kin foster homes vary widely in the amount of screening, both from one state to another and even within the same state. It often seems sensible to allow relatives to care for a child who must be taken out of the parental home, especially in crisis situations when there is no time to do careful research. If the child is to stay in the home for more than a few days, there usually is an extensive check to make sure that the home is suitable. But requirements may not be as stringent as they are for state or private foster parents, or overloaded case workers may simply be too rushed to investigate closely.

Parafosters are often simply friends or acquaintances with whom the parent(s) decide to leave the child. Frequently there is no formal arrangement, although if the parent who leaves the child is under supervision by a child protective agency, there may be a record on file somewhere. There is no way of knowing how frequently this type of fostering takes place or how many children are mistreated, but while 11 of the 24 foster home deaths in our files were in state or private foster homes, 7 of the remaining 13 victims were with parafosters and 4 were with kin fosters. Of the other two cases, one victim was adopted and slain by the state-selected couple who had previously fostered him; and the other, although a foster child, was abducted, sexually molested, and slain by an unknown perpetrator.

Parafosters may be overlooked entirely and never investigated if child protective agencies are not aware that a child has been left with someone other than a parent. When state agencies know about the placement, however, they are usually expected to make the same kind of investigation as that given to other types of foster homes. The case of Dyneeka Johnson, a 5-year-old girl who was killed in 1989, falls between the regular state foster program and the informal parafoster — that is, the state agency workers did not select Dyneeka's foster parents from their carefully checked list because Dyneeka's mother asked the state to place the child with her friends. They should have checked the foster parents as carefully as any chosen by them, but they did not.

Carol Johnson of Newark, New Jersey, was 25 and still unmarried, although by 1989 she had given birth to four children, three of whom were no longer in her care. That year she asked the state to give Dyneeka to the care of Stacy Smith (25), a childhood friend who had a live-in male partner, Willy Grant (39). Both Stacy and Willy had criminal records and had been convicted on drug charges. The state workers who placed Dyneeka apparently failed to investigate either Stacy's or Willy's background. When Dyneeka died (the cause of her death was not given in the *New York Times* article), Stacy was charged with manslaughter and endangering; Willy was charged with murder. Five workers in the Division of Youth and Family Services were either suspended without pay or demoted and two more were reprimanded; one of them was a former vice president of Union Local 1037 of Community

Workers of America. This disciplinary action caused other union members to walk off the job; the agency was trying to make them scapegoats, they said. One of the seven workers disciplined stated that "it's amazing there are so few deaths" because case workers are so overloaded and foster homes are in such short supply that it is not possible for workers to protect children properly. On the other hand, the agency director accused the workers of failing to carry out established policy and procedures. No follow-up on this case was reported in the *Times* (Case 440).

The few foster cases in our files tend to follow the pattern of the rest of the victims. There were more males killed than females (54 percent to 46 percent) (Table 1.24), 3 years of age or less was still the most dangerous period for children (Table 1.25), and the numbers decreased for every three-year age group after that (Table 1.25). The numbers are so small that they do not allow any broad generalizations about the overall safety of foster homes, but they do indicate that they, too, are not entirely safe.

Family Preservation

Many states legally require child protective agencies to make every effort to preserve the family — that is, if a child is removed from the home for some reason, the case workers must try to make it possible to reunite the child with the parents. Richard Gelles has written at length about the problems that can result from this policy (Gelles, 1997). Our files indicate that removing a child from an abusive or neglectful home for a time and then returning him may increase the danger to the child. The first few weeks after the return appear critical. Thirty-nine percent of the deaths in our files of children who were removed and then returned occurred during the first ten weeks that the returned child was home (Table 1.26). But a returned child is at risk during the entire first year. Even when the courts mandate frequent supervisory visits, most child welfare agencies are too overloaded to comply, or parents resist intervention. Our figures suggest that returned children need to be given very high priority for close supervision by case workers, particularly during their first few weeks back home.

The percentage of children age 3 and under who are killed after being returned home is even larger than it is in the full sample. Sixty-five percent of children returned to the home and then killed were 3 or under, compared to 47 percent of the children 3 or under in the full sample (compare Tables 1.27

and 1.1). There were no children in the 10-to-12-year-old group killed after being returned home. We have no idea why these differences occur. The small size of the sample, however, means that the figures may simply be a statistical artifact; a change of one or two victims in any age group would alter the percentages substantially.

While more males were killed than females, the difference from the full sample is not great considering the sample size (Table 1.28). The fact that so few of our total of 1,098 victims were reported killed after being returned home is difficult to interpret without some idea of the total number of abused children who are removed and then returned to their families. Newspaper articles may not mention the fact that the child was previously taken from the home. Gelles indicates that the problem is far greater than our figures suggest but also that there are ways to determine which families pose the greatest risks to a returned child. This topic should be investigated in more detail.

Summary

During this chapter the question was raised as to whether it was possible to identify potential victims or perpetrators. The answer would appear to be that no single factor will serve, but in combination several of them can suggest when a child is at higher or lower risk. Although all studies of child abuse indicate that women physically abuse children far more frequently than men, our data show that men are more likely to kill than women (Table 1.19). Of the 820 perpetrators whose gender was given, 68 percent were males, and 32 percent females. In the 110 cases classified as "sudden attacks" involving loss of control or sudden rages, males were responsible 78 percent of the time, females only 22 percent. In 106 cases classified as "sustained abuse," however, when newspaper articles indicated that physical abuse had gone on for some time before the killing, males were held responsible only 57 percent of the time, while the female responsibility jumped to 43 percent.

In some situations the effect of gender is particularly clear. When the escalation of an argument was involved — that is, when there was a quarrel that became more serious and violent — the perpetrators were overwhelmingly male. Out of 31 perpetrators, there were only two females. Out of 34 identified perpetrators who killed newborn infants, as expected, most were women. Only four males were identified as killing newborns: two who were charged with the female, and two who acted alone. Since males are almost always the perpetrators in cases of sexual assault, it is also no surprise that males are the killers in almost all cases of sexual abuse murders.

In the 66 cases where the perpetrator had mental or emotional problems, however, the total was more evenly divided between males and females, with 54.5 percent of the perpetrators male, 46 percent female. The total is also more evenly divided in cases where the perpetrators made bad decisions. Out of 48 cases, 46 percent were males, 54 percent females. However, since the overall percentages of known perpetrators include 68 percent males and only 32 percent females, in both the circumstances of mental or emotional problems and bad decisions, the percentage of females is higher than expected and that of males lower.

In 1992 there were 101,000 family foster homes in the United States, down from 142,000 in 1978 (*National Advocate*, 1994). Given the smaller number of foster homes in 1992, and the number of total non-foster family homes, even our slim data suggest that children in foster homes run a risk, although perhaps not as great as children in their own homes. The point must be made that just as not all family homes are dangerous, neither are all foster homes. The difficulty is that the dangerous ones are very dangerous indeed, and the problem lies in attempting to determine which ones they are. As with family homes, there are several types of foster homes, which differ in the amount of supervision and background checking that they receive.

Although the number of children killed after they are returned to their homes is small (fortunately, we do not have many such cases in our files), the data indicate so consistently that the first year home is the time of greatest danger that the warning must be heeded. This concern is expressed strongly by one of the experts in the field, Richard Gelles, in his recent *The Book of David*. More effort must be made to protect returned children, and more creative and effective mechanisms for improving parenting and protecting children also need to be developed. The subject is discussed again in Chapter 8.

Children under age 3, removed from the home because of neglect or abuse and then returned to one or both parents; children in a disintegrating or broken marriage; children whose family members are involved with drugs as users or dealers or both; children living in high-crime areas; and children in families whose members are involved in violent conflict with other family members, with neighbors, or with acquaintances, are particularly at risk. But it is vitally important to remember that even children who meet all of the above criteria are not always killed. Any statistical discussion of child homicide and fatal abuse may be misleading. Indeed, most children do not die. And most parents, even inadequate ones — rich or poor, urban or rural, regardless of race, in whatever region of the country, whatever their education or occupation — do not kill their children and do not abuse them. All of the factors combined provide only a relative assessment of risk, not an absolute certainty. We need to use case reviews more extensively to try to identify more precisely the combination of factors that place a child's life at greatest risk.

Tables for Chapter 1

Table 1.1 Victim's Age at Last Birthday When Known*

Age	Frequency	Percent
0 - 3 Years	493	47.0
4 - 6 Years	194	18.5
7 - 9 Years	187	17.8
10 - 12 Years	174	16.6
TOTAL	1,048	99.9

*There were 50 victims whose ages were not known.

Table 1.2 Gender of Victims*

Gender	Frequency	Percent
Male	542	52.6
Female	488	47.4
TOTAL	1,030	100.0

*There were 68 victims whose gender was not given or not known.

Table 1.3 Victims' Age by Victims' Gender

Gender	0–3	%	4–6	%	7–9	%	10–12	%	Total	%
Male	258	54.1	95	50.0	93	50.3	93	53.8	539	52.6
Female	219	46.0	95	50.0	92	49.7	80	46.2	486	47.4
TOTAL	477	46.5	190	18.5	185	18.0	173	16.9	1,025	100.0

*There were 3 males and 2 females with ages unknown, 68 victims with gender unknown.

Table 1.4 Known Gender of All Perpetrators*

Gender	Frequency	Percent
Male	602	69.1
Female	269	30.9
TOTAL	871	100.0

*There were 14 perpetrators whose gender was not given and 107 cases with unknown (but at least one) perpetrators, for a minimum total of 992 perpetrators.

Table 1.5 Known Age of Perpetrators in Five-Year Increments*

Age Group	Frequency	Percent
14 and under	45	6.2
15–19	116	15.9
20–24	172	23.6
25–29	148	20.3
30–34	107	14.7
35–39	80	11.0
40–44	37	5.1
45–49	14	1.9
50 and over	11	1.5
TOTAL	730	100.2

*There were 155 perpetrators whose ages were not given and 107 cases with unknown perpetrators for a minimum total of 992 perpetrators, since all 107 had at least one perpetrator.

Table 1.6 Age of Perpetrators in Five-Year Groups, by Gender*

Age	Male	%	Female	%	Total	%
14 and under	38	86.4	6	13.6	44	6.0
15 to 19	79	68.1	37	31.9	116	15.9
20 to 24	122	70.9	50	29.1	172	23.6
25 to 29	103	69.6	45	30.4	148	20.3
30 to 34	73	68.2	34	31.8	107	14.7
35 to 39	47	58.8	33	41.3	80	11.0
40 to 44	28	75.7	9	24.3	37	5.1
45 to 49	13	92.9	1	7.1	14	1.9
50 and over	8	72.7	3	27.3	11	1.5
TOTAL	511	70.1	218	29.9	729	100.0

*There were 91 males and 51 females whose ages were unknown, one under 14 whose gender was not known, 13 perpetrators whose gender and age were both unknown, and 107 cases where the perpetrator was unknown. These are not included in the calculations to make the distribution of perpetrators with known age and gender clearer.

Table 1.7 Number of Victims by Age of Perpetrator*

Age	One	Two	Three	Four	Five+	Total	%
14 and under	38	4	3	0	0	45	6.2
15–19	99	12	4	0	1	116	15.9
20–24	151	17	3	1	0	172	23.6
25–29	115	24	4	4	1	148	20.3
30–34	84	7	9	4	3	107	14.7
35–39	56	19	2	3	0	80	11.0
40–44	27	4	3	2	1	37	5.1
45–49	9	3	1	0	1	14	1.9
50 and up	10	1	0	0	0	11	1.5
TOTAL	589	91	29	14	7	730	100.2

*There were 155 perpetrators whose ages were not given, and 107 cases where no perpetrator was identified. There is one more perpetrator in the 14-and-under group than in Table 1.6 because the perpetrator's gender was unknown and therefore could not be included in Table 1.6.

Table 1.8 Psychological or Drug Problems of Perpetrator

Problems	Perpetrators	Percent
None mentioned	314	58.8
Psychological, mentioned*	157	29.4
Suicide, no note**	41	7.7
Drugs or alcohol	22	4.1
TOTAL	534	100.0

*This includes previous visits to mental health professionals, specific diagnoses, statements by neighbors, or suicides with notes indicating emotional problems.
**Suicide with no note left probably indicates emotional problems but was classified separately.

Table 1.9 Psychological or Drug Problems of Perpetrator by Number of Victims Killed

Problems	Number of Victims	Percent
None mentioned	285	43.2
Psychological, mentioned	250	37.9
Suicide, no note	69	10.4
Drugs or alcohol	56	8.5
TOTAL	660	100.0

Table 1.10 Known Employment Status of Perpetrators*

Status	Frequency	Percent
Under 18	108	30.0
18 or older in college	5	1.4
In poverty**	81	22.5
Employed†	145	40.3
Other‡	21	5.8
TOTAL	360	100.0

*In 508 instances where someone was charged there was not enough information to determine employment. In 17 instances the newspaper mentioned a former employment. In addition, in 107 cases no perpetrator was known.

**Includes 36 people specifically called "unemployed" in the newspaper articles, 33 on welfare, and 12 living in homeless shelters.

†Includes 50 perpetrators living with another person who was employed (see Table 1.11).

‡Includes those described in the sources only as "working": robbers, hired assassins, gang members et al., with no specific occupation mentioned.

Table 1.11 Gender of Perpetrator, and Employed Person, Living Together

Status	Perpetrators	Percent
Female perpetrator, male employed	21	42.0
Female perpetrator, both employed	3	6.0
Male perpetrator, female employed	7	14.0
Male perpetrator, both employed	5	10.0
Both were perpetrators*	14	28.0
TOTAL	50	100.0

*There were seven couples: in four, only the male worked; in one, only the female worked; and in two, both worked.

Table 1.12 Types of Occupations of Perpetrators*

Type of Occupation	Perpetrators	Percent
Laborers (minimum skill/education)	70	42.2
Technicians (technical training)	32	19.3
Managerial (supervising/owners)	15	9.0
Professional (advanced degrees)	13	7.8
Other**	36	21.7
TOTAL	166	100.0

*Includes the occupations of the working individuals counted in couples in Table 1.11.
**Includes people simply said to be "working" and people in illegal occupations.

Table 1.13 Victims Killed According to Method Used*

Cause	Number of Victims	Percent
Shooting	243	24.3
Beating**	232	23.2
Stabbing/slashing	150	15.0
Suffocating	145	14.5
Burning	73	7.3
Drowning	47	4.7
Other†	111	11.1
TOTAL	1,001	100.1

*Insufficient information on the cause of death of 97 victims.
**Includes shaken child syndrome cases.
†Includes causes of death too infrequent to be listed separately, such as poison, injection, etc.

Table 1.14 Method Used by Perpetrator(s) in Killing*

Method Used	Frequency	Percent
Beating	266	29.6
Shooting	196	21.8
Stabbing/slashing	123	13.7
Suffocating	105	11.7
Burning	49	5.4
Drowning	41	4.6
Other	120	13.3
TOTAL	900	100.1

*There was insufficient information on method in 92 cases.

Table 1.15 Method Used by Gender of Perpetrator*

Method Used	Male	%	Female	%	Total	% Total
Beating	172	69.4	76	30.6	248	31.0
Shooting	143	91.1	14	8.9	157	19.6
Stabbing/slashing	83	79.0	22	21.0	105	13.1
Suffocating	57	62.0	35	38.0	92	11.5
Burning	26	59.1	18	40.9	44	5.5
Drowning	17	42.5	23	57.5	40	5.0
Other	60	52.6	54	47.4	114	14.2
TOTAL	558	69.9	242	30.3	800	99.9

*There were 44 males and 27 females with insufficient information on method, and 14 perpetrators whose gender was not given. One of these stabbed, three beat, eight shot, and two killed their victims by other methods.

Table 1.16 Comparison of Methods Used by Individual Mothers, Fathers, and Lovers*

Method	Mothers	%	Fathers	%	Lovers	%	Total	%
Beating	18	17.6	44	43.1	40	39.2	102	31.6
Shooting	10	16.4	43	70.5	8	13.1	61	18.9
Suffocating	22	56.4	13	33.3	4	10.3	39	12.1
Stabbing/ slashing	15	42.9	15	42.9	5	14.3	35	10.8
Drowning	19	67.9	5	17.9	4	14.3	28	8.7
Burning	7	58.3	5	41.7	0	0.0	12	3.7
Other	28	60.9	15	32.6	3	6.5	46	14.2
TOTAL	119	36.8	140	43.3	64	19.8	323	100.0

*There were 20 mothers, 6 fathers, and 2 lovers whose methods were unknown.

Table 1.17 Number of Victims According to the Circumstances of the Killing*

Circumstances	Victims	Percent
Violent abuse**	453	46.2
Wrong place/time†	133	13.6
Mental/emotional	106	10.8
Sex abuse /cover-up	65	6.6
Bad decisions	58	5.9
Serial killer	56	5.7
Other‡	44	4.5
Newborn	38	3.9
Escalating argument	27	2.8
TOTAL	980	100.0

*The circumstances were unknown for 118 victims.
**Includes sustained abuse and violent attack.
†Includes attacks not aimed at child, crime cover-ups, family target, and "accidents."
‡Includes cases too infrequent to list separately, and 9 mercy killings.

Table 1.18 Circumstances by Victim's Age in Three-Year Groups*

Circumstances	0–3	4–6	7–9	10–12	Total	Percent
Violent abuse	271	90	50	26	437	47.0
Wrong place/ time	28	30	26	38	122	13.1
Mental/ emotional	39	19	25	13	96	10.3
Sex abuse / cover-up	11	8	24	18	61	6.6

Serial killer	29	5	6	16	56	6.0
Bad decisions	33	6	4	6	49	5.3
Other	15	9	11	9	44	4.7
Newborn	38	0	0	0	38	4.1
Escalating argument	4	5	7	11	27	2.9
TOTAL	468	172	153	137	930	100.0
Percent of Total	50.3	18.5	16.5	14.7	100.0	

*There were 50 victims where the ages of the victims were unknown.

Table 1.19 Circumstances According to the Known Gender of the Perpetrator

Circumstances	Male	%	Female	%	Total	%
Violent abuse	117	61.9	72	38.1	189	23.0
Sudden attack	86	78.2	24	21.8	110	13.4
Sustained abuse	60	56.6	46	43.4	106	12.9
Mental/ emotional*	36	54.5	30	45.5	66	8.0
Witness/ family target**	59	95.2	3	4.8	62	7.6
Other†	42	68.9	19	31.1	61	7.4
Sex abuse/ cover-up	51	98.1	1	1.9	52	6.3
Bad decisions‡	22	45.8	26	54.2	48	5.9
Newborn	4	11.8	30	88.2	34	4.1
Escalating argument	29	93.5	2	6.5	31	3.8
Wrong place/ time#	29	93.5	2	6.5	31	3.8
Serial killer	20	66.7	10	33.3	30	3.7
TOTAL	555	67.7	265	32.3	820	99.9

*The female column includes three diagnosed cases of postpartum psychosis.
**Includes perpetrators whose victims were witness to a crime or were members of a targeted family.
†Includes circumstances too infrequent to list separately, nine of which were called mercy killings, with 3 male and 6 female perpetrators, and cases called accidents, with 7 male and 1 female perpetrators.
‡Includes cases where drug use caused perpetrators to forget about a child's needs, and cases where medical help was not sought for a child because of religious reasons.
#Includes only those perpetrators whose target was not the victim or the victim's family.

Table 1.20 Known Relationship of Victims to Lone Perpetrators

Relationship	Number of Victims	Percent
Parent	423	50.9
Paramour	82	9.9
Adoptive	7	0.8
Foster	17	2.0
Friends, neighbors, in-laws	92	11.1
Other biological kin	63	7.6
Strangers	74	8.9
Step kin	21	2.5
Other*	52	6.3
TOTAL	831	100.0

*Includes baby sitters, nurses, co-workers or employees of parents.

Table 1.21 Relationship of Individual Perpetrators to Victims by Perpetrator Gender

Relationship	Male	Female	Unknown	Total	%
Parent	142	133	0	275	47.3
Step relative	16	3	0	19	3.3
Paramour	64	1	0	65	11.2
Foster relative	5	5	0	10	1.7
Biological relative	38	10	0	48	8.2
Adopted relative	2	5	0	7	1.2
Neighbor, friend, in-law	69	2	1	72	12.4
Stranger	52	2	0	54	9.3
Other	21	9	2	32	5.5
TOTAL	409	170	3	582	100.1

Table 1.22 Relationship of Victims to At Least One Individual in Perpetrator Groups

Relationship	Number of Victims	Percent
At least one biological parent	72	48.0
Adopted family	3	2.0
Biological kin	4	2.7
Foster	7	4.7
Friends, neighbors, et al.	23	15.3
Step family	2	1.3
All strangers	30	20.0
Other	9	6.0
TOTAL	150	100.0

Table 1.23 Household Situation Where Known, by Cases

Household	Cases	Percent
Broken, blended*	272	43.1
Biological parents**	164	26.0
Outsiders†	195	30.9
TOTAL	631	100.0

*Households with a single, divorced, or estranged parent, stepparent, or adopted parents.
**Households where the partners were married or had been living together long enough for both to be parents of the victim.
†The household arrangement was not relevant because the victim was killed in the course of another crime, such as a robbery, or by people who were never members of the household.

Table 1.24 Gender of Children Killed in Foster Homes

Gender	Victims	Percent
Male	13	54.2
Female	11	45.8
TOTAL	24	100.0

Table 1.25 Age by Gender of Children Killed in Foster Homes

Gender	0–3 Years	4–6 Years	7–9 Years	10–12 Years	Percent
Male	6	1	4	2	54.2
Female	4	5	1	1	45.8
TOTAL	10	6	5	3	100.0
Percent of Total	41.7	25.0	20.8	12.5	

Table 1.26 Time Victims Were Home Following Return After Removal

Time Home	Victims	Percent
Less than 10 weeks	9	39.1
11 to 19 weeks	0	0.0
20 to 32 weeks	3	13.0
33 to 36 weeks	0	0.0
37 to 45 weeks	2	8.7
46 to 51 weeks	3	13.0
Less than one year, not specific	4	17.4
Time home not given	2	8.7
TOTAL	23	99.9

Table 1.27 Age by Gender of Victims Killed After Returning Home

Gender	0–3 Years	4–6 Years	7–9 Years	Percent
Male	10	1	2	56.5
Female	5	4	1	43.5
TOTAL	15	5	3	100.0
Percent of Total	65.2	21.7	13.0	99.9

Table 1.28 Gender of Victims Killed After Returning Home

Gender	Number of Victims	Percent
Male	13	56.5
Female	10	43.5
TOTAL	23	100.0

Table 1.29 Relationship of Household Killers to Victims (Cases)

Relationship	Cases	Percent
Biological parents	295	61.2
1 biol. parent plus others*	37	7.7
Close kin (not parents)**	39	8.1
Lovers and past lovers†	66	13.7
Step relatives‡	19	3.9
Adopted relatives	10	2.1
Foster relatives	16	3.3
TOTAL	482	100.0

*Includes mothers with lovers, with stepparents, with a grandmother of the victim, with an acquaintance; fathers with stepmother, father who was also a stepfather to some victims.

**Includes grandparents, siblings and half siblings, maternal or paternal siblings, grandparents' siblings.

†Includes mother's lovers and former lovers, a grandmother's lover, a godmother's lover, and two father's girlfriends.

‡The term "relatives" includes parents, siblings, uncles, and cousins of the step, adopted, or foster families.

Table 1.30 Household Killers Who Were Non-Relatives (Cases)

Relationship	Cases	Percent
Mother's lovers (alone)	53	36.1
Mother's lover w/mother	24	16.3

Former lovers and friends*	15	10.2
Biol. mother and stepfather	8	5.4
Biol. father and stepmother	1	0.7
Stepparent relatives	19	12.9
Adopted relatives	10	6.8
Foster parents	12	8.2
Foster siblings	2	1.4
Parafosters	3	2.0
TOTAL	147	100.0

*Includes two older males identified as "baby sitters," two others identified as "friends" who were taking care of the victims in the absence of the mother, and two father's girlfriends.

Table 1.31 Killers in the Nuclear Family (Cases)

Relationship	Cases	Percent
Biological mother	132	42.7
Biological father	142	46.0
Both	21	6.8
Full siblings	10	3.2
Half siblings	4	1.3
TOTAL	309	100.0

Table 1.32 Killer's Rationale for the Killing

Rationale	Frequency	Percent
Discipline	30	7.4
Mercy killing	13	3.2
Religious	30	7.4
Revenge	19	4.7
Remove witness*	83	20.6
Meant well	10	2.5
Accident	35	8.7
Anger at child	74	18.4
Anger (generalized)	17	4.2
Crazy	20	5.0
Other	72	17.9
TOTAL	403	100.0

*This category was automatically assigned when the victim was sexually assaulted or was killed in the commission of some other crime. The rest were based on reported statements made by the accused.

Table 1.33 Perpetrator's Relationship to Victim by Victim's Age*

Age	Parent	%	Kin	%	Non-Relative**	%	Total
0–3	288	58.5	23	4.7	181	36.8	492
4–6	89	45.6	12	6.2	94	48.2	195
7–9	57	30.5	13	7.0	117	62.6	187
10-12	32	18.4	13	7.5	129	74.1	174
TOTAL	466	44.5	61	5.8	521	49.7	1,048

*There were 50 victims with ages unknown.
**Includes adoptive and foster relatives, step relatives, nonrelated in-laws, friends, neighbors, and strangers.

Table 1.34 Criminal and Child Maltreatment History of Perpetrators

Perpetrator History	Perpetrators	Percent
No criminal record	9	1.9
No record mentioned, long article	296	61.0
Criminal record	73	15.1
Record with Social Services	63	13.0
Criminal, Social Services record	7	1.4
Perp. age 14 or less	37	7.6
TOTAL	485	100.0

Table 1.35 Criminal and Child Maltreatment History of Perpetrator by Number of Victims Killed

Perpetrator History	Victims	Percent
No criminal record	10	1.8
No record mentioned, long article	339	61.2
Criminal record	118	21.3
Record with Social Services	52	9.4
Criminal, Social Services record	6	1.1
Perp. age 14 or less	29	5.2
TOTAL	554	100.0

CHAPTER 2

Multiple Killers: Mass Murderers and Serial Killers

Most of the perpetrators in our files killed only one or two children each. A few, however, killed a number of people, either at once or over a period of years. The term "multiple killer" is used here for serial killers, spree killers, and mass murderers. Although they represent a small percentage of the killers of children, these exceptions receive more notoriety and cause greater public concern than the more common perpetrator who has only one victim.

Most of the books and articles written about mass murderers and serial killers deal with males. Only a few authors in the decade of the 1990s have paid attention to female mass murderers or serial killers, and most of those studies do not focus on the ones with children as their victims. *The Death of Innocents* (Firstman and Talan, 1997) is an exception, since it details the discovery and prosecution of serial killers of the children in two different families. The book concentrates on the difficulties of distinguishing between SIDS (sudden infant death syndrome) and the murder of infants; one of the serial killers is a male, the other a female. Because of the general shortage of information about child killers, it is important to indicate what our data can add about female mass murderers as well as about serial killers, who are not always the male sexual predators usually depicted in the popular and scholarly literature.

Part of the reason for the lack of information lies in the definitions of "mass murderer" and "serial killer." The whole topic of societal violence is rife with contending definitions that have hindered understanding and the development of effective methods for dealing with the issues. Both serial killers and mass murderers are multiple killers — that is, they both kill more than one victim. We looked at all multiple murderers, regardless of whether they could be labeled spree killers, mass murderers, or serial killers. We found two different but overlapping perpetrator populations in our files: 1) those who had reportedly only killed children in our sample — that is, children age 12 and under killed between 1977 and 1993; and 2) those who killed people outside our sample's age and time frame in addition to the victims in the sample. Tables 2.1 and 2.2 summarize the gender characteristics of the multiple killers. The discrepancies in specific categories in the two tables occur because some individuals moved out of one category into another. For example, there were 26 females in Table 2.1 who killed two children in the sample, but only 24 females who killed two victims. Two of the women counted in the two-victim category in Table 2.1 are in the three-victim category in Table 2.2 because along with the two children in the sample they each had another victim — either someone older, or someone killed before 1977. The overall total of both male and female killers rose when victims outside the sample were counted. There were 176 perpetrators who killed two or more children when only those in our sample were counted; there were 299 people who killed both victims in our child sample and others outside the age or time range.

None of the multiple killers whom we counted includes people responsible for car accidents, such as the drunken driver who smashed into a church bus in Kentucky in 1988 and killed twenty-seven people, at least seven of whom were children age 12 or younger. Although the driver was clearly at fault in that case and was charged with murder, he had no intention of killing anyone. The mass murderers and serial killers counted here deliberately killed their victims.

Mass Murderers

The criminology literature agrees that the term "mass murderer" refers to perpetrators who kill more than one victim at once, or at least within hours of each other. This category eliminates serial murderers, whose killings are weeks, months, or even years apart. But what is the lower limit of victims who have to be killed to qualify someone as a mass murderer rather than simply a killer? Here, the criminology literature is not consistent. An article by Holmes and Holmes (1992:53) uses three victims as the lower limit, while an article by Park Dietz (1986:480) uses five wounded and three killed. Dietz chose his figures based on statistics for violent crime. The Bureau of Justice Statistics for 1983 indicated that only 1.7 percent of the cases of violent crime involved three victims, and only 1 percent involved four or more. Dietz therefore decided that the least restrictive definition for mass murder would be "the willful injuring of five or more persons of whom three or more are killed by a single offender in a single incident." We tabulated all cases where perpetrators killed more than one victim (Tables 2.1 and 2.2), however, in order to learn what characteristics were correlated with the number of victims. We counted only people who successfully killed more than one victim and did not include those who tried but failed. A little more attention is given to killers with four victims, as being a compromise between three and five. Certainly, the number of victims used in any definition of mass murder is admittedly arbitrary. The figure becomes meaningful only when or if a discernible pattern emerges in the characteristics of victims, killers, or the circumstances surrounding the crimes.

There is one pattern that seems significant. Tables 2.3 and 2.4 show the frequencies for known mass murderers only; serial killers and cases with unknown perpetrators are omitted. Using the figure of four victims as a definition of a mass killer, an interesting pattern appears: 13 males and 6 females who killed four or more victims killed only those in the sample (Table 2.3). Table 2.4, however, shows a major leap in male killers, from 13 to 76 male perpetrators who killed four or more victims including adults and children older than age 12, but only eight women did so.

One result of including victims outside as well as inside the sample is that the number of perpetrators increases, from 57 to 144 (Tables 2.3 and 2.4). As the number of victims increases, however, the number of perpetrators decreases. This is true both for the killers of children in the sample, and those who killed adults and older children as well. The drop is especially sharp in the case of the children age 12 and under (from 38 to 6 compared with 60 to 37). Dietz reports a similar drop in violent crime from the Bureau of Justice Statistics (1986:480).

The mass murderers counted in Table 2.4 who killed four or more victims often killed members of their extended family along with their spouses and children. Males killed in-laws, more distant relatives, and even people outside the family or household who were in some way involved in their lives, as in the cases of Gene Simmons and George Banks (described below). Most of the women who included victims other than children age 12 and under limited themselves to family members.

In our records the largest number of victims intentionally killed by a single mass murderer was seventeen, fifteen of whom were related either by blood or marriage to the killer, R. Gene Simmons (age 47). The other two victims were his co-workers. Simmons had been in trouble before the murders. He fled from New Mexico with his family some time before 1987, to escape three indictments for incest with his daughter Sheila. He may have fathered one of her children. Since the New Mexico police could not find him, they dropped the charges.

In 1987, when the killings occurred, the family had been living in Arkansas for about five years. According to the police reconstruction, Simmons probably began by strangling his sleeping children on Christmas Day. Presents were wrapped and under the tree. He apparently started with Sylvia (6), who was his granddaughter and possibly also his daughter from the incestuous relationship with Sheila. Simmons next killed his remaining minor children: Eddie (14), Loretta (17), Marianne (11), and Rebecca (8). Then he killed his wife and Sheila, who was now married to Dennis McNulty, by whom she had had a child, Michael (21 months old). Simmons killed Dennis and Michael, his grown son William, William's wife Renoda and their 20-month-old son William Jr., as well as another grown son, Ronald Gene Jr., his wife Becky, and their 3-year-old daughter Barbara. In sum, Simmons murdered seven of his children, three grandchildren, and one child who might have been both a child and a grandchild. He also killed his wife, one son-in-law, and two daughters-in-law.

As soon as businesses were open on the day after Christmas, Simmons went into town, shot a secretary at a law office, killed a man in an oil company office where he had worked, wounded two more at a grocery store owned by an officer of the same company, and wounded another woman at a motor freight office. He barricaded himself with a hostage at the freight office but was finally talked out by police. The president of the freight company said that the wounded woman had rejected Simmons's "amorous affect" (affections?). After the killings, Simmons, a former Air Force master sergeant, never offered any explanations or answered questions by police or news media personnel. He spoke only to his lawyers, who honored confidentiality.

Simmons was convicted and sentenced to death. He asked that the sentence be carried out as soon as possible. It was not. Although he waived appeals, saying, "Let the torture and suffering in me end" — a statement never explained in any of the articles about the case — the defense got a change of venue and appealed. Simmons was tried again, convicted, and sentenced to death once more, but a priest claimed that he was incompetent when he waived his appeals right, and so the defense appealed again. The State Supreme Court rejected the appeal but the Federal Court in Little Rock considered the case. The U.S. Supreme Court blocked Simmons's first execution date, but he was finally put to death in 1990, three years after the multiple killings (Case 381).

The killer with the next largest number of victims was George E. Banks. At the end of September 1982, Banks shot thirteen people with an AR-15 semi-automatic weapon, killing twelve of them. Seven of the victims were children under age 12, five of whom were his own. Banks, 40 years old, was a prison guard who had been on sick leave since the beginning of September. He thought he was being poisoned and that there was a conspiracy against him; he had sought help at a mental clinic but was turned away on the grounds that he was "not overtly suicidal or homicidal." Earlier, he had served seven and one-half years in jail for robbery. The prison knew his record when he was hired in 1980, but he was described as a "good employee." After the killings, one doctor diagnosed him as "terminally paranoid" and incompetent, but another said that he was competent to stand trial.

Despite the fact that he had killed five of his own children, he was described by people who knew him as a "good father" and a highly religious man, with a mail-order minister's degree. Eight of the victims were killed in the Wilkes-Barre, Pennsylvania, house where Banks lived with three women. Two people were killed nearby but outside the house, and four more were murdered in a mobile home in Jenkins Township about five miles away. Two other children in the mobile home hid in a closet and were unhurt. Banks held off police for eight hours, but his mother finally persuaded him to surrender. Banks had been having a dispute with Sharon Mazzillo, who lived in the trailer park, over the custody of Kissmayu (5), his son by her and one of the children killed. Banks also killed Sharon; another of her children, Scott (7), whom Banks had not fathered; and Sharon's mother.

Witnesses earlier had seen Banks abusing the three women whom he had killed in the Wilkes-Barre house that they shared, but previously he had never hurt the children. Someone said that he "doted on kids, but beat up on women." Each of the women had borne him children; he killed them all as well as one of the women's 11-year-old child, whom he had not fathered. Banks also killed an adult male who lived across the street. All of the women were white. Banks himself was said by the newspaper articles to be illegitimate, the son of a white mother and an African-American father. In addition to the women with whom he was or had been living, Banks was married to an African-American woman in Ohio. He was quoted in articles as saying that he killed people "because he loved them" after he "awoke from drug and alcohol abuse," although he claimed he was neither drunk nor drugged at the time of the murders. He also said that the killing spree was the culmination of forty years of racist hatred. The news articles reported that he resented both his mother's people and his father's. Banks was convicted and sentenced to death, a sentence confirmed by the Pennsylvania Supreme Court, which ruled that he was legally sane and competent to stand trial (Case 178).

Several of the individual male mass murderers in our records killed ten victims. One case involved jealousy, greed, and attempted robbery, with some drug dealing thrown in. In April 1984, Christopher Thomas (34) of Brooklyn planned to steal money and drugs from Enrique Bermudez, a small-time convicted drug dealer for whom he occasionally worked. Thomas then planned to use the same money to pay off a debt owed to Bermudez. To pay back a debt with money stolen from the person to whom the debt was owed must have seemed very clever to him. Also, Thomas wrongly believed that Bermudez was having an affair with Thomas's estranged wife, so he wanted revenge. Thomas wiped out everyone in the Bermudez home at the time except for an 11-month-old infant. His estranged wife did not live there, and Enrique Bermudez was not at home, so neither of them was injured.

Thomas was already in jail on sodomy charges for raping a relative when he was charged with the Bermudez murders. Despite the ten deaths, he was eventually acquitted of murder by the jury because, according to the newspaper article, they believed that he was under the influence of drugs or "strong emotion" at the time of the killings. He was convicted of manslaughter and sentenced to a minimum of eight and one-third to a maximum of twenty-five years on each of ten counts, the sentences to be served consecutively. Under New York State law, Thomas will be eligible for parole in twenty-five years after entering prison. His lawyers had pleaded for a "humane sentence" and did not believe that they received one, so they planned to appeal, but no additional articles about the case had appeared in the *New York Times* up to 1993 (Case 264).

In April 1989, in Glen Ellen, California, Ramon Salcido, a 28-year-old fork-lift operator in a winery, killed nine people: his wife, his parents-in-law, their other children, his own children, and a co-worker. One of his children survived his attempt to kill her. He was drinking heavily beforehand and went on a cocaine and alcohol binge afterward as he fled. According to the newspaper, the police traced him through his use of his credit card. He was convicted in October 1990 and sentenced to death in November, but the case was appealed. In the appeal, the defense asked for a manslaughter or second-degree murder verdict because "drugs had him in a psychotic depression." An article reporting the filing of an appeal in February 1991 was the last on the case in the *New York Times* before the end of 1993 (Case 457).

Ramon Concepcion is an example of an individual male mass murderer whose case had some unusual elements. In May 1993 in Harlem, New York City, Ramon killed three children and three adults. The first victim was Maria Rodriguez (27), his former lover; after an argument, he stabbed her in the back. Then he beat and strangled her mother, Bienvenida Rodriguez. Maria's son by an earlier relationship, 11-year-old Billy Getz, may have tried to come to his mother's assistance; he was strangled with electrical cord. His sister, Jennifer Getz (5), was beaten and strangled to death. Finally, Maria's youngest child, Linda Javier (18 months), was beaten to death. Ramon then slept in the apartment overnight and went to a Yankees baseball game the next day. When he returned to the apartment about six in the evening, he met Rufino Lopez, Bienvenida's lover. They fought, and Ramon killed Rufino by stabbing him ten times in the head, four times in the back, and twice in the chest. On Sunday night, Ramon slept in the apartment again. About 6:15 on Monday morning he poured paint thinner on the beds and started a fire. Then he hurried to work in the mattress factory where he was a machine operator.

His relationship with Maria had been a stormy one from the start. He had forbidden the Getz children to see their paternal grandmother, Angelas

Miranda, although Angelas claimed that she did not know why. According to the newspaper article, Ramon was very jealous. He bothered Maria so much that she fled to Puerto Rico with Linda, the baby, and had only returned a month before the attack. Maria and her mother had filed four complaints against Ramon for harassing them and for breaking windows. Again, according to the paper, Maria wanted to "improve herself" — she was trying to get off welfare and had just earned her GED — and Ramon did not like it. The newspaper said that Ramon's neighbors and co-workers described him as a "sweet man" and were surprised when he was arrested. He was charged with six counts of second-degree murder. There was no article in the *New York Times* on the outcome (Case 782).

While jealousy and generalized rage seem to motivate some mass murderers, depression can also play a role. Neil Schatz Sr., a 55-year-old county commissioner in Sullivan, Missouri, owned a construction company, but all was not well. He recently had lost a close election as the Republican candidate for a seat in the Missouri House of Representatives. He was struggling with depression and taking medication for a heart ailment. In March 1992 he killed himself, two children, and three adults with a twelve-gauge shotgun after a family gathering in a rural farmhouse about sixty miles southwest of St. Louis. The children, Brett Schatz (8) and Ryan Lamb (3 months), were his grandsons. Neil Sr. also killed his son, Neil Schatz Jr., who was Brett's father, and his daughter Cindy Schatz Lamb, who was Ryan's mother, as well as his own wife, Sarah, and finally himself. His mother, who lived next door, found the bodies. There was no additional information in the *New York Times* (Case 745).

Most female mass murderers did not kill as many victims as the males did. One mother who had eleven victims, all her children, had left them alone in the house and there was a fire; the children then died of smoke inhalation (Case 174). Three women also killed their husbands, but most female mass murderers killed only their childern. One example is Jeanne Anne Wright (25) of Camden, New Jersey, who was unmarried and six months pregnant with her fifth child in November 1983. She had grand mal epilepsy and, according to her mother, was "like a little girl who has never grown up" but was a "good mother." Her first three children were by one man who, according to Jeanne, abused both her and the children. Recently she had begun to worry that he was going to come and kidnap the children, her relatives said. Although she was upset at what she saw as her inability to care for her children, she thought that they would be better off dead than returning to their father. The children were Janah (7), Emilio (5), Johnathan (2), and Juan (almost 1). On November 11, Jeanne took all the children down to the river where she sat on a plank with them for some time "trying to think." Finally she "placed" them in the river as they slept. She indignantly denied "pushing" them off a bridge into the water. She reported them missing on November 13 and at first said that a man in a white car had taken her and the kids to the railroad trestle near the bridge. People searched there for the bodies. Police, however, thought that there were inconsistencies in her story and on December 14, after the bodies of Juan and Johnathan were found, Jeanne was indicted for murder. Emilio's body was not discovered until February 1984, and Janah's body was never found. Jeanne pleaded not guilty, and the court-appointed attorney said that she would pursue an insanity defense but then accepted a plea bargain. Jeanne was sentenced to four concurrent life terms with no possibility of parole for thirty years. Even the district attorney admitted that a death sentence would not have been appropriate because of Jeanne's history and mental state, although thirty years with no possibility of parole was hardly a light sentence (Case 260). This case could also have appeared in Chapter 4, on mental and emotional problems. It is an example of the complex and multiple factors that enter into the attempt to understand mass murderers as well as into the entire issue of the murders of children.

There was only one article in the *New York Times* about a second female mass murderer, Gail Trait, who killed her four children on July 17, 1978, in Buffalo, New York. That article detailed her conviction on four counts of second-degree murder in the deaths of the unnamed children: a 2-year-old boy and three girls ranging in age from 4 to 9. She had pleaded insanity, but the jury apparently did not agree. The *Times* did not mention her sentence or give any additional details. The Buffalo newspaper, however, was more informative: the three girls were Kylia (8), Amina (6), and Inez (4); the 2-year-old boy was named Demario. Their mother, Gail Trait (26), had been separated from their father for about two years. She was a student at Erie Community College, a liberal arts major specializing in social sciences, and had recently moved with her children into her mother's apartment. The children, who had been in the custody of the Erie County child welfare officials, had been returned to her two weeks before they were killed.

Gail's defense attorney attempted to convince the jury that she was insane at the time of the crime. Several psychiatrists for the defense and the prosecution testified, those for the defense saying that she was a paranoid schizophrenic and those for the prosecution saying that she had killed in anger and knew what she was doing. The jury believed the prosecution psychiatrists, and Gail was convicted in December 1979. She was sentenced to twenty-five years to life in prison on February 25, 1980, but on June 15, 1988, New York State's high court refused to block an April 8, 1988, ruling granting her a new trial. This last *Buffalo News* article said that she had killed her children in a voodoo rite, which had been mentioned when she first was arrested but which the police said was "unfounded." We have no record of additional articles, and she was still in prison in June 1988 (Case 57).

The most recent case of a female mass murderer in our files is that of Maria Isabella Amaya in Port Chester, New York. In May 1990 she killed four of her children: William (11), Jessica (8), Christopher (6), and Edward (3). Maria stabbed the children and herself while her husband was at work. She was in critical condition in the hospital at the time the articles were written. The family had emigrated from El Salvador "a decade ago," according to the newspaper. Her husband was a maintenance worker at the Westchester County Medical Center. They had lived in the house in Port Chester for three to five years (two articles differed on the amount of time that the family had spent there). Maria had been treated for mental problems, had been hospitalized, and was on medication; moreover, she had an appointment that she did not keep with a psychiatrist on the afternoon of the killing. Her husband became concerned when she missed the appointment, so he went home and there found the bodies. There was no information in the articles as to whether she ultimately succeeded in her suicide attempt (Case 615).

All the mass murderers described above acted as individuals. Four women, however, were charged together with a male or males. In one instance, the couple left the children locked in a room and a steam radiator valve broke (Case 70, described in Chapter 7). In two cases, the victims were not relatives. In one case, the perpetrators were acquaintances trying to collect money; they stabbed two adults and one child (Case 608). In the other case, which follows, a group of people — one a woman — became mass killers.

Alice Lundgren is one of the few female mass murderers in our files who killed both children and adults. Alice (39) was convicted of five counts of conspiracy, complicity to commit aggravated murder, and kidnapping; she was sentenced to five consecutive life terms. Her husband, Jeff Lundgren (39), was convicted of five counts of murder and sentenced to death. Their son Damon (19) was convicted of four murders but acquitted on the fifth; he was sentenced to four consecutive sentences that added up to a minimum of 120 years. The three were founders of an offshoot Mormon religious sect. Their victims — all members of the Avery family: Dennis, Cheryl, and their three children, Karen, Rebecca, and Trina — were also members of the sect. None of the three newspaper articles about the case reported the method used to kill the Averys. The articles also differed on the children's ages: one said that they were 5, 7, and 13, respectively; the other reported them as 7, 13, and 15. In either case, at least one is in our sample of children age 12 and under. The Lundgrens and the Averys had been living in a commune in Ohio in 1989, and, according to Alice Lundgren, her husband criticized the Averys as insufficiently zealous. The Lundgrens were sentenced in 1990 but, because of mandatory appeals, Jeff Lundgren had not been executed by 1993, the last year for which we collected data (Case 494).

In the final case, perhaps the woman should not have been counted as a mass murderer since, according to letters sent both to a newspaper and to a television station in Lebanon, New Hampshire, the man did the actual killing although the woman participated in the planning. In 1986, Caroline Hull, the widow of a disabled Vietnam veteran with three children, wrote suicide letters saying that she and her lover, Michael Dean, another disabled Vietnam veteran, killed themselves and the children in frustration over the treatment that veterans and their families were receiving. She wrote the letter as if these acts had already happened. Her lover was to shoot all of them, set the house on fire, and then kill himself. That is apparently what happened. The pair gave sleeping pills to Jeremy (5), Theresa (4), and Kenneth (11) before Michael shot them. Michael had moved in with Caroline after her husband, whom Michael had known, died about two years earlier. The letter said that they were both tired of fighting a system they wanted to forget. Michael was receiving a 70 percent psychiatric disability pension. Family members told reporters that both Caroline and Michael were very concerned about the

Reagan administration's cutbacks because the Veteran Disability benefits were the only income they had (Case 339).

Concern for a bleak economic future contributed to Caroline and Michael's tragic end, and it played a role in the Almarez case as well. In 1980, Stella Delores Almarez (29) of Norfolk, Nebraska, shot two of her four children and stabbed the other two, then tried unsuccessfully to kill herself with a shot to the head. Although she was married, she and her husband were planning a divorce, and she said that she was depressed at the thought of having to raise her children on welfare. She was found not guilty by reason of insanity, sent to a mental health center for five years, and unconditionally released in 1985 (Case 482).

For a variety of reasons — some clear and others less so — mass murders attract a great deal more attention and concern from the public than do individual killings, unless the victim of the single killing is famous or related to a celebrity. Because of this interest, speculation as to the motives for mass killing has prompted a number of books. One, Elliott Leyton's *Hunting Humans* (1986), suggests that race or class hatred motivates mass murderers. In the Banks case, George Banks claimed race hatred as his reason, but in the other cases described, race was not a factor. Other writers have suggested economic woes as a major factor; and, in the last two cases described, economic concerns were expressed by the perpetrator. In the other cases, even when the killer was suffering from depression, it was not necessarily brought on by economic troubles. Also, insanity may well be a factor in some cases. No single telling factor emerges, however. The mass murderers seem to be distinguished from the perpetrators who kill only one child in the study population mainly by the number of victims. They tend to be somewhat older than the killers of one victim, but that may simply be because older perpetrators have had time to produce more children and thus have more available victims.

As stated before, the lack of a clear, straightforward definition is one of the problems in studying mass murder. The Dann case bears this out. According to our files, Laurie Dann killed only one child, 8-year old Nicholas Corwin, of Winnetka, Illinois, in 1988 (Case 403). She is, however, one of the few females who can be considered a would-be mass murderer who acted alone and did not kill members of her own family. Her situation is an example of the difficulty in choosing a lower limit for mass murderers. According to *Murder of Innocence*, by Joel Kaplan et al., "If she had been successful . . .

[Laurie] would have fatally poisoned at least fifty people, shot to death at least a dozen schoolchildren, incinerated three members of [one] . . . family . . . and burned down two schools with 440 children inside" (1990:298). The article in the *New York Times* in our records was in response to a civil suit against her parents and mentioned only that she had fired on a second-grade class, killing Nicholas and wounding five other children, then wounded a seventh person, barricaded herself in a house, and committed suicide. Kaplan's book, of course, is much more detailed than the newspaper article and explores Laurie's background as well as her possible state of mind at the time of the crimes. While the *Times* article did not even hint at a motive, it suggested that she had long-standing emotional problems. The book, however, makes it clear that she was mentally ill, had had problems for which she was treated for years, and, on the day of the killing, was out to get everyone who had ever, in her mind, done her any kind of an injury.

Laurie apparently committed suicide because she could not escape being caught, not because she was filled with remorse over what she had done. She tried to get away from the scene of the shooting, unlike most of the suicides in our records, but failed to go far before she was trapped. When she realized that the house was surrounded, she killed herself. We do not count her as a mass murderer in our analyses because, as mentioned, we counted only successful killers of three or more victims. Nevertheless, her case illustrates the arbitrary nature of whatever limit is chosen for labeling mass murderers. Should individuals who attempt to kill many people, but fail, be studied as mass murderers? If mass murderers are indeed different from people who kill only one victim, then the people who try to kill more should probably be included in any study even when they fail in their attempts. If those who tried but failed were counted in this study, our files would have several more female mass murderers but only a few more males. This issue is discussed again in the next to last chapter.

Serial Killers

According to Philip Jenkins, "This type of crime has attracted enormous public attention. . . . Both in fiction and in true crime, there were considerably more publications in the three years from 1991 through 1993 than in the 1960s and 1970s combined" (Jenkins, 1994:2). He suggests that "serial murder has increased significantly in the United States in the last three decades . . .

but even today, this type of violence accounts for only about 1 percent of American homicides, and possibly less" (1994:13).

Serial killers, like mass murderers, are defined in a number of ways. According to Jenkins, there are three types of multiple murder: 1) mass murder, committed in a brief period in one place; 2) spree killings, carried out over a few days or weeks; and 3) serial murder, "which implies that the killings are spread over months or years with a cooling off period intervening" (1994:21). Jenkins argues that the term "should simply mean multiple acts of criminal homicide committed over a period of time," but he points out that the common usage is more limited although "the reasons for excluding some types of behavior are quite arbitrary" (1994:23). An example of the arbitrary nature is the FBI standard, which limits serial killers by several criteria; one is that "he must claim three or more victims in at least three separate incidents" (King, 1993:11). Why three victims? And why three separate incidents? This definition, along with others, is so specific in the qualifications for serial killers that it excludes many multiple murderers who kill over time. For example, some definitions limit serial killers to males who kill for the thrill alone (Giannangelo, 1996:5), which allows the cases the author uses to fit his hypotheses. While this is a valid subclass of serial killers, leaving out so many people who kill more than once over time adds little to our understanding of the phenomenon. Jenkins defines serial killers as those who have killed "at least four victims, over a period greater than seventy-two hours. Excluded are cases where the offender acted primarily out of political motives or in quest of financial profit" (Jenkins, 1994:23).

Eliminating political assassins and criminal hit men from our discussion makes sense. These people have been well studied and seem to be relatively well understood. But why limit the killings to four, as Jenkins did, or to three, as the FBI standard does? Gary King's book discusses Wesley Allan Dodd as a serial killer even though his three victims (all in our files) were killed in only two "incidents." In one of the incidents, Dodd killed two brothers. If one of the brothers had survived, would Dodd then not be a serial killer? Three seems as arbitrary a number as four. Our study includes spree killers (in which the killings occur in different places and over a period of days or weeks) with serial murderers, and classifies cases like those committed by Simmons and Banks (which took place in different locations but were clearly part of one "incident") with mass murderers. It defines serial killers as Jenkins did but lowers the number of victims to more than one instead of four. There is no good reason why serial killers should not include perpetrators with only two victims, so long as those two were separated by a period of weeks or months and meet the other qualifications in Jenkins's definition.

Jenkins's definition also allows the inclusion of women and other people who kill for nonsexual motives, as ours does. Again, this inclusion seems sensible. Limiting the gender of serial killers to male and the motivation to a sexual one would exclude over half the perpetrators (including all the women) in our files who killed their victims over time. The more limiting definition tends to feed a false association made by some news media and law enforcement groups between homosexuality, pedophilia, and serial killing. It also supports the false association of serial killings with men as killers and women as victims, promoted by some women's associations (Jenkins, 1994:139 passim). To understand what makes people kill more than once, we need to look at everyone who does so. Such an examination reveals that there is not just one type of serial killer, but several.

Individual serial killers may have more victims than mass murderers but since they kill them over a longer time, they are not so easily detected. Several deaths may occur before anyone realizes that a serial killer is responsible. It was a year before people generally accepted the idea that some of the Atlanta child murders were the work of a serial killer. This delayed recognition is particularly true when the victims are not sexually molested, as was the case in Atlanta, since the general public tends to think of sexual deviance as the primary motive for serial killers. A number of the women in our records escaped detection for years both because of the stereotype that does not include women, especially mothers, as serial killers and because of the frequent omission of an autopsy when a child dies. The difficulty of distinguishing SIDS from deliberate smothering adds an additional complication when a baby under 6 months of age dies (Firstman and Talan, 1997: passim).

We have records of thirty serial killers in our files: twenty males and ten females (Table 2.5). According to Jenkins, "serial killers are considerably more diverse than is suggested by some recent claims. Women and racial minorities are quite well represented, while sex-killers do not hold quite the monopoly they appear to" (1994:14). Of course, so long as people exclude all but sex-killers from their definitions, the sex-killers will certainly have a monopoly. That is one reason to adopt the more inclusive definition.

What about the serial killer who murders children? Serial killers often specialize (Sears, 1991:48). Ted Bundy killed young women but not usually children. He came into our files because one of his victims happened to be a 12-year-old girl; all the others were older. The Atlanta child killer, on the other hand, specialized in young boys, most of whom were under 12. He is believed to have killed at least twenty youths although he was only tried and convicted for two, neither of which was the proper age for our sample (Sears, 1991:43).

Prosecutors frequently do not try killers for the deaths of all of their victims. Sometimes, prosecuters may be given an option of trying the accused another time with a different case if they do not succeed in getting a conviction the first time. In other situations, a prosecutor may wish to try only the case or cases with the best evidence. Whatever the prosecutor's reason for trying Wayne B. Williams, the accused Atlanta child killer of 1979–1981, on only two counts, the police closed the cases of eight victims in our files when he was convicted.

Most studies, including Donald Sears's *To Kill Again* (1991), analyze only male serial killers. Yet in our records one-third of the serial killers of children are female. Consequently, some attention to possible differences in patterns between male and female serial killers is important, and differing patterns do occur. Six of the ten female serial killers were mothers of their victims (Table 2.6), which does not fit the pattern for male killers analyzed by Sears, who pointed out that male killers usually pick strangers for their victims (1991:ix). Most of the male serial killers in our records fit the pattern described by Sears. Thirteen of the twenty male serial killers were strangers to all or most of their victims, but only one of the female killers was.

Sears reports that "most of the victims of serial killers are picked up off the street" (1991:47). For the male killers in our files that may be true since thirteen of the twenty (65 percent) killed strangers. The female serial killers, however, had access to victims in various ways. As noted, six of the ten women killed their own children. Of the remaining four female serial killers, one was a nurse (Case 202 described below), one was the girlfriend of the children's father (Case 209), and one was a baby-sitter.

Because there have been highly publicized cases recently in which a baby-sitter was accused of killing a child, parents may be overly anxious about hiring baby-sitters. In the years 1977 to 1993, however, our files record only one female serial killer who sat for her victims' parents. She was also a relative of at least four of the children. Christine Falling, in Blountstown, Florida, had five children die in her care between 1980 and 1982. She was 17 when the first child, Cassidy Johnson, a 2-year-old girl, died. It was only after a fifth child, Travis Coleman, a 10-week-old boy, died in 1982 that Christine was charged with killing Travis and two other children. According to newspaper articles, she told her sister that she had killed five children. When she went to trial, she feared that she might be found guilty and sentenced to death, so she accepted a plea bargain in which she admitted that she had killed three of them. In return for her guilty plea, she was sentenced to life imprisonment, with eligibility for parole in twenty-five years.

One article (*New York Times*, July 26, 1982) quoted Christine as saying that she blacked out and had epileptic seizures "when she gets too tense." The article also reported that she was a school drop-out, and as a child had tried to commit suicide by slashing her wrists. At age 3 she was left in an orphanage by parents who did not want her. She had a juvenile record, but because the record was sealed, the *Times* could not say what was in it. The deaths of four of the children had initially been diagnosed as resulting from natural causes: one, of encephalitis; two, whose bodies were autopsied, of myocarditis, an inflammation of the sac enclosing the heart; and one, from a reaction to an immunization injection (Case 112). Since Christine was a relative of four of the children whom she claimed to have killed, she is hardly an example of the hired stranger. Those cases are quite rare in our records.

In the only case where the victims were strangers to the female serial killer, the woman possibly should not be counted with the others. She went on a killing spree with a male partner in 1984, and the choice of victim was apparently made by her partner. He chose strangers for the most part, which is characteristic of male serial killers (Case 297).

Child killers who are strangers to their victims are the ones most likely to escape detection, particularly if they stop at one victim. Serial murderers may be caught eventually, either for the serial crimes themselves or for some other law violation. The evidence for the murders may be uncovered during the investigation of the other crime. A number of serial killers, however, are never caught, possibly because there is no traceable connection between the killer and the victim despite intense police and public efforts to find one (King, 1993; Jenkins, 1994; Douglas and Olshaker, 1995, 1997).

Regarding age, most of the male serial killers in our records fit the Sears profile closely. The females vary from the pattern more than do the males (Table 2.7). According to Sears, "Almost all known serial killers are between the ages of twenty and thirty-five when they commit their crimes" (1991:45). The majority of serial child killers in our records, eighteen of the thirty (60 percent), are between age 20 and 35, thus fitting the pattern. Thirteen of those eighteen are male, however, and only five are female; thus, 65 percent of the twenty males fit the pattern, but only one-half of the ten females do. Of the five males outside the pattern, two are 19 and the other three are over 35. The age of two males was not given in the newspaper articles. Of the five females outside the pattern, one is 19, two are 17, and two are 40 or over (Table 2.7). The number of serial killers in our records is so small that it is difficult to determine whether this difference in ages is significant.

Do male serial killers kill more boys or more girls? How about female serial killers? Our sample is too small to give a definitive answer, but the figures are suggestive (Tables 2.8 and 2.9). Seventy-two to 90 percent of the male serial killers specialized in victims of a particular gender, depending on whether all victims are included (72 percent) or only the children in the sample (90 percent). In the latter situation, six of the males killed only female children, twelve killed only male children; only two men killed children of both genders. If children killed before 1977 (the start of our data base), children over age 12, or adult victims are included, nine male serial killers killed only males, five killed only females, and six killed both genders. Ted Bundy, who killed only one child in our sample group, was a heterosexual who specialized in killing females (Case 47). Wesley Dodd (Case 450, described below) was a homosexual who specialized in killing males. Leonard Lake and Charles Ng (Case 283) were heterosexuals who killed both males and females.

Female killers were also gender selective. When only children in our sample are counted, seven of the ten women killed only female children, none killed only male children, and three killed children of either gender (Table 2.8). If children over 12, those killed before 1977, and adult victims are counted, the figures change as with male killers. Under those conditions, six of the female killers murdered children of both genders and only four specialized in female children; even with the expanded number of victims, however, no female serial killers killed only male victims (Table 2.9). There is no information on why this gender distribution occurs, and it might not hold true with a larger sample. In addition, serial killers who specialize in adult victims may be different from those who kill children. The subject is worth more investigation.

Another interesting area of information worth further study is the method used by the serial killers in our files. Not one of them shot their victims (Table 2.10). The most frequent method was strangling or smothering (40 percent). Twenty-three percent used more than one method, which was not so frequent in the general perpetrator population. Even with those employing multiple methods, smothering occurred most often, and no one shot any victims. The only reason suggested is that shooting is a less intimate form of killing, and the serial killer is perhaps more emotionally involved in the murder process than are other child killers.

Although some serial killers may continue their crimes for years, and some are never caught, on occasion discovery is rapid. In September 1989, in Vancouver, Washington, William Neer (10) and his brother Cole (11) were found stabbed to death in a wooded section of David Douglas Park. They had told their father that they were going to pick up golf balls to sell for pocket change. In our records the killer was first listed as "unknown." In late October, their murderer, Wesley Allan Dodd (28), killed another boy, Lee Iseli (4). Dodd was caught trying to abduct still another boy in November. During the investigation of that crime, it became clear that Dodd was involved in a number of other cases, most involving only sexual molestation, but he had killed Iseli and the Neer boys (King, 1993:176–215). Although Dodd claimed to have molested scores of children, he apparently only killed these three and was caught after the third. Dodd was executed in January 1993, and the last information out of newspapers that we have about the case is from Newsbank, in a *Seattle Times* article by Jack Broom in January 1994 (Case 450). Since Lee Iseli was in our files, we were able to identify Dodd as the Neer perpetrator in our records based on the later articles about the Iseli case, and we combined the cases under one identification number.

The Dodd-Iseli case is reasonably typical of male serial child killers. The killer has a sexual motivation, specializes in one gender (with Wesley Dodd it was young boys, but often it is young girls), and continues until he is caught. In prison he may, as Dodd did, admit that, if released, he would continue his vicious behavior. He used that argument to oppose any alteration in the death sentence. Dodd also chose hanging because, he said, that is the way he killed the Iseli child.

Sometimes the solution to a crime takes place years after the event. *The Death of Innocents* (Firstman and Talan, 1997) focuses on two cases of serial child killers — one the father, the other the mother — that were successfully prosecuted years after the deaths. Although the book was published in 1997, the crimes are not in our files because they took place before 1977. The authors emphasize the reluctance of jury members, prosecutors, and detectives to believe that parents, especially mothers, would kill their own children. This problem of refusal to believe guilt is discussed at greater length in Chapter 8.

A number of cases in our files also illustrate the problem. An article in the *Omaha World-Herald* on May 24, 1990, reported that Texas authorities were investigating Diana Lumbrera (32) for the death of five of her children and one cousin's child, all killed between 1976 and 1984. She was eventually accused of seven murders and convicted of the most recent one, 4-year-old Jose, who was killed on May 1, 1990, and two others, killed earlier, to which she pleaded no contest. One of the cases, Joanna (3 months), who was killed in November 1976, is not in our sample because she died before our starting date of January 1977. The other six children are included in our tables. The newspaper articles gave the cause of death for three of them: Jose was suffocated; Melissa (3), who died in 1978, choked on vomit, according to an autopsy; and in 1980, Diana told Ericka's parents (her cousins) that Ericka was choking, then drove to a hospital forty miles away although the newspaper implied that she could have obtained help much closer. Christopher (5), who died in 1984, was said to have a blood ailment.

Diana Lumbrera had dropped out of school in the seventh grade. She married for the first time at age 14; and by 1990, when Jose was killed, she had been married three times. According to the newspaper she had no known mental problems, although she had fainting spells when she was under pressure. The county attorney said that she had two motives for the murders: greed (she had a $2,300 life insurance policy on Jose and also wanted to decrease the $40 per week she was paying for baby-sitting); and sympathy (she told people that one of her sons had leukemia and that her father had died in a car accident). Neither story, according to the newspaper, was true. Diana was convicted and received three life sentences (Case 638). There was no article on the case in the *New York Times* and no additional information from the *Omaha World-Herald*. The reluctance to think of women, especially mothers, as serial killers of their children may have been partly responsible for the time that elapsed between the first killing and the one that finally led to her arrest. One unidentified official expressed horror that anyone could continue killing for such a long time without being caught. The next case is an even more dramatic example.

Mary Beth Tinning, of Schenectady, New York, was accused of killing eight of her own children plus one adopted child. Only four of the children are in our victim count because the rest were killed before 1977. The first one killed, on January 3, 1972, was Jennifer, less than 2 weeks old. After Jennifer died, Tinning killed Jennifer's brother Joseph (2) that same month. Then, in March, she killed their sister Barbara (4). After those deaths, no child born to her lived more than five months. Michael, however, who was in the process of being adopted, was 2 years old when he was killed in 1981. The articles on the case never raised the question of why someone with her record was allowed to adopt a child. Yet despite all the deaths, up to the time she was charged, her record was officially clean. There were autopsies on all the children and complete investigations of three, which resulted in a diagnosis of "natural causes": respiratory failure and brain abscess, brain edema, crib death, SIDS, cardiopulmonary arrest, and viral pneumonia.

Tinning was tried for the death of Tami Lynne, 3 1/2 months old, who died on December 20, 1985. Employees of St. Clare's Hospital called police when Tami was brought in dead. People said that they were suspicious of all the deaths, but even Tinning's husband never confronted her. According to one newspaper article, when he was questioned, he answered, "When you have a legitimate cause of death, where do you go from there?" However, Tinning confessed that she had killed Tami because the baby was always crying; "I couldn't do anything right." She also confessed to killing Timothy, 14 days old in 1973, and Nathan, 5 months old in 1975, by holding a pillow over their faces. Her defense lawyers insisted that the confession was coerced and that the deaths were, as diagnosed, from natural causes. Nonetheless, the jury found her guilty of second-degree murder, and she was sentenced to twenty years to life on October 1, 1986 (Case 473). In this case, it seems possible that an undiagnosed postpartum psychosis might legitimately have been considered as a defense, since the killings seemed to start so soon after the birth of Jennifer in 1972. None of the articles mentioned that possibility, however, and the defense team did not bring it up since they were claiming that the deaths were from natural causes.

The cases of female serial killers demonstrate that the male serial sexual killer is only one subtype of serial killers. Although the motivation for many male serial killers may be sexual, the motivation for female serial killers and a minority of male serial killers is not. If postpartum psychosis or neurosis is not a factor for the women, however, it is difficult to say what the motivation might be. One of the more bizarre rationales suggested involved a nurse, Genene Jones Turk (32), in Texas. The investigation began when Chelsea Ann McClellan, 15 months old, died in September 1982 from an injection of succinylcholine, which can cause convulsions, and a curare-like drug, unidentified, which is a muscle relaxant. Genene Jones was indicted in Kerr County in May 1983 for the death of Chelsea Ann. Genene had been working for a Dr. Holland but was fired about ten days after Chelsea Ann died, apparently because she could not explain holes in the cap of a succinylcholine vial that she had reported missing and then subsequently found. Dr. Holland turned the case over to the authorities. Before she worked for Dr. Holland, Genene had been employed by the Bexar Medical Center. After the investigation into Chelsea Ann's death, officials reviewed forty-seven infant deaths that had occurred at the center between 1978 and 1982 while Genene worked there. They found twelve of the deaths "very suspicious," according to the newspaper. Forty-two of the forty-seven deaths had taken place in the intensive care unit, and five in the general pediatrics ward.

Genene Jones was divorced and had two children, a boy (11) and a girl (6). While the investigations were going on, she married a 19-year-old nurse's aide, Garron Ray Turk. Genene Jones Turk was charged with giving the drug to children in order to appear as a miracle-worker when she could block the action of the drug and stop the convulsions or other symptoms. She, of course, denied giving injections that caused convulsions. The prosecution included six other injury cases in the indictment, and the district attorney said that the investigation was continuing into "at least ten" more. One other death mentioned in the newspaper articles was that of Jimmy Pearson, a retarded 7 year old who died after Genene gave him an injection. Jimmy was being taken to the hospital by emergency personnel who said that all of his vital signs were normal until after the injection, when he had a "seizure," according to the newspaper. Genene insisted that he was having one before the injection. One witness at the trial stated that the reason for Genene's behavior — including the fatal case of Chelsea Ann — was that Genene hoped to prove an intensive care unit was needed in Kerrville, where she lived. She had tried to persuade the state to establish one there but had been turned down because there were not enough cases.

The prosecution of Chelsea Ann's death and the investigation into the other cases were hampered because the Bexar county hospital destroyed nine thousand pounds of pharmaceutical records, some of them under subpoena. The acting executive director said that the hospital pharmacy director had ordered the destruction of all the records from 1974 through January 21, 1982, as part of "normal protocol." Fifty thousand pounds of records kept by the University of Texas, which supplies the county hospital with staff members, were also ordered destroyed by the director, but a tip allowed the prosecutor's office to intervene and save forty boxes of documents that "might be relevant to the case." Hospital officials called both incidents of record destruction "coincidence." Despite all the difficulties that the prosecution had with the case, Genene Jones Turk was found guilty in February 1984 and sentenced to ninety-nine years. She will be eligible for parole in 2004 (Case 202).

Another female killer who apparently had an unusual motive was Paula Sims. She did not abuse her children — she just killed them, and only the girls. In 1990 she was convicted of killing her two daughters, one in 1986 when the newborn was 13 days old, and the other in 1989, when the infant was 6 weeks old. In each case the mother claimed that the child was kidnapped by a masked gunman while her husband was at work and that the kidnapper was the same person both times, even though the family had moved to another community after the first killing. According to the newspaper, the prosecution said that she had smothered both children and, at least in the case of her second child, kept the body in the freezer until she could dispose of it in a trash can across the state line. Her son, Randy, who was born between the births of the two daughters and was 2 at the time of the second death, was unharmed. Randy was placed in his father Robert's custody after the arrest of his mother. Robert said that Paula had apologized to him for having given birth to a girl after the first child was born. Although the defense asserted that "the person who did this is still out there," the jury found Paula Sims guilty of first-degree murder, obstructing justice, and concealing a homicide. There was no article about her sentence (Case 348).

Non-Serial Killers Who Sexually Abuse

Male serial killers are not the only killers who sexually abuse their victims. This section is included here because of the close association in the minds of many people between serial killers and sexual abuse. Yet not all male serial killers sexually abuse their victims, and not all sexual abusers who kill are serial killers. Sexual abuse in general is currently a topic of great public concern, and this concern is well founded. Parents who caution their children about going anywhere with strangers for any reason are as wise today as they were in the past.

Killing accompanied by sexual abuse of the victim provides an exception to the statistics that show parents, either acting alone or together, as the principal killers of children. Most sexual abusers are male, but they are not usually the fathers of the children whom they kill. In addition to the sixteen (out of thirty) serial killers who sexually molested their victims, we have 52 other perpetrators who sexually assaulted their victims but who were not serial killers (Table 2.12). Only one of them was a woman. Out of the 67 male molesters with known relationship to their victim (including sixteen male serial killers who sexually molested their victims but are not counted in Table 2.12), only four (6 percent) were the fathers of their victims. Of the 16 male serial killers who sexually molested their victims, thirteen were strangers, one was a family acquaintance, and two were neighbors.

Several reasons have been suggested for the small number of fathers who are both sexual assaulters and killers. Fathers who sexually molest their children may be able to bully them into keeping quiet, so they do not have to kill them to silence them. Sexual abuse may also stem from misdirected affection; they "love" their child (usually a female) and do not want to kill her. The child's affection for the offending parent may inhibit her willingness to denounce her abuser; and if the father is aware of the affection, this knowledge affords him enough security so that murder is not necessary to silence the victim. There might be more fathers among the sexual killers if the perpetrators were known in cases where they are currently unidentified in newspapers. Twenty-six (50 percent) of the 51 non-serial male killers who sexually assaulted their victims were strangers, but in the data base as a whole, only 9 percent of the individual perpetrators were strangers (Table 1.20). Friends, parental lovers, more distant relatives, and neighbors make up the remainder (41 percent) of killers other than fathers who also sexually abused their victims (Table 2.12). Sixteen of the twenty male serial killers sexually molested their victims, while four did not. Of the sixteen, eleven were strangers, the relationship of one was not given, and four were acquaintances or neighbors. Of the four serial killers who did not sexually molest their victims, one was a stranger, one was an in-law, one was the father of both victims, and the other was a father of one victim and the mother's lover of the other one. None of the female serial killers sexually molested their victims. The topic of sexual molesters who are not serial killers but who do kill their victims has not received much attention. Not much is known about them.

Since so many killers who also sexually assault their victims are strangers to them, identification and prosecution are difficult. In the following example, the wrong people were convicted. Although the real killer was eventually caught, the men originally charged, especially Ernest Holbrook, may have suffered from stereotypes associated with their socioeconomic status — that is, in much of the literature on murders, especially in the popular press, the assumption both explicit and unwritten is that most killers are found in the lower socioeconomic levels of our society. The news media personnel tend to react with astonishment and shock when an accusation of murder is leveled against someone in a more affluent and well-educated segment of the population.

In 1981, near Akron, Ohio, Tina Maria Harmon (12) was sexually attacked and strangled. Ernest Holbrook (19), a poor agricultural worker, and his friend Herman Ray Rucker, whose age and occupation were not given in the article, were tried and convicted although there was no physical evidence linking them to the crime and both passed lie detector tests. The main evidence against them came from two witnesses, Curtis Maynard, Ernest's cousin, and Susan Sigler, an acquaintance. Both said that during a night of drinking, Ernest and Herman claimed that they killed Tina because she had resisted their advances. The defense attorneys tried to show that these accusations were lies, but the jury convicted the two men, and in the summer of 1982 they were sentenced to life imprisonment. Then the two witnesses against Holbrook and Rucker got into trouble. Susan Sigler was convicted of filing a false rape charge in a neighboring county. In addition, she lied on a marriage application, stating that she had been married only once before and that her husband was dead when actually she had been married four times and her former husbands were alive. Moreover, Curtis Maynard had been on probation for a series of felony convictions at the time of the trial and was arrested on theft charges shortly afterward. While he was in jail on the theft charges, he recanted his testimony against both Holbrook and Rucker, saying that the police had pressured him into lying. According to the newspaper article, Maynard was borderline retarded.

Rucker was granted another trial on the basis of the new information about the witnesses and was acquitted after only two hours, but Holbrook's request for a new trial was denied. No reason for the denial was given in the articles. While both men were confined, at least two other children in the area of the first crime were killed, one of whom was Krista Harrison. Other girls in the area reported that they had been approached by a man but escaped. Krista (11) was sexually attacked and murdered in July 1982; her body was found in an old garage on a rural road. Robert Buell (age not given), a former City of Akron Planning Department employee, was charged with the crime. During his trial, experts testified that the carpet fibers found on Krista's body and on the body of Tina Harmon matched the carpeting in Buell's van; moreover, a carpet maker testified that very little of that carpeting had been sold in Ohio. Buell was convicted and sentenced to death. According to the newspaper article in 1984, the Wayne County prosecutor said that the evidence linking the two crimes and linking Buell to them was so strong that he could not use it to convict Buell without also freeing Holbrook. He joined Holbrook's attorneys in seeking a new trial. Holbrook was finally freed in May 1984. There were no additional articles about the case in the *New York Times* (Case 150).

A more typical example of a sexual abuse murder (although the victim is a year younger than most) is the case of 6-year-old Latisha Goodman. She was playing with her cousins outside her aunt's house in New Jersey on a Sunday afternoon in July 1993 when a man approached them and offered them money to leave with him. Latisha did so. The other children ran into the house to alert adults, who called police at 5:15 in the afternoon. Latisha's body was found that evening under the porch of an abandoned house on a street behind her aunt's home. David Cooper (22) had been seen sleeping there and was arrested. He was charged with aggravated sexual assault and kidnapping. David had been released on May 17 from a correctional facility where, since May 1991, he had been serving a four-year sentence on a drug-related conviction. The *New York Times* had not reported the outcome of the case by the end of 1993 (Case 783).

Another case, also in 1993 and also in New Jersey, involved Divina Genao, a 7-year-old girl. She was with her older sister and other children in front of her house when Conrad Jeffrey, a man in his forties, "began playing with the kids." He offered them quarters if they would race each other in the streets; and when they ran off, he grabbed Divina. Her sister sped off to tell their mother, who called police. Jeffrey, who had a long police record and was currently on parole, lived nearby and police went immediately to his home. One officer, unidentified in the article, said, "We know this guy . . . he had no business being out on the street." The police broke in, but Divina was already dead. Only twenty minutes elapsed between the time when the police were called and when they found her. Another resident of the roominghouse where Jeffrey lived said that she had seen him with Divina two days before the crime. When she asked who the girl was, he replied that she was the daughter of a friend and walked away (Case 781). There was no additional information.

One case of sexual molestation and murder that involved the father was that of Trisha McRoy (11), who was smothered in Tyler, Texas, in 1981. It took two years of investigation before the case went to court. Ultimately her father, Eugene McRoy (38), was charged. He confessed that he sexually molested her, killed her, and dumped her body in a nearby lake, with the help of his wife, who gave the authorities the first information that her husband was guilty of the murder. She was not charged, and police said that he had been a suspect during the entire investigation. According to the newspaper, she said that he had threatened to kill her, too, if she did not help him dispose of the body. An unusual factor in this case was that McRoy was blind (Case 156).

Public concern about sexual abuse most often focuses on the family, where the majority of nonfatal sexual abuse cases occur. But damaging as that particular type of abuse may be, at least most of the children abused by a parent live to have a chance to straighten out their lives. Trisha McRoy is one of the rare exceptions. The child sexually abused by a stranger, a neighbor, or a friend is less likely to survive.

Summary

The cases of mass killers and serial killers raise troubling questions. Such killers are not a recent phenomenon, nor confined to the United States. London's Jack the Ripper was a serial killer, and there are other historical examples of both mass murderers and serial killers. Do these individuals differ from the killer who stops at one or, at most, two victims? And, if so, how? Most multiple killers of either type are male, but some are female. To learn more about the dynamics that make a multiple killer it is essential to examine the cases of all examples, not just a select few.

Male and female serial killers have different patterns. Males often kill strangers, tend to specialize in a certain sex, age range, or physical appearance, and often have a sexually based motivation. Females do not. Instead, females who kill children know their victims. Indeed, even those who kill only adults usually know their victims (Cauffiel, 1992; Linedecker and Burt, 1990; Rule, 1988).

It is difficult to know how these cases could be prevented. Very few multiple murderers give hints to the people around them that they are going to kill a lot of victims. Even when they do, any people who are alarmed often have no recourse, or their alarm is not shared by whatever authorities with whom they communicate, as was the case with Laurie Dann. Although her former husband spoke to police, her parents, and others about the problems she was having and his concerns about her behavior, he was ignored (Kaplan et al., 1990). Similarly, people who expressed concern about the cases analysed in *The Death of Innocents* had a difficult time convincing anyone that a problem even existed (Firstman and Talan, 1997).

Mass murderers and serial killers are not a major social problem. The number of their victims is far smaller than those killed in industrial accidents or on the highways, but the mystery that surrounds them causes uneasiness in all of us. We think that we need to know more about them. Elliott Leyton believed that intensive biographical studies would reveal answers, but they are difficult and time consuming. Such studies might repay the effort, however.

Tables for Chapter 2

Table 2.1 Multiple Killers* of Victims in Child Sample** by Killer's Gender

Number of Victims	Male	Female	Unknown	Total	Percent
Two	77	26	7	110	62.5
Three	34	6	1	41	23.3
Four	9	5	2	16	9.1
Five and up	6	3	0	9	5.1
TOTAL	126	40	10	176	100.0

*Includes both mass murderers and serial killers.
**Victims in child sample are children 12 or under killed between 1977 and 1993.

Table 2.2 Multiple Killers* of Victims In or Out of Sample by Killer's Gender

Number of Victims	Male	Female	Unknown	Total	Percent
Two	80	24	18	122	40.8
Three	53	8	5	66	22.1
Four	41	7	4	52	17.4
Five and up	47	7	5	59	19.7
TOTAL	221	46	32	299	100.0

*Refers to multiple murderers, mass murderers, or serial killers in our files who killed at least one child in our sample.

Table 2.3 Known Mass Murderers Only by Number of Victims in Sample, by Perpetrator Gender

Number of Victims	Male	%	Female	%	Total	%
Three	33	86.8	5	13.2	38	66.7
Four	8	61.5	5	38.5	13	22.8
Five and up	5	83.3	1	16.7	6	10.5
TOTAL	46	80.7	11	19.3	57	100.0

Table 2.4 Known Mass Murderers Only by Number of Total Victims by Perpetrator Gender

Number of Victims	Male	%	Female	%	Total	%
Three	52	86.7	8	13.3	60	41.7
Four	41	87.2	6	12.8	47	32.6
Five and up	35	94.6	2	5.4	37	25.7
TOTAL	128	88.9	16	11.1	144	100.0

Table 2.5 Gender of Serial Killers*

Gender	Frequency	Percent
Male	20	66.7
Female	10	33.3
TOTAL	30	100.0

*There was one male killer who claimed that he was a serial killer, but police could never find any of the bodies of people he claimed to have killed other than the one, a child, he was charged for. We did not count him as a serial killer.

Table 2.6 Relationship of Serial Killer to the Victims

Relationship	Males	%	Females	%	Total	%
Parent*	2	10.0	6	60.0	8	26.7
Parent's lover	0	0.0	1	10.0	1	3.3
Acquaintance	1	5.0	1	10.0	2	6.7
Neighbor**	3	15.0	0	0.0	3	10.0
Stranger	13	65.0	0	0.0	13	43.3
Other†	1	5.0	1	10.0	2	6.7
Not known	0	0.0	1	10.0	1	3.3
TOTAL	20	66.7	10	33.3	30	100.0

*The father was also a mother's lover to one of his victims, and one of the females was also in an unspecified relationship to one of her victims. Each is counted only once in the table.

 **One of the neighbors was also a stepfather to one of his victims. He is counted only once in the table.

†The male killed members of his wife's family; the female was a baby-sitter to her victims.

Table 2.7 Ages of Serial Killers by Gender

Age	Male	Female	Total	Percent
Below 20	2	3	5	16.7
20 to 35	13	5	18	60.0
Above 35	3	2	5	16.7
No information	2	0	2	6.7
TOTAL	20	10	30	100.1

Table 2.8 Gender of Child Victims Killed by Each Gender of Serial Killer

Gender of Victim	Killer Male	Killer Female	Total	Percent
Female only	6	7	13	43.3
Male only	12	0	12	40.0
Killed both genders	2	3	5	16.7
TOTAL	20	10	30	100.0

Table 2.9 Gender of All Victims Whatever Age Killed by Each Gender of Serial Killers

Gender of Victim	Killer Male	Killer Female*	Total	Percent
Female only	5	6	11	36.7
Male only	9	0	9	30.0
Killed both genders	6	4	10	33.3
TOTAL	20	10	30	100.0

*If the children whom female serial killers are suspected (but not convicted) of having killed are counted, there would be 2 less females who killed only female victims and 2 more who killed victims of both genders, thus reversing the figures.

Table 2.10 Methods Used by Serial Killers by Gender

Method	Males	%	Females	%	% of Total
Stabbing/slashing	1	5.0	0	0.0	3.3
Beating	1	5.0	1	10.0	6.7
Strangling/smothering	7	35.0	5	50.0	40.0
Multiple methods *	5	25.0	2	20.0	23.3
Other **	1	5.0	1	10.0	6.7
Method not given	5	25.0	1	10.0	20.0
TOTAL	20	100.0	10	100.0	100.0

*The multiple methods included two drownings, four suffocations, three beatings, two stabbings, and two "other"—a hanging and a poisoning—all by the 7 perpetrators.
**The "other" methods used were injection of a deadly muscle relaxant by the female, and throwing the victim off the roof by the male.

Table 2.11 Serial Killers by Number of Victims, Any Age or Time, by Perpetrator Gender

Number of Victims	Male	Female	Total	Percent
Two	7	4	11	36.7
Three	1	0	1	3.3
Four	0	1	1	3.3
Five and up	12	5	17	56.7
TOTAL	20	10	30	100.0

Table 2.12 Sexual Abusing Killers with Known Relationship to Victims*

Relationship	Male	%	Female	%	Total	%
Parent	4	80.0	1	20.0	5	9.6
Paramour	4	100.0	0	0.0	4	7.7
Biological kin	3	100.0	0	0.0	3	5.8
Neighbor, friend, other**	14	100.0	0	0.0	14	26.9
Stranger	26	100.0	0	0.0	26	50.0
TOTAL	51	98.1	1	1.9	52	100.0

*Serial killers are not included in this table.
**Includes a member of a foster family.

CHAPTER 3

Juvenile Killers: Children Out of Control

Our files show 105 perpetrators who are under 18 years old. The victims of ten of them are counted in the "wrong place/wrong time" category—that is, the perpetrators apparently had no intentions of killing the specific victims who died. Consequently, it did not seem appropriate to include them in the calculations of factors that were designed to shed light on the perpetrators who did mean to kill their specific victims. Three of the juveniles probably did not intend to kill anyone. One of these was a 3-year-old boy who shot himself playing with an unlicensed gun, and no one was charged in this case (Case 175). A 4 year old also shot himself, but his father was charged as the perpetrator because he had left the gun lying around. This incident demonstrates some of the difficulties in classification. Because the father was identified as the perpetrator, this case is not counted with the juvenile perpetrators, although the victim is counted in the "wrong place/wrong time" category (Case 688). The case could have been placed in the "bad decisions" category, but the possibility that the father made a deliberate decision to leave the gun where the 4 year old could find it seems unlikely. The perpetrator in the second of the three cases where it is probable that no killing was intended was a 13-year-old boy who accidently shot his cousin while playing with a gun (Case 232), and the third was a 17 year old who shot a neighbor while showing off his new gun (Case 777).

The other seven juveniles may have intended to kill someone, but not the persons who died. All seven belonged to gangs, and they hit victims who were not gang members when they shot at members of other gangs. Four juvenile perpetrators were individuals who each belonged to a different gang that was engaged in a firefight and killed an innocent bystander (Cases 238, 707, 715, and 808). The other three — ages 13, 17, and 17 — were reputed members of one gang who sprayed a playground with gunfire, killing a 9-year-old boy. The newspaper regarded this case as probably another incident of an innocent victim caught in gang-war crossfire (Case 604). Most of the statistical tables of juvenile killers do not include these ten whose victims are counted in the "wrong place/wrong time" category.

Concern about juvenile crime is currently high because it has increased alarmingly — by 600 percent since 1960, according to some authorities (Bradley, 1997:4) — although violent crime in general has gone down in the last few years. In 1995, James Alan Fox, dean of the College of Criminal Justice, Northeastern University, said that homicides by males age 14 to 17 increased 165 percent at the same time that the adult crime rate was dropping. In an article in the *Lexington Herald-Leader*, Fox was quoted as saying, "Since 1984, the number of teen agers committing murder with guns has quadrupled." The homicide rate for girls was unchanged, as was the rate for juveniles using other weapons (Sniffen, 1995:A4, A8). An editorial in the *Lexington Herald-Leader* in June 1997 quoted from the national Bureau of Justice Statistics report, "Privacy and Juvenile Justice Records: A Mid-Decade Status Report," that gun homicides committed by juveniles have tripled since 1983. Between 1985 and 1994 the juvenile crime rate increased 145 percent, according to the editorial, while the adult rate fell 30 percent in the same period (*Lexington Herald-Leader*, June 7, 1997). Regardless of which of the articles is more accurate, a significant increase is undeniable. It is perhaps of interest that the seven gang members mentioned above who killed innocent bystanders appeared in cases in the 1990s. The slight decrease in juvenile violent crime in 1996 did not cause public concern to diminish because the decrease was not continued in 1997 or in the first part of 1998.

As a result of this concern for the rising juvenile murder rate, a number of books and articles have been written recently about juvenile killers (Benedek and Cornell, 1989:29–36; Ewing, 1990a; Ewing, 1990b). Do young killers differ from adults? Do the juveniles who kill children age 12 and under differ from juvenile criminals in general or from juveniles who kill only adults? What should be done with juvenile killers? And how should they be prosecuted or punished? These are only a few of the questions that are currently being asked. Most of the juvenile killers discussed in the books cited above killed adults. If they also killed children, this fact was mentioned only incidentally. As a result, our data are not strictly comparable with the existing literature, but there are some interesting similarities.

Juveniles — as stated, individuals under 18 years of age — still commit only a fraction of the homicides in our society despite the increase in the decade of the 1990s. In 1986 they represented less than 9 percent of the total arrested nationwide for murder, although they were arrested for 33.5 percent of property crimes (Benedek and Cornell, 1989:7). In our records, perpetrators age 14 or younger make up 6 percent of our total of 730 perpetrators whose ages are known. The 105 juveniles in our files make up 14 percent of the perpetrators whose ages are known. Table 3.1 lists 95 juvenile killers under 18 in our records by their age (excluding the perpetrators whose victims are counted under "wrong place/wrong time"). Notice the sharp break in frequency of perpetrators between 13 and 14 year olds. It is rare to find killers under 13, and only 12 year olds have as many as five perpetrators in the files. There are thirteen 14 year olds, however, compared to three 13 year olds. From age 14 onward, the numbers of perpetrators increase almost each year, with 17 year olds represented by twenty-two individuals. The figures presented by Benedek and Cornell agree with the sharp rise in the early teen years, noting that "in 1986 only 12 children age 12 or under were arrested for homicide," but the numbers increased "to 134 thirteen-to-fourteen-year-olds" (1989:7). Criminal justice statistics do not usually count killers under age 14. Our data suggest that this omission may be a mistake. Although there are not many under 14, in any specific case police would be wise not to ignore the presence of younger children when considering suspects.

The major shift in perpetrator frequency between the ages of 13 and 14 suggests that juveniles experience a significant life-style change at this juncture. That age correlates, at least in most states, with the start of high school or the last year of middle school. It also is associated with the onset of puberty and all the physiological and emotional changes that accompany that process. Young people are becoming more independent and thinking more seriously about mates, careers, or both. Peer pressure may weigh heavily upon them — to join gangs, to experiment with adult forms of amusement, and to rebel against conventional rules or authority. These pressures are present at earlier ages, of course, but they often intensify sharply at about ages 13 and 14. Whatever the reasons, the sudden increase in frequency of killers is a real one, and more investigation into the factors involved is clearly needed.

The youngest killers in our records are only 4 years old. There are two of them, both males (Table 3.3). It can easily be said that they did not know what they were doing, had no intention of killing, or did not understand what killing meant. One 4 year old was part of a group of four, with older children (9, 10, and 13) who beat a 6-year-old boy to death. His mother had left him at a playground while she visited a relative. The victim had a speech and hearing difficulty, and the newspaper speculated that he failed to respond effectively to the children when they tried to interact with him; and, infuriated, they killed him. There was no indication in the article of how active a role the 4 year old took in the actual beating (Case 305).

The other 4 year old may not have known what killing really meant, but he knew what he was doing. In 1991 in Queens, New York City, the boy shot his 2-year-old sister. He got his father's rifle from a gun rack on the living-room wall. Usually he would not have been able to reach the rifle, but his parents had pushed the couch against the wall under the gun rack because they had been entertaining guests. The rifle was not loaded, but the boy knew where his father, a supervisor for a supermarket chain, hid the ammunition. According to the investigating officer, the boy had learned how to load the gun from watching television. When he pulled the trigger, the gun was pointing down and a bullet hit his sister, who was in a baby seat on the living-room floor. The Queens district attorney said that no criminal charges were warranted (Case 667).

As Tables 3.2 and 3.3 indicate, juvenile perpetrators are similar to adults in the preponderance of male killers: 22 percent of the killers were female and 76 percent male. There were no female killers under 11 years of age, although there were sixteen males who were 10 years old and younger. There were two 11-year-old females, none age 12, and one age 13. Starting with age 14, as with the males, female killers are more frequent, and they, too, are most numerous by age 17. Eight 17-year-old female perpetrators are recorded in our files. There are no easy explanations as to why boys begin to kill earlier than do girls, just as there are no easy explanations as to why males in general are more likely to kill than females.

For children who are older than 4, there are some preliminary indications that they intended to kill either because they were angry at the victim or were removing a witness to some crime. Take, for example, the case of Cameron Robert Kocher, almost 10 years old. In 1989 in rural Pennsylvania near Stroudsburg, the Polk Township elementary school closed for a snow day. Cameron's mother worked as a sewing machine operator and his father as a day laborer, so they left Cameron with neighbors, the Rattis, as they had done before. Jessica Carr (7), the child of another neighbor, was also there. The Rattis had a Nintendo game, and the children played "Spy Hunter." Jessica was very good at the game, a birthday present.

Although Jessica was two years younger than Cameron, she won, which made him angry. The children created such a mess playing that Mrs. Ratti made them stop. That also angered Cameron, who complained that he was being punished although the mess was not his fault. He went home. There he got the key to his father's gun cabinet and picked out a .35 Marlin with sling and scope. In the ammunition drawer he found the proper bullets for the gun and loaded it. Then he went to a bedroom, climbed on the bed, opened the window, and took out the screen. Jessica and Shannon Ratti, the 13-year-old daughter of the Rattis, were outside in the yard, snowmobiling. Cameron later said that he was playing hunter and could not see anything but snow; he "touched something and the gun went off." Jessica was hit in the back. After the shot, Cameron carefully removed the spent cartridge, hid it in a box of bullets, replaced the rifle, and relocked the cabinet before Mr. Ratti called him to come back because "a sniper" was loose. The Rattis had called for help and carried Jessica into the house. Cameron walked past the room where Jessica lay dying and turned on the Nintendo game. According to the newspaper, he said, "if you don't think about it, you won't be sad."

Because of his age there were lengthy debates about what to do with him. Cameron was a good student, on the honor roll at school; he had no behavioral problems with the neighbors, and was a Cub Scout. His father had taught him how to shoot the high-powered rifle. Ultimately, in 1992, when he was 13, he pleaded no contest in a plea bargain. Jessica's mother reluctantly agreed to a misdemeanor charge of involuntary manslaughter, although she said that it "wasn't an accident." The plea included several conditions: Cameron's family could not have any weapons at home, and Cameron himself could not have a gun until he is twenty-one. He apparently did no jail time since he was home with his parents until the trial and received a Nintendo game for his tenth birthday, April 16, a little over a month after Jessica was killed (Case 432).

Juvenile perpetrators, particularly the younger ones, were often not identified by name in the newspaper articles. Some were even younger than the Kocher boy. Two brothers, one 9 and the other 7, killed Barbara Parks, an 8-month-old girl in Clearwater, Florida, in April 1983. They were the children of Barbara's baby-sitter, and they said that they acted out the violence they saw in their mother's pornography magazines. Legal authorities and child welfare officials in Florida had trouble deciding what to do with the boys. The older one was convicted of first degree murder, and the younger one was convicted of aggravated sexual assault in a plea bargain. They were sent to the Camelot Care Center for emotionally troubled youths, which is near Chicago, where they were to stay under the supervision of the Florida Department of Health and Rehabilitation Services indefinitely but not beyond their nineteenth birthdays. Three years later, the Florida Supreme Court overturned the older child's conviction on the grounds that there should have been a competency hearing to see if he understood the crime. The defense wanted a dismissal because he was "too young to be tried." This was the last information (in 1986) that appeared in the *New York Times* through 1993 (Case 254).

Very young killers pose serious ethical problems for members of American society. In some states, killers under age 14 cannot be prosecuted as adults, regardless of the circumstances of their crime; and in various states, children under a particular age (which differs from state to state) cannot even be charged with a crime (Ewing, 1990b:3). When a child of 6 or 7 commits a serious crime such as murder, the community is thrown into turmoil. No matter what the law states, people disagree.

Although the numbers vary somewhat, the killing methods used by juveniles are similar to the ones used by adults. Twenty-three percent chose guns (Table 3.5) compared to 22 percent of all killers (Table 1.14). Charles Ewing (1990b:11) states that a majority of juvenile killers use firearms, but the largest percentage of juveniles in our records (27 percent) beat their victims to death, again paralleling all killers (30 percent). The difference between our figures and Ewing's may relate to the fact that all the juveniles in our records killed children. A juvenile confronting an adult might feel impelled to use a gun to counter the greater strength of the adult but would not find it necessary to use one against a younger child.

Ewing also says that "gun use in juvenile homicides is lower in younger age groups and seems to increase steadily with age" (1990b:11). Our records do not agree with this statement, either. One of the 4-year-old killers in our records used a gun, as did four other children under 13. Seventeen year olds did not use guns any more often than did 14 year olds. In fact, the percentage of gun users was higher for 14 year olds (four of thirteen, or 31 percent) than for 17 year olds (four of twenty-two, or 18 percent) (Table 3.6). Again, the difference is probably due to the age of the victims.

Although the literature on juvenile homicide suggests that juveniles most often kill strangers, the ones in our files killed members of their own families. For example, one case involved a blended family. Robert Gates (39) had divorced his wife Kristi about ten years before the crime occurred. She lived in California, he in New York. Their sons, Wiley (17) and Robert Jr. (19), lived with their father. Robert Sr. operated a trucking company that salted roads in winter. He lived in a log cabin off a dirt road with his two sons, his girlfriend, Cheryl Brahm, and Jason Gates (3). Jason was Robert's nephew and had lived in the cabin since his parents, Robert's brother and sister-in-law, were killed in a car crash the year before.

Wiley was a good student, a computer buff, and the vice president of his senior high-school class; he played the cornet in the school band. On December 13, 1986, his grandmother, Vivian Gates, who lived nearby, called police and said that Wiley had come home and found the bodies of Robert Sr., Robert Jr., Cheryl, and Jason, all shot. Wiley was arrested, and police said that he made a full oral confession on December 14. Then Damien Rossney (16), a junior in the high school, was also arrested and charged with murder; he was also accused of hindering the prosecution because Wiley had left the murder weapon with him. Police stated that Damien and Wiley had conspired for two months to murder Wiley's family. According to the police, Wiley hated his father and resented Cheryl. Another classmate, Miles, said that Wiley had intimated in late September or early October that he had a plan to kill his father.

Wiley subsequently recanted his confession and said that he had confessed out of loyalty to his friends, but police said that he wanted a $100,000 inheritance. Three psychiatrists testified that he was psychotic and that his confessions were false. Wiley was ultimately convicted of conspiracy but acquitted of murder, primarily because of a technicality. He was sentenced to eight and one-half to twenty-five years on the conspiracy charge. Miles was given immunity for his testimony, and Damien's lawyers were seeking dismissal of the charges against him at the time of the last newspaper article (Case 333).

Wiley presumably used a gun, but 27 percent of the juvenile perpetrators beat their victims to death. An example is the case of Derrick Robie, a 4 year old who in 1993 was beaten and choked to death by Eric Smith (13), in Savona, New York, a small town southeast of Rochester. Derrick was on his way to a recreation program when he was lured into some woods and killed. Eric had just been sent home from the playground for disobeying rules and apparently chose his victim at random. Four years earlier, Eric had strangled a neighbor's cat; when his father heard about it, he "came out of the house and booted him so hard it lifted him off the ground," according to one newspaper article. Although Eric was to be tried as an adult, he would be punished as a juvenile, so the maximum sentence would be nine years. The case had not gone to trial by the end of 1993 (Case 803).

Another more typical example is the case of Maurice Adolphe Jr. In 1980, in Spring Valley, New York, Maurice, 10 months old, was beaten to death. He died of injuries to his head and body from a "blunt instrument." The body also had bite marks, however, and the police arrested Maurice's 12-year-old stepbrother after "a check of teeth marks." In a plea bargain the charge was downgraded from second-degree murder to first-degree assault. The stepbrother, not named in the newspaper because of his age, pleaded guilty to assault by biting. The article gave no reason why the stepbrother had attacked Maurice nor any additional details, and there was no information about the sentence given to the perpetrator (Case 97).

In another example, three boys, all 8 years old, died from blows to their heads inflicted by two 17-year-old boys and one 18 year old. The killings took place in West Memphis, Arkansas, in 1993. The three victims were found with their hands and feet bound. The 18 year old, Michael Echols, was a high-school dropout who liked "to rule" and, according to one article, also said that he would do whatever he could to hurt people. The other two killers, one of them also a high-school dropout, "hung out" with Echols. Their trial was set for February 1994 (Case 775).

Twenty percent of the juvenile killers, compared to 12 percent of all killers, stabbed or slashed their victims. One of the youngest juveniles was a 10-year-old fifth grade student in Brooklyn, New York City, not named in the article. In June 1993 he stabbed 12-year-old Charles Mapp, who died ten minutes after he reached the Woodhull Medical Center. Witnesses said that the 10 year old had argued with Charlie's 8-year-old sister and then got into a shouting match with Charlie, who was sitting on some steps with his friend. The 10 year old ran into the first-floor apartment where he lived, came back out with a steak knife, and stabbed Charlie. A police sergeant told the newspaper that Charlie's last words in the hospital were, "Please, Mommy, help me." Then he died. There was no additional information (Case 792).

In 1979 in Newark, New Jersey, another 10 year old stabbed 8-year-old Robert Kratic. Robert had been playing in a touch football game and had called the 10 year old (who was not named in the newspaper article) a sissy. The judge who held the preliminary hearing said that the boy must remain in custody until the trial. He was to be tried in Juvenile and Domestic Relations Court because New Jersey law did not permit offenders under age 14 to be tried as adults. Here, too, there was no additional information (Case 87).

Most of these cases were the result of childhood quarrels that a decade or so ago would have been settled with fists or name calling. The next one, however, is different. A high-school student wiped out his entire family with an ax. In February 1988, in Rochester, Minnesota, students told high-school teachers that Rick Brom was saying that he had killed his parents. The teachers notified authorities, who went to the boy's suburban home in a quiet, well-to-do area where they found the bodies in nightclothes. Rick had killed his father, his mother, his 14-year-old sister, and his 9-year-old brother. Friends said that he had been arguing with his father, who did not want him listening to a tape that he had purchased. The day before the killing, Rick had told a friend that he would kill his parents, and on the next day he said that he had done so. He pleaded not guilty by reason of mental illness, but the jury rejected the insanity defense and sentenced him to life with no parole for fifty-two and one-half years (Case 398).

Those who did not beat, stab, or strangle their victims used a variety of methods. For example, in 1981, in Queens, New York City, parents brought two boys, ages 7 and 9, into the 101st Precinct station. The newspaper did not identify the boys because of their ages. They had pushed two 4-year-old boys, who drowned, into Jamaica Bay from an embankment in Queens Park. Until the parents went to the police, the deaths were believed to be accidental. There was no further information (Case 139).

In the Bronx, New York City, in 1983, 15-year-old Susan Hobson set fire to her home because she was angry with her parents, who were "on her back about school." Susan's mother was caring for two children, a 4 year old and a 16-month-old baby. Susan's father rescued the 4 year old but could not save the baby. There was no additional information (Case 224). This case also could have been included among those in the "wrong place/wrong time" category because the victim was probably not the target.

Most of the juveniles in our records acted alone (66 percent), although the ones who acted with others are a substantial minority (Table 3.4). Ewing states that juveniles who kill family members usually act alone, while those who kill strangers or acquaintances are more likely to act in groups (1990b:10). Only 18 percent of the perpetrators in Ewing's figures killed family members, the rest killing strangers or acquaintances (1990b:7). In our figures, 46 percent killed relatives or household members, and almost 15 percent of the juvenile perpetrators whose relationship to their victims was known were parents of the children killed (Table 3.7). The fact that all our perpetrators killed at least one child age 12 or under probably accounts for the difference from Ewing's figures.

Summary

Members of the behavioral science community, legal experts, and law enforcement personnel continue to debate why these young people kill and what should be done with them. There seems to be little consensus about how often neurological or biologically caused brain malfunctions are usually responsible. Benedek and Cornell do not believe that the evidence is strong and reject only monocausal explanation (1989:10–18, 28–29). That leaves genetic and social behavioral factors as the main arenas for discussion. The last two chapters of this volume look at varieties of explanations or suggested solutions and what our data may indicate.

Since psychological studies show that juvenile killers rarely have brain abnormalities, the evidence suggests that we, as members of society, have to look closely at what we are teaching our young people. Not only were guns used by the juveniles in our records, but younger children also resorted to some means of lethal violence without guns to settle arguments. Victims were beaten with knives, fists, feet, and any solid objects at hand, but small children were also pushed into water and dropped out windows or thrown off roofs. We are simply not teaching young people that violence is wrong and should never be the first solution to a problem.

The message that young people receive in most forms of public entertainment today is a violent one. Live and televised sports, newcasts, music, videos, video games, and movies as well as mystery or adventure programs all include violence. Whom are we kidding when we say that children do not learn from such exposure? When basketball, football, hockey, and even baseball games erupt in fights, what message does this send to young people who are routinely told that sports build character? What kind of character are we building?

Tables for Chapter 3

Table 3.1 Age of Perpetrator at Last Birthday for Killers Under Eighteen

Age	Frequency	Percent
Four	2	2.1
Seven	4	4.2
Eight	2	2.1
Nine	4	4.2
Ten	4	4.2
Eleven	3	3.2
Twelve	5	5.3
Thirteen	3	3.2
Fourteen	13	13.7
Fifteen	18	18.9
Sixteen	15	15.8
Seventeen	22	23.2
TOTAL	95	100.1

Table 3.2 Gender of Known Perpetrators Below Eighteen

Gender	Frequency	Percent
Male	72	75.8
Female	21	22.1
Not mentioned	2	2.1
TOTAL	95	100.0

Table 3.3 Gender of Perpetrators Under Eighteen by Age

Age	Male	Female	Unknown	Percent
Four	2	0	0	2.1
Seven	4	0	0	4.2
Eight	2	0	0	2.1
Nine	4	0	0	4.2

Ten	4	0	0	4.2
Eleven	1	2	0	3.2
Twelve	5	0	0	5.3
Thirteen	2	1	0	3.2
Fourteen	9	3	1	13.7
Fifteen	14	4	0	18.9
Sixteen	11	3	1	15.8
Seventeen	14	8	0	23.2
TOTAL	72	21	2	100.1

Table 3.4 Number of Perpetrators Below Eighteen, Alone or With Others*

Age	Alone	Two	Three	Four	Total	Percent
Four	1	0	0	1	2	2.1
Seven	1	2	1	0	4	4.2
Eight	1	0	1	0	2	2.1
Nine	1	2	0	1	4	4.2
Ten	2	0	1	1	4	4.2
Eleven	2	0	1	0	3	3.2
Twelve	4	0	1	0	5	5.3
Thirteen	2	0	0	1	3	3.2
Fourteen	9	3	1	0	13	13.7
Fifteen	15	1	1	1	18	18.9
Sixteen	12	3	0	0	15	15.8
Seventeen	13	3	3	3	22	23.2
TOTAL	63	14	10	8	95	100.1

*There were two groups of four, one with three people age 17 and one 15. The other group ranged in age from 4 to 13 with one 9 and one 10. The numbers in the table refer to individuals; when they are not divisible by the number in the group, it means that one or more groups had older individuals in them.

Table 3.5 Known Method Used by Juvenile Perpetrators

Method	Frequency	Percent
Stabbing/slashing	17	19.8
Beating	23	26.7
Suffocating	4	4.7
Drowning	6	7.0
Burning	4	4.7
Shooting	20	23.2
Other	12	14.0
TOTAL*	86	100.1

*The method used was not given in the newspaper articles for 9 juveniles.

Table 3.6 Methods Used by Juveniles by Age

Age	Stabbing/ Slashing	Beating	Suffo- cating	Drowning	Burning	Shooting	Other	Do Not Know	Total
Four	0	1	0	0	0	1	0	0	2
Seven	0	1	0	1	0	0	1	1	4
Eight	0	1	0	0	0	1	0	0	2
Nine	0	1	0	1	0	1	0	1	4
Ten	2	2	0	0	0	0	0	0	4
Eleven	0	1	0	0	0	1	0	1	3
Twelve	1	3	0	0	0	1	0	0	5
Thirteen	0	2	0	0	0	0	1	0	3
Fourteen	1	2	1	1	2	4	2	0	13
Fifteen	4	3	2	1	2	3	2	1	18
Sixteen	6	2	0	1	0	4	1	1	15
Seventeen	3	4	1	1	0	4	5	4	22
TOTAL	17	23	4	6	4	20	12	9	95

Table 3.7 Juvenile Perpetrators' Known Relationship to Victim

Relationship	Perpetrators	Percent
Biological parent	12	14.8
Stepparent or paramour	3	3.7
Foster, adoptive, or baby-sitter	2	2.5
Other biological relative	20	24.7
Neighbor, friend, acquaintance	39	48.1
Stranger	3	3.7
Other	2	2.5
TOTAL*	81	100.0

*The relationship was not given for 14 of the juveniles.

Table 3.8 Juvenile Perpetrators' Relationship to Victims by Age

Relationship to Victims	4–8	9–13	14	15	16	17	Total	Percent
Biological parent	0	0	1	3	3	5	12	12.6
Stepparent or paramour	0	0	0	1	0	0	1	1.1
Foster, adoptive, or baby-sitter	0	1	0	0	1	0	2	2.1
Other biological relative	2	3	2	4	3	6	20	21.1

Neighbor, friend, acquaintance	5	12	7	6	4	5	39	41.1
Stranger	0	1	0	0	0	1	2	2.1
Other	0	1	0	0	0	1	2	2.1
Insufficient information	1	1	3	4	4	4	17	17.9
TOTAL	8	19	13	18	15	22	95	100.1
Percent of total	16.8	40.0	27.4	37.9	31.6	46.3		

CHAPTER 4

"Crazy" Killers: Saving Children from Pain

Mental and emotional illnesses are highly sensitive issues. Their definitions and causes are hotly debated by physicians, psychologists, biologists, and the general public. Some of the debate stems from the very old argument about nature versus nurture. In one sense, the argument is moot because everyone has both a genetic heritage and an environment that shapes them. It is always a matter of degree as to which has more effect on the adult personality, and the question probably is only answerable on a case-to-case basis.

Lawyers, legislators, medical doctors, psychologists, psychiatric social workers, biologists, and people in general use the terms "crazy" or "insane" in a variety of ways. Individuals so labeled tend to behave in ways different from other people in the same circumstances. Their actions, words, or beliefs deviate sharply from what is seen as "normal," and they are unable to control what they do or to change their bizarre perceptions of the world. Sometimes the cause of their illness is at least partly genetic, sometimes the problem can be controlled with medication and counseling, yet sometimes nothing seems to be of any use. There is clearly a continuum from normal individuals who are creative or unusual in their behavior, through those who are often called "eccentric" (such as Dennis Rodman) to people who are dangerous to themselves and to others. The border between sanity and insanity is a difficult one to draw; indeed, it is drawn in different places by laws, by medical personnel, and by specialists in a number of fields. This chapter treats killers who were reported to be deeply depressed and despairing of the future, those who successfully used insanity as a defense in their trial, and those who were diagnosed as psychotic. This classification and approach is neither perfect nor the only one possible, but it is useful for the purposes of this book.

Killers Who Are Desperate

In the first group of cases discussed, the perpetrators were apparently prompted by fear for themselves or for the children whom they killed. This group, representing only 1.1 percent of all perpetrators, consists of child killers who seemed overwhelmed by their life circumstances. Their cases are among the saddest. Newspaper articles often reported that these accused killers were severely depressed, but there is no evidence that this was a clinical diagnosis or that insanity was a successful defense in their trials. People in general, including reporters, are apt to use the term "depressed" for individuals who are sad or unhappy regardless of whether the term applies in a medical sense. The depression of the people whom we included in this group had an identifiable immediate cause: loss of a job or a realistic fear of losing it; marital discord with an impending separation or divorce; financial problems that threatened the loss of their home; and health problems, especially those affecting the children to the extent that the killer could reasonably plead that he or she was motivated by love and wanted to keep the children from suffering. Their fears may have been exaggerated, but they were not irrational or even, in some cases, unreasonable. If the perpetrators in this category claimed insanity as a defense, however, it was unreported. These people seem different from killers who appeared completely out of touch with reality, those who were acquitted for reasons of insanity, or those who had diagnosed psychoses.

It is an unhappy fact that children who are physically or mentally challenged may add just the right amount of stress that pushes a parent over the edge. When the difficulties of caring for a seriously challenged child continue month after month, despair may mount steadily until the caregiver can no longer cope. Daly and Wilson state that killing abnormal infants is a biologically reasonable practice because such children are unlikely to be successful in passing along a valuable genetic heritage (1988:49–51). Even the problem of caring for normal children can wear down unemployed or single parents to the point where their despair of ever being able to escape from an intolerable burden leads them to kill. Some of the deaths recorded in our files fit this picture. Occasionally, however, stress does not have to build over time. When a child's devastating problem, either physical or mental, becomes overwhelming, an individual may react immediately and violently.

In 1983, Chicago veterinarian Daniel McKay (35), who had been married for ten years and had a 6-year-old daughter, learned that his wife was pregnant with a son. The pregnancy was a stressful one, and Daniel was present in the delivery room when the boy was born seriously deformed—a "cleft palate and clenched fists, both correctable," plus several internal defects such as a dislocated heart, malfunctioning lungs, missing testicles, and webbed fingers. He begged the doctors not to use heroic measures to keep the infant alive, but they ignored his pleas. The physical appearance of his malformed son apparently drove Daniel over the edge. The father snatched up the boy while the doctors were still working on him and dashed him to the floor, killing him. Daniel said that he could not bear to see his wife and newborn baby suffer. He pleaded temporary insanity but was tried for murder three times, with a hung jury each time, before the prosecution finally gave up (Case 250).

Physical or mental abnormalities may create a burden perceived as overwhelming by some mothers, despite articles in the popular press extolling families who continue to care for a disabled child regardless of professional advice to institutionalize him. The situation with the Bernsteins is an example. Their son Eric was 9 weeks premature when he was born in Broomall, Pennsylvania, on July 1984, suffering from a respiratory disease. He was also retarded. His mother quit her job as a court stenographer to devote full time to his care. She and her husband publicly asked for teams of volunteers to help in teaching their son so that he would not have to be institutionalized. Three hundred people responded, and the parents chose seventy to help Eric learn to crawl. In an interview in February 1986 she said that they were making progress, but apparently she was growing increasingly despondent. After the crimes she said that she considered suicide, but instead, in May 1987, she shot Eric while her husband was at work. Her defense lawyer argued that she could not cope any longer (Case 362). The outcome was not mentioned in the *New York Times*.

The desperation of unemployed single women left to raise children without the help of a husband can increase risks for those children even when they have no mental or heath problems. Brigitte Jefferies (27), who lived with her children and her mother in a New York City housing project, usually took good care of her kids, according to her mother and neighbors interviewed by the newspaper. But one day in May 1986 the mother, Mildred Howard, returned home in the afternoon and found the two girls, Rasheeda Howard (8) and Tesia Jefferies (4), dead. Mrs. Jefferies had apparently asphyxiated them with plastic bags. She told authorities that she was depressed over having to care for them. There had been no previously reported incidents of problems or abuse (Case 338).

Marital problems, especially a pending separation or divorce, often cause one spouse or the other to despair. Women in particular dread the loss of income unless they happen to have a well-paid job themselves, and sometimes the fear that they may have to turn to welfare is enough to lead them to kill their children. In one such case, the numbers of victims in our files would be larger if it were not for the unexpected intervention of outsiders. A fire truck in New York City was returning to its station from a false alarm in 1989 when firefighters saw a child dangling from a tenth-floor window and another being pushed out. They stopped the truck; and while some of the men raced up to the apartment, others tried to catch the children. A 7-year-old girl fell to her death before they could get into position, but a police officer broke the fall of a 3-year-old boy, who was injured and in critical condition at the time of the newspaper article. The other three children of Meenah Abdul-Salaam were saved. The firefighters found her apartment, although they broke into two others before reaching the right one. Mrs. Abdul-Salaam had barricaded the bedroom door, which the firefighters also broke down. She screamed at them that she was giving her children to God. She told her 1 year old, "Go, go, Allah is waiting for you!" The 7-year-old girl who died had tried to climb back through the window, but her mother had pushed her off the ledge.

The mother was taken to St. John's hospital for psychiatric evaluation. Neighbors were shocked. Mrs. Abdul-Salaam, a devout Muslim, had lived ten years peacefully in the same apartment, and the children were well behaved. But recently she had had marital and financial problems. She had ordered her husband out. Although she had received one eviction notice for nonpayment of rent, she managed to pay that month's rent, but the building superintendent did not know whether she had paid the current month's. Police assumed that she intended to jump after all the children had fallen to their deaths. The newspaper did not follow up on this case, so we are left in ignorance of what finally became of the mother and her remaining children (Case 426). Lacking any other information, we can suppose that this was a case where a series of hardships overwhelmed an otherwise stable individual.

Another woman, also worried about how to care for her six children, threw them into Buffalo Bayou near downtown Houston, Texas, in 1986. Again, according to the newspaper reports, outsiders intervened. A city employee jumped in and saved all but two of the children. In this case, authorities apparently decided that the mother, Juana Leija (29), needed help. She was given ten years' probation under the care of Harris County Mental Health and Mental Retardation officials (Case 341). There was no additional information. This case and the next one illustrate the variations in the ways that different states deal with mothers under emotional stress who kill their children.

Twenty-five-year-old Jeanne Anne Wright of Camden, New Jersey, was not so fortunate as Juana Leija. No one rescued her children, and the law treated her much more harshly. As described in Chapter 2, Jeanne was unmarried and six months pregnant with her fifth child in November 1983. She had grand mal epilepsy. Worried that the abusive father of her first three children was going to kidnap them, she took all four children down to the river and "placed" them in the water as they slept. Indicted for murder, Jeanne pleaded not guilty but then accepted a plea bargain. She was sentenced to four concurrent life terms with no possibility of parole for thirty years (Case 260).

After a marital or relationship split when the mother does not take the children but leaves them with their father, sometimes similar tragedies occur. Men also feel the desperation of trying to raise children alone with inadequate resources. King Bell (33), a Vietnam veteran and an auto worker, had been laid off and was unemployed for three years, but just a month before the killing, a friend helped him land a job. Then his wife decided to divorce him and left. He grew increasingly upset and worried about his ability to keep and care for the four children: Kingston Edmond, Berkima, Bertina, and King Edward III, whose ages ranged from 1 to 6. On August 21, 1981, in Indianapolis, he lined the children up on a bed and shot them all in the head, then covered them with a blanket. Later found scrawled on a basement wall in chalk was the phrase, "Jesus take them all to heaven," and a sign on another wall said, "The family that prays together stays together." Neighbors noted that Bell was "a great one for praying."

After he killed the children, he went looking for Clarence Barnett, a friend of his wife. Carrying a shotgun, Bell caught up with Clarence, who was in his parked car outside the YMCA, and shot but did not manage to kill him. Then Bell went after his estranged wife, Birtha (21), who was staying with her mother, Mary Alice Kirby (54). He killed them both. Police arrested him as he came out of the Kirby house with the shotgun (Case 138). Although Bell is a mass murderer, his concern about being able to raise his children alone appears to be the important factor in this killing. Jealousy may also have played a role, although Bell's reason for trying to kill Barnett was not discussed in the newspaper article.

Another case where financial problems seemed to play an important part in a family tragedy is that of Da-pei Wu (37), who emigrated from China with his wife around 1986. He found work in New York City's garment district, sewing buttons on clothing. For almost seven years the family lived a quiet life and none of its members was ever in trouble with the law. The couple had two girls born in the United States, Renee (2) and Lauren (5). In 1992, Wu's employer fired him. Wu was not fluent in English; and in 1993, after six months of unemployment, he still did not have a job. He experienced periods of mental instability, which might have been either a cause or an effect of his joblessness. On January 18, 1993, he bought a knife. According to the newspaper article, he told police that he had heard "voices" telling him that his entire family would be tortured if they were still alive on January 23, the beginning of the Chinese Year of the Rooster.

Da-pei Wu loved his family; indeed, "in his own mind, he was saving them," the captain of the 110th Precinct told reporters. So on January 21, Wu stabbed and bludgeoned to death his wife, Hui Ming, and his daughter Renee. He changed his clothes, took Lauren out of school, went home, and killed her, too. Wu tried to kill himself by electrocution, using the exposed wires from the radio, but all he managed to do was to blow some fuses. A neighbor called police after she asked him where the children were and he explained how he had been told to kill them. Police found him pacing the floor. All three bodies were in a bedroom, lined up and covered with a blanket (Case 771). There is no indication of previously abusive behavior in this family.

The desire to save children from pain or life's difficulties is the professed rationale of some other killers. The first example detailed here is Carolyn Lloyd (34), who claimed that she wanted to protect her son from suffering. In 1981 she lived in Shadow Creek, Kentucky, a middle-class subdivision near Louisville. Her son, James Allen (4), had recently been evaluated for speech problems and retardation. She was told that he might not be able to go to kindergarten because he was "slow." When she did not seem to understand, the social worker explained that "slow is the same as mentally retarded." Her defense lawyer said that this news was too much for her on top of her father's recent death and her off-again, on-again marriage. She had married Tom Lloyd, the boy's father, in 1971, divorced him in 1973, and reunited in 1974. In her statement to police, Carolyn said of the boy, "What chance did he have? I didn't want to hurt somebody, just to help somebody. I tried to drown him. I thought that might hurt him." So instead, she shot him in the head while he was in the bathtub because "it would be fast"; then she called an ambulance. Before she shot her son, she had called an emergency hot line and asked for help. She had "felt a sense of doom" ever since the evaluation center had told her that her son was retarded. Despite the testimony of psychiatrists, police, family, and social workers, the jury did not accept Carolyn's insanity defense and found her guilty (Case 520).

In Greenwich, Connecticut, Linda Sandor (43) suffered from Marfan's syndrome—a genetic disorder of connective-tissue development that usually affects the skeleton, heart, and eyes—and was losing her sight because of it. Linda's children, Scott (11) and Michelle (14), had inherited the disorder and already wore heavy corrective lenses. Her distress over their vision as well as over the deterioration of her own eyesight had caused her to try suicide earlier in the year. On Thursday, September 2, 1982, she bought a gun. Late Friday morning her stepson, Richard, found her body and the bodies of both of the children in their bedrooms, each shot once in the head. The children were still in their nightclothes, but Linda was fully dressed, with the gun lying beside her. She apparently had shot them and herself just after her husband, a building contractor, left for work at 8 o'clock. The newspaper article did not mention how Richard happened to find the bodies. Although Linda left no note, the article said that there was no evidence of foul play and the police believed that she killed the children and herself to spare them from suffering (Case 213).

The same fear that led to the Sandor killings played a major role in another case. In 1991, Maryanne Leute (30) took her 7-year-old son, Howard, and jumped off the roof of their apartment building in the Bronx, near the New York Botanical Garden. She left no note but was known to have been "very depressed over the last two days." Neighbors said that apparently she thought that she and her husband had HIV, the precursor to AIDS. Her husband worked for the Sanitation Department and had already gone to work on the morning that she jumped with her son. No additional information was given in the newspaper article (Case 677).

While all incidents of child murder are upsetting, a case review occasionally reveals details that are out of the ordinary. The next case is an example — the method was gentler than usual, but the results were the same. In Philadelphia in 1990, Dr. Anthony Paul (49) decided to kill himself. He was a "highly regarded specialist in gastro-intestinal cancers" who had emigrated to the United States from Sri Lanka with his wife about 1972. His two children, a 17-year-old girl and a 12-year-old boy, were born in the United States. On a Monday afternoon, Dr. Paul left the Fox Chase Cancer Center early. He told the receptionist that he had left a packet for his assistant, but not to give it to her until Tuesday. When the assistant opened the envelope on Tuesday morning, she found a suicide note and some money. She notified the police, who broke into the doctor's home in the "affluent Chestnut Hill section" and found the family assembled in the master bedroom. They all had IVs in their arms leading from plastic bottles that hung on picture hooks on the wall. Precisely what was in the bottles was never stated in the newspaper articles. In his note, Dr. Paul said that "we lived together, we loved together, we die together." He blamed himself for the situation, which was not revealed by the police. There was no alternative, he wrote, for his wife, who was suffering from arthritis and depression, or for their daughter, who was retarded and helpless. He was not sparing his son, Dr. Paul continued, because he was afraid that the boy would be sent to a foster home and thus become a "social misfit." He also gave instructions on how to treat his daughter's asthma should she happen to survive. He had carefully swabbed everyone's arms with alcohol before inserting the needles (Case 643).

Unlike most of the people in a later chapter who made poor decisions that resulted in unexpected and undesired death, these perpetrators meant to kill their victims. In these cases, however, their apparent motivation was either love or despair. They did not want their children or their mates to suffer, or they were overwhelmed with the difficulties that they foresaw for themselves or their children in continuing to bring them up. In fact, they believed — or said they did — that the children would be better off dead than living the future which they saw for them. Is there any way that these tragic deaths could have been prevented? Possibly. If the perpetrators had a more extensive support system or more information about the resources available to them, if they had been able to reach out for help, or if the people who were interacting with them had been more knowledgeable about the signs of despair, then the victims might have been spared.

Killers Who Claim Insanity

About 9 percent of the perpetrator population either successfully claimed insanity as a defense, were diagnosed at some point as psychotic, or were treated by specialists in psychological disorders. Unfortunately there is little research into the number of such people in the general population who have children. For many of them, their problems are more of a burden to themselves than to others. They may parent their children as well as or better than people who have no apparent emotional disturbances. Nonetheless, some pose a real danger to themselves and to the people in close contact with them, who often include children.

Children are also killed by people who claim insanity at a trial, although they fail the legal definition of insanity. These people usually know right from wrong but kill anyway. The question of how much of their behavior is by choice and how much results from irresistible compulsion is hotly debated in legal, psychological, and law enforcement circles. Some law enforcement personnel doubt the strength of any claimed compulsions (Douglas and Olshaker, 1995; idem, 1997). Others, who are often psychiatrists or psychologists employed by defense lawyers, affirm that it is a sufficent excuse for murder. Experts who are not in the hire of either the prosecution or the defense are rarely asked for their opinion, or, because of confidentiality restrictions, may not be given sufficient information to make a judgement. Moreover, juries believe one expert or another in a manner difficult to predict — there are cases in the files in which jury members might not have given enough credence to the insanity plea, and others where perhaps they gave too much.

Childbirth

The strain of pregnancy and giving birth may result in a form of mental illness called postpartum depression or psychosis. Its precise cause is still debated. Most cases are shortlived, but occasionally a mother's postpartum psychosis may put children at risk. In 1982 a woman was tried for smothering two of her children and attempting to do the same to a third. She took that third child to a neighbor and said that the baby had stopped breathing. The neighbor, who was a nurse, resuscitated the baby and called for help. The child was placed in a foster home. At the trial for the murder of the two children and the attempted murder of the third, the mother was acquitted in all three cases on the grounds of postpartum psychosis and was ordered to undergo thirty days of outpatient observation. Since she was a former pediatrics nurse in a New York City hospital, the hospital reviewed 438 deaths that had occurred during the fifteen years she had worked there but found no suspicious ones connected to her (Case 480).

Unattended births may well involve some form of emotional disturbance. One of the authors of Kentucky's *Epidemiological Study of Abused and Neglect-Related Child Fatalities FY 1991–1995* (Delambre and Wood, 1997) suspected that many of the women who gave birth unattended were probably so traumatized by the experience that they went through a period of time when they did not fully realize what they were doing (Private Conversation). Almost all of the deaths of newborn infants in our files occurred after unattended births. For example, in New Jersey, in 1991, Michelle Schnitzer, a 20-year-old college student, gave birth to a seven-pound full-term baby girl in the bathroom at her home. She stabbed the infant with cuticle scissors 175 times in the head, face, chest, and neck and then tossed her out the window. Michelle's parents had not known that she was pregnant. At the trial, her attorney said that she was voluntarily undergoing psychiatric treatment, but whether before or after the birth was not made clear (Case 690). A similar case occurred in Chicago in 1992. Kimberly Keller (19) stabbed her newborn son to death with scissors only moments after he was born at home. Once again, the birth was unattended. This killing was cited in the *Chicago Tribune* in 1993 as part of its series reporting all the nonnatural deaths of children age 14 or younger that had taken place in one year, but there were no more details (Case 705).

Religion

A number of perpetrators included with the mentally ill gave religious justifications. In 1980 in Denton, Texas, Patricia Ann Frazier cut out her 4-year-old daughter's heart to save herself and the world from the "demons" who, she believed, possessed the child. She was declared not guilty by reason of insanity, and a hearing was held to decide if she should be committed to a mental institution. There was no follow-up article in the *New York Times* on the outcome of the hearing (Case 106). On Christmas Day in 1983, Steven Johnson (28) of Randallstown, Maryland, picked up a knife and seized his 14-month-old son, Steven Jr. He declared to his wife that he was God and that his son was "Jesus Christ reborn." Then he said, "Steven, the two of us are going to have to die for the sins of the world" and began to stab him. When his wife tried to stop him, he slashed her shoulder. She fled to call police, but by the time they arrived, Steven Sr. had decapitated the boy (Case 243). There was no more information on the outcome of this case in the *New York Times*.

In 1978 in Manhattan, 11-month-old Irving Williams was asleep in a playpen in his parents' bedroom. His father suddenly leaped out of bed, ran into the kitchen for a knife, and began hacking at the baby. The mother was cut trying to protect him; she then ran for help. The baby was killed. When police arrested the father, he said that "according to his Muslim religion he should have taken the head of the child." The only religious tenet from followers of Islam concerning beheading refers to the destruction of demons (Private Conversation). There were no additional articles in the *New York Times* (Case 58). In a similar case in 1985, also in New York City, Lillie Etienne (41) asphyxiated her two daughters, Lillie (2) and Christine (3), by pressing down on their chests and praying. She said that she was trying to rid her daughters of the voodoo spirits placed in them by her estranged husband. She was convicted and sentenced in 1988 to twenty-five years to life (Case 474).

In 1985 in St. Joseph, Missouri, Richard Wells, a 36-year-old construction worker, brought his 4-year-old son Christopher to the hospital with a slashed throat. He told people at the hospital that he had "sacrificed" the child. The boy's mother, Richard's ex-wife, said that he was a "perfect" father and she could not understand what had happened. Richard wanted to attend the boy's funeral, but the sheriff would not allow it because of death threats received by his office (Case 556). There were no additional articles in the *New York Times* about Wells.

At five in the morning in July 1993 in Corpus Christi, Texas, a fisherman was stopped by a woman who told him that she had just killed her son. She said that he had a dragon inside him. The body of the 4-year-old boy was found wrapped in a sheet in the back of a pickup truck. The dead child was holding two teddy bears with family photographs and a Bible placed beside him. There were piles of ritual objects and recently constructed altars near the truck. When police arrived, the 37-year-old woman was quoting Scripture, although the *New York Times* article did not state which passages. She was taken to the psychiatric unit of the Memorial Medical Center (Case 805). There was no additional information in the *Times*.

Another case with religious overtones also had some unusual elements. Samuel Andrews (27), a Muslim "who called himself Samson Solomon Mohammed," had lived with Arlene Ware, in her early twenties, and her two children, Kimberly (4) and Fred (2), in Pittsburgh for about eighteen months. Arlene was six months pregnant with his child. On January 9, 1980, he took his family hostage in their home. During the siege he demanded a ship to Iran and also that all Jehovah's Witnesses be gathered at Three Rivers' Stadium; the newspaper article did not say why. The siege lasted thirty-nine hours. Then, on the morning of January 11, Samuel's (or Samson's) house burst into flames. The police broke in, and Samuel shot all the hostages and then himself. Arlene was only wounded, but the baby, who was delivered by Caesarean section, was three months premature and died. The police said that the fire may have saved Arlene's life because it separated her from Samuel (Case 130).

Religious motivation may be claimed by perpetrators in an attempt to establish a basis for an insanity defense. In 1981 in the Bronx, New York City, Noel Archibald reported that his child, a 2-year-old boy, was missing. Noel said that the boy had disappeared while they were at an off-track betting establishment in the Bronx. Two days later, however, Noel turned himself in to the police: "voodoo activity and the Devil had put certain lights on him and spoke to him telling him to do what he did." He had strangled the boy, stuffed the body in a pillowcase, put it in a plastic bag, and thrown it into the Harlem River. At the time of the newspaper article the Harbor Patrol had not yet found the body (Case 136). There was no later item in the *New York Times*. Since we have no information on the outcome of the case, we do not know whether an insanity claim was accepted by the jury.

At times, even when a history of mental illness is present, jury members do not believe that the perpetrator is as insane as he claims. An example is William C. Mauro, who killed his 7-year-old son in Arizona in the late 1980s. (The exact year was not given in the sources.) He declared that he killed the boy because the child was possessed by a devil. His defense was insanity, and, according to the newspaper, he had a history of mental illness. However, the prosecution produced a recording made during a visit from his wife in which he told her not to talk unless her lawyer was present. The jury, with this claim that he was not insane, believed the prosecution, convicted Mauro, and sentenced him to death. Mauro appealed, citing the Miranda rule, because he had not been told that the visit was being recorded, and the sentence was overturned. The state appealed to the State Supreme Court, which reinstated the conviction and the death sentence with the ruling that Miranda did not apply since the conversation was not an interrogation (Case 379). There were no additional articles in the *New York Times* by 1993.

A confusing series of reports was given in the *Louisville Courier-Journal* about another case in 1977. Trula Bush and Willa Mayes were charged in the death of 6-year-old Donald (or Daniel) Bush. Trula's age was given as 35 in one newspaper article, 40 in another, and the victim's name was alternatively given as Donald or Daniel. The child died of "the highest concentration [of salt] in the blood we have ever seen," according to the doctors who attended him. He had been fed almost entirely on saltwater for an unspecified amount of time "to get rid of demons," the women said. Five other children from the same home were hospitalized. An individual identified by the newpaper as "Reverend Charles Tachau" performed funeral rites and said that demons had killed the child. Trula claimed that they were members of a cult called the True Spirit of Saint Jude, but some people said that the cult had disbanded while others thought that it had held services earlier in the year. According to one article both Trula and Willa were rumored to be able to hex people. Willa Mayes was sentenced to ten years and Trula Bush to only two because she cooperated with the state (Case 496).

People who use religious justifications for killing children are not necessarily household members. In 1983 in Grand Haven, Michigan, Maris Karklins, a 42-year-old draftsman, was convicted of killing his friend and co-worker Mary Jane Paulson, her husband Robert, and their three daughters, Cynthia (18), Carla (13), and Case (8). The bodies were found on March 13, 1982, in their burning home. Karklins, who called himself a "hit man for God," said that Robert and his daughters were "demons"; he also killed Mary Jane to "save her" from her family. He claimed to have killed a number of other people, but the newspaper articles do not confirm that assertion. He was sentenced to five life terms and said that he would appeal, but the *New York Times* did not record any appeal (Case 210).

Killers Who Are Mentally Ill

A third group consists of killers who were undoubtedly mentally ill — people with diagnosed or obvious emotional problems that often required hospitalization but who did not claim any religious justification for their actions. These perpetrators sometimes used bizarre methods to kill their victims. For example, there is the case of Bartley Dobben (36), a foundry worker in Muskegon, Michigan. Bartley, diagnosed as paranoid schizophrenic and given medication to control his "desperate religious vision" and bizarre behavior, had a long history of mental problems. The treatment worked well enough so that he married, but he began having "visions" again after his second child was born. He and his wife quarreled. She tried to have him committed and got a court order to keep him away from her and the children. In less than a week after it was issued, Bartley was fined for disobeying the order. However, when he promised to take his medication, the judge waived the forty-five-day jail sentence that could also have been imposed.

Bartley regularly attended Emmanuel Fellowship Church, and, according to the *New York Times* article, its "self-ordained pastor," Rood Vaughn, persuaded him to reconcile with his wife; according to Bartley's relatives, Vaughn also persuaded him to stop taking his medication. While driving to Thanksgiving dinner in 1987 with his wife and the two boys, Joel (2) and David (13 months), Bartley stopped the car at the foundry where he worked. He left his wife in the car and took the children inside. The explanation that he gave his wife is not mentioned in the article; perhaps he told her that he wanted to show them his worksite. He put the boys in a transfer ladle used to move molten metal and heated it to 1,300 degrees. The children died of burns and suffocation. Bartley was found guilty but mentally ill, and he was sentenced to life without parole. If he gave a religious justification for the murders, it was never mentioned in the *Times* articles (Case 368).

The case of Renee Green (29) is complicated. She was a troubled woman who was in and out of hospital psychiatric units for several years with what the doctors labeled "emotional instability," according to the press. On November 7, 1984, she was reported to New York City's Human Resource Agency for child neglect. That same day, she went to the Lincoln Hospital emergency psychiatric unit seeking admission. Because Lincoln had no bed for her, she was transferred to Bronx-Lebanon hospital on November 9. There, a staff doctor examined her but refused to admit her because she was not having hallucinations, was not agitated, and appeared to be "no homicidal risk, no suicidal risk." She did not keep her follow-up appointment on November 12, and no one apparently tried to find out why. A social worker visited Renee on the day that she came home from Bronx-Lebanon and reported that the children were safe and the environment was appropriate. Unfortunately, both the staff doctor and the social worker were wrong. On the evening of November 28, according to neighbors, Renee began to fight with her sister, Lenora Davis. Both women lived in their mother's apartment with their children. The neighbors did not know what the quarrel was about, but it continued into the next day. Sometime during the morning of the 29th, Renee stabbed her sister in the shoulder and cut the throat of Lenora's 2-month-old son, Clinton. Lenora fled the apartment to get help. When police arrived, Lenora warned them that Renee had hostages in the apartment. By then, Renee had killed her own 3-year-old son, Clayton, and was sitting in a room with her 3-month-old daughter, Dorothea, unharmed, in her arms. Lenora's baby, still alive but bleeding badly, was in the same room in his bassinet.

The police called in a hostage negotiation team. They squatted on the fire escape and talked with Renee from noon till about 1:20, when an emergency medical team lowered themselves on ropes from the roof to the third-floor apartment and crept in through a window. As soon as they entered her room, Renee started to "squeeze" Dorothea, who was still in her arms. A team member sprayed the contents of a fire extinguisher into Renee's face and she released the baby. Another team member snatched Lenora's baby from the bassinet and gave him CPR as he rushed the boy to the hospital, but Clinton was dead on arrival. While Renee had been talking to the negotiating team and a reporter who was with them, she kept threatening to kill herself. She told them that her family called her a heifer and a witch and fed her chopped meat like an animal. There was no newspaper follow-up (Case 293).

A contributing factor in the Green case is the problem of patient treatment in overcrowded and underfunded facilities. If the Lincoln Hospital emergency psychiatric facility had had enough room, Renee would not have been sent to another hospital in the first place. It is possible that the time involved in transferring her from one hospital to another allowed the acute phase of her disorder to pass, so an accurate appraisal of the risks involved was not made and Renee was not admitted for treatment. Similarly, as can occur in certain types of mental disorder, Renee was probably not obviously disturbed during the social caseworker's visit. The failure of two systems that missed the chance to prevent these deaths is part of a troubling pattern that is discussed in the last chapter of this volume.

In the next case, none of the systems that failed Renee had even a chance to intervene. In 1986, Carol Ann Washington (28) from Detroit stowed away on a cruise ship to the Bahamas with her 18-month-old daughter. She was apprehended, and both she and her daughter were confined to a guarded cabin, where she strangled the little girl. She said that she feared crew members would enter the cabin and sexually abuse her and the child. She told police that she had previously been a mental patient. At her trial, Carol was found not guilty by reason of insanity and was sentenced by a federal judge in Miami to an indeterminate period for care, treatment, and observation for mental illness (Case 353). It is unreasonable to expect the crew members who apprehended and confined Carol to have identified her precarious mental state.

Some people in the "mental illness" category, like Renee Green, recognized their irrational condition and tried to get help, but they were turned away by overcrowded, understaffed facilities. In other cases, people close to the perpetrator recognized that he or she had a psychological problem but did not realize how serious it was and believed that reasoning with the individual would be sufficient. Patrick McCord thought of calling the Nebraska Psychiatric Institute when Cathy, his 3-year-old daughter, came running to him, shouting, "Mother's going to kill me!" His wife, Shawna, was chasing after the child with a .44 Magnum. Patrick disarmed Shawna and "had a long talk with her." He told her that if she could not convince him that she did not need help, then he would have her committed. She had only chased Cathy because the child had misbehaved and "I wanted to scare her," she argued. Shawna had been very depressed after Cathy's birth, but a social caseworker had told Patrick that she would be better after she recovered from the birth. She had improved but continued to have bouts of depression; in fact, she had tried suicide twice during the eight-year marriage and was being treated for emotional problems. Their youngest child, Colleen, was only 4 months old.

Shawna's explanation about the pistol reassured Patrick, and he did nothing further. That was on Thursday, August 25, 1983. On Saturday night, they visited Patrick's brother, and Shawna seemed to be in good spirits. After they returned home, Patrick lay down on the couch to watch television while Shawna and the children went into the air-conditioned bedroom to go to sleep. Patrick fell asleep too, and when he woke up at 5:15 A.M. and decided to go to bed, he found the bedroom door locked but forced it open with a coat hanger. Both children had been stabbed to death and Shawna was in critical condition; she had swallowed PineSol as well as a gun-cleaning substance. In the hospital she said that she was depressed because she was home all day with the kids and could not find a job. When she was growing up, as the second oldest child of twelve in her family, the responsibility of raising the ten younger children had often fallen on her. Her father was in the military and the family had moved a lot. Her husband had also moved often in his jobs, but now he was a swing-shift engineer for the Omaha Public Power District and seemed likely to remain in one place. Their neighbors in a small town near LaPlatte, Nebraska, said that they were "nice people." Shawna was held in police custody while it was determined whether she would face court action on a second-degree murder charge or be brought before the mental health board (Case 544). No additional information was found.

Even when individuals are correctly identified as mentally ill and are hospitalized, the public is not always safe if these patients are bent on violence. In 1989 in Middleton, Connecticut, Jessica Short (9) was stabbed to death on the street by David Peterson (37). He was a patient at the Connecticut Valley Hospital, where he had been committed after a finding of insanity on criminal charges. He had been declared not guilty of stabbing attacks in 1971 and 1988 by reason of insanity. On the day that he stabbed Jessica, he had had an outburst of violence but, instead of being confined to a ward, Peterson was allowed outside unsupervised. He walked away from the hospital grounds, boarded a bus, went downtown, and bought a knife. He used it on the first person he saw, who happened to be Jessica. Her family sued the state, which eventually settled out of court for $1.5 million. Peterson was declared innocent once again because of insanity and was confined, this time, to a maximum-security mental hospital (Case 461). This case could have been included in the category of victims who were in the wrong place at the wrong time. Since the death was preventable, however, had Peterson been treated as he should have been, it is appropriate to include it here, among the mentally ill.

Summary

When mental illness has been studied crossculturally, the results tend to show that all populations have a rate of five to seven per thousand who do not seem to be able to abide by the rules of the society and are out of touch with reality as other members know it. This rate seems to hold true even in societies that accept the idea of visions and other direct communication from the supernatural (Murphy, 1976:1027). The *Encyclopedia of Mental Health* states that 20 percent of "our population" at any time is affected with some form of specifically diagnosable psychiatric disorder (1993:x). The *Federal Register* for March 28, 1998, sets the figure at 23.9 percent having some form of diagnosable psychiatric disorder and 5.4 percent having a serious mental disorder (62 #60:14928–32). The proportion of mentally ill perpetrators in our files is smaller than the proportion of people in the general population who suffer from specific diagnosed psychiatric disorders. Yet our figures for perpetrators with a serious mental disorder are higher than the proportion in the population at large.

Unlike the victims in some of our other categories, the children killed by perpetrators suffering from mental illness or emotional disturbances might have been saved if one of the following had occurred: 1) that family, friends, or neighbors not only had noticed the odd or unusual behavior but also had intervened effectively (although laws often prevent forceful intervention); 2) that proper diagnosis and subsequent treatment had been provided by the medical community; or 3) that adequately staffed facilities with sufficient space had been available. Our failure as a society to address systematically the needs of the mentally ill has led, on occasion, to tragic results.

CHAPTER 5

Violent Abuse and Sudden Attacks: Outbursts of Rage

Family, friends, and neighbors are the people most often involved in killing children. When a lone perpetrator was identified, only 9 percent of the victims were killed by strangers. Violent abuse of some sort accounted for 47 percent of the victims in our files (Table 1.18). The general category of "violent abuse" includes cases where the killings clearly resulted from sudden attacks and those where death resulted after physical abuse was carried out for a long time. Perpetrators who commit sudden attacks accounted for 13 percent of the known killers in our files (Table 1.19). These sudden outbursts of rage come with little or no prior warning. Sometimes there is an obvious trigger for the anger, but in other cases, particularly when the perpetrator refuses to discuss the crime or commits suicide, the trigger may never be known. In one sense, almost all of the recorded deaths of children, except those that are the culmination of long-continued abuse, could be considered the results of sudden attacks.

In our classifications, however, "sudden attack" is limited to a subcategory of violent abuse, and we have included only cases where the perpetrator had continuous or frequent contact with the children with no previous indications of violence toward them—or, at least, none reported. Most of the cases of multiple murders described in Chapter 2 are counted in the "sudden attack" category. Those described in this chapter serve to indicate how these events can happen with little or no warning, although one cannot rely entirely on the assumption that there have been no previous incidents of abuse simply because none was reported. Some of the cases that we did not classify as such appear to be sudden attacks, but without the specific statement to that effect in the news article or any clear evidence of previous abuse, we included the case in the indeterminate category. The killers in these ambiguous cases accounted for 23 percent of the perpetrators (Table 1.19) and are discussed at the beginning of this chapter.

Violent Abuse

The violent abuse cases that cannot be classified as sudden attacks or sustained abuse (discussed in Chapter 6) include a wide variety of perpetrators and methods. For example, Matthew Ayers (3) was drowned in Binghamton, New York, on January 30, 1991, by Donald Kenyon (23), his mother's lover. Donald had beaten the boy earlier that day and put him in the bathtub "to discipline him." There, Matthew drowned. Matthew's mother, Terri Ayers (20), denied any wrong-doing on Donald's part, stating that the couple "loved each other very much. I don't see where Don did nothing wrong" (Case 659). Terri married Donald just two weeks after her son's death. Her reaction typifies the response of some biological parents (usually women) in a new relationship, which is deemed more important than the safety of the child from a previous mating. We have a number of examples where mothers ignored or denied the evidence of abuse by a current lover who was not the father of the children being harmed. The newspaper reports in this case failed to indicate whether Donald's beating of Matthew was an isolated incident or whether Matthew was a victim of sustained abuse.

There are, unfortunately, many more examples. In 1988, Allen Swinton, a 2-year-old boy, died in Brooklyn from a punch to the chest hard enough to kill him. Verna Swinton, Allen's mother, was at work at the time. Kenneth Norris, the 24-year-old man living with Verna, said that it was an accident; he was engaged in "rough play" with the boy and got too rough. The newspaper article did not indicate whether he was the boy's father. Another child in the home (not identified by name, gender, or age) was taken away by the Bureau of Child Welfare. Kenneth was charged with manslaughter. There was no later information (Case 423). This case is another example that could be considered in a different category. Hitting a 2 year old hard in the chest is a bad decision. Since the statement about rough play could have been offered as an excuse for behavior that was by no means play, however, this ambiguous category of general violent abuse seemed more appropriate.

One more case where the death resulted from what may have been a new partner is that of Monique Fleming. In 1990 her male friend, Kim Maynor (21), shared her apartment in Harlem, New York City. Monique worked while Kim took care of her 2-year-old child, Monae. On Monday night, October 22, Monique found her daughter dead in her crib. Kim had beaten the little girl on the head and shoulders because she would not stop dancing to a music video (Case 623). The newspaper articles contained no information on the duration of the relationship between Kim and Monique, or whether Kim was Monae's father, or whether he had abused Monae earlier.

A depressingly similar story is found in the case of the Rodriguez child. Sylvia Rodriguez and Giovanni Piquaad had moved into an apartment in University Heights, the Bronx, New York City, in September or October 1991. The other residents in the building said that they were "always fighting." One of them had heard Sylvia cry out, "Don't hit me!" On January 9, 1992, Sylvia brought her 18-month-old daughter, Adriana, into the Montefiore Medical Center with head injuries. Giovanni had thrown her headfirst against the wall when she blocked his view by crawling in front of the television set. The child died the next night (Case 748). The newspaper did not make it clear whether Giovanni was the father of the child or whether he was married to the mother. The article strongly suggests that he abused Adriana's mother, but whether he had previously abused Adriana is never mentioned. If Giovanni had not abused the child earlier, this case would be classified as a "sudden attack," but since there is no clear information, it was placed in the general "violent abuse" category.

Even if a mother does not live with her new male friend, the child may be at risk if the mother leaves the child with him while she runs errands. For example, Penny Fortner decided to leave her 5-month-old baby daughter, Ashley Hoffman, with Charles LaChapell Jr. (30), a man whom she had been dating for about four months. They had separate apartments in Council Bluffs, Iowa, but sometimes he baby-sat with Ashley. On September 10, 1984, he stayed with her while her mother went to the grocery store. Ashley was sleeping when Penny left. She had not been gone long when the child woke up and started to cry. Charles tried to quiet her, but Ashley refused her bottle and her toys and kept on crying. For several seconds, Charles shook her, her head bobbing back and forth; when he put her down, she arched her back and stopped breathing. She died in the hospital on the next day (Case 547). Once again, this incident could be a "sudden attack," or even "bad decision," but without more information about any previous mistreatment of the child, the classification of "violent abuse" is more appropriate.

Some of the newspaper accounts of the following cases raise the possibility that physical abuse preceded death, but without some statement of involvement with social services or mention of bruises, the cases were left in the less specific "violent abuse" category. For example, in October 1987, Lucille Taloute (20) called 911. She said that a masked man broke into her Brooklyn apartment and beat her and Tracy, her baby. A 2-year-old girl's body was found in the bathroom. Lucille's husband, a 31-year-old gypsy-cab driver, was not at home. Later, Lucille changed her story and said that a friend beat them; still later she changed her story again and said that she had accidently dropped the child. The autopsy showed that the little girl had been asphyxiated. On November 16, about two weeks after Tracy's death, Lucille was arrested and charged with murder. There were no further articles in the *New York Times* (Case 386). This case is another example of a perpetrator strategy that turns up surprisingly often in our files — claiming that the child's killer was a masked stranger. Our records show a number of perpetrators who attempted to place the blame on some unknown individual who broke into the house or kidnapped the child on the street, although child killing by strangers is actually rare.

This next case was also difficult to categorize. The perpetrator, Frank DeCorleto Sr. (34), had a history of violent behavior. In August 1977, in East Hartford, Connecticut, he shot his 4-year-old son, Frank Jr. The father had been released from prison in 1963 after serving eight years for killing a former girlfriend, whom he shot because she thought he was crazy. He subsequently married Kathy DeCorleto, who gave birth to Frank Jr. She later divorced Frank Sr., who won custody of the boy after a bitter year-long battle. Kathy was afraid to continue to fight for custody of the child because Frank had threatened her with a gun. At the time of the killings, she told newspaper reporters, "they let him go and they let him take my son. . . . I told them in court this would happen again. Nobody listens." After the divorce, Frank Sr.

had married a 22-year-old woman and worked as a baker's helper until October 1976. Unable to find work, in August 1977 he stole silver from a library and was holding it for ransom. When the police went to the house to investigate the silver theft, Frank Sr. took his wife and Frank Jr. hostage, claiming that he was angry because no one would give an ex-con a job. The standoff ended when Frank Sr. killed his wife and son and then turned the gun on himself. No one accused him of abusing his son (Case 9). While this case could have been placed with those where the perpetrators were motivated by despair, none of them showed the rage displayed by Frank DeCorleto.

In 1988 in the Bronx, 26-year-old Thomas Butts brought his 1-month-old baby, Ikeya, to the hospital. There she was pronounced brain dead. Earlier, when she would not stop crying, Thomas shook her violently (Case 401). Violently shaking an infant is likely to cause spinal and brain damage, which many adults apparently do not realize. Too many children die or are permanently disabled as a result of this ignorance. There are a number of similar cases in our files such as the one of Clark Poldevaart, a 22-month-old boy who died in 1991 of brain injuries from a severe shaking given by his 19-year-old baby-sitter, Joan Ann Stuhrenberg. At first, she said that he had fallen, but the autopsy revealed the characteristic signs of shaken baby syndrome, and Joan was charged with first-degree murder and child endangerment. There were no later articles (Case 880).

Some cases classified as general violent abuse were so complex, one wonders if the facts were ever properly sorted out. Our Case 774 began on September 11, 1988, when Kayesean Blackledge was born in Brooklyn, New York City, to a 15-year-old single mother, Kaaron Blackledge. Two months later, a neglect petition was brought against Kaaron and her mother, with whom she and Kayesean were living. Kaaron was fighting with her mother and had had some trouble with the law (the newspaper article was not specific). Child Welfare authorities investigated Dana Blackledge, a relative, for a possible kin foster-care program placement. Kayesean was placed with Dana, a nurse at the Woodhull Medical Center in Brooklyn, and did well there. In late 1992 or early 1993, Dana married Stephan David Poole, an enforcement agent with the New York City Sanitation Department, whom she had met through a singles advertisement. The family moved to Jersey City, New Jersey, across the river from New York City. All seemed to be going smoothly until May 20, when a bruised, pajama-clad boy's body was found in a trash-compactor bag at the base of a garbage chute in a Brooklyn housing project. When police finally identified the body and looked for the mother, they found Dana, who had been hospitalized with stab wounds since May 20, the same day that Kayesean's body was found. Dana said that she had refused her husband's sexual advances, so he had bound her wrists and stabbed her. She escaped and ran naked from the apartment, flagged down a passing car, and was taken to the police station. When the police returned to the apartment, Stephan Poole and the boy were gone.

A nationwide search resulted in Stephan's arrest in Texas. He claimed that he had attacked Dana because he found out that she was a transsexual. Kaaron, the dead child's mother, insisted that Dana had never been a male, but Kaaron's mother (Kayesean's grandmother) insisted that she had turned over custody of Kayesean to her brother, not her sister. Dana had had a sex change operation in a Brooklyn hospital in 1981. Surgery that police believed was connected to her sex change had left her with a scar on her neck. She was about to collect a $500,000 insurance settlement because of it. Police believed that the opportunity to inherit the insurance money was Stephan's real motive in stabbing Dana. They reopened an investigation into the death of Stephan's first wife in 1989 because there had been an insurance settlement involved there, too. Kayesean, who had been taken from the apartment by Stephan, was killed because he would not stop crying. Stephan was arraigned on two counts — intentional murder and murder with depraved indifference, a technical legal category of crime in New York — because Kayesean may have been alive when he was thrown into the trash compactor. In 1994, Stephan confessed to killing Kayesean and was sentenced to twenty-five years to life (Case 774).

The Hollins case is complex and raises an important issue: Is a fetus legally a person? States vary on the definition, and this whole issue is discussed at greater length in Chapter 8. Here, in this case, the 6-to-7-month fetus was killed when the father pushed it clear into the abdomen of the mother. The doctor who surgically removed the two-pound fetus from the mother's body said that it probably died about five minutes after the injury. The case occurred in June 1981 in Monticello, Kentucky, and continued in the courts until 1983 when the Kentucky Supreme Court ruled that homicide is not possible unless the fetus is "born alive." Prosecutors needed proof that life existed separate from the mother. An earlier investigation of this case was complicated by the fact that Barbara Hollis, the mother, gave two versions of what happened. At first, she stated that her husband did not want the baby and assaulted her in a barn after he had fled her parents' house with her and their 2 year old, but later she said that she accused him because she was angry about losing the child. Running from her parents' house, she said, had caused her to go into labor and he tried to help. The fetus had been pushed through the uterine wall into the abdominal cavity under the rib cage (Case 518).

Sometimes greed leads to a killing, and complexities can arise after the case is over. In 1981 in Los Angeles, Clifford Lee Morgan (57) hired two men to kill his wife and child. The stabbed bodies of his wife and 8-year-old Mitchell Morgan were found in their home on May 21. The men (whose names were not given in the *New York Times* article) were convicted and sentenced to death in February 1982. Clifford Morgan was convicted in September 1983, but he died of bone cancer before the sentencing phase of the trial began. According to the article, since he was never sentenced, his conviction never became official. In December 1984 the *Times* said that a judge was to call a hearing to decide whether to sentence the man posthumously since insurance money was involved. In California, as in many other states, criminals and their heirs cannot profit from a crime. Clifford Morgan's heirs were trying to obtain the insurance money on the grounds that the conviction was not official, but the heirs of his murdered wife believed that they were the ones who should collect the money. The hearing was scheduled for January 15, 1985, but the *New York Times* never published the result (Case 286). The *Los Angeles Times* of January 16, however, reported that at the hearing Judge Fratianne formally declared Morgan guilty, thus completing the trial, so his heirs could not inherit. The judge held that an actual sentence was not necessary if he pronounced Morgan guilty. The California Court of Appeals upheld the decision, but the case could still be considered by the California Supreme Court. Over $900,000 is at stake.

The next case was classified as general violent abuse, although it might have been a sudden attack. In 1987, Nicholas Christopher (3) was stabbed with a butcher knife. His mother Charisse (28) and his sister Lacie Jo (2) were slashed to death. Nicholas survived, although the police found him holding in his intestines with his hand when they arrived. The killer, Pervis T. Payne, a 20-year-old male, was a family acquaintance whose girlfriend lived next door to the Christophers. Pervis worked as a painter and carpenter, was mentally handicapped, and had no prior police record. On the night of the killings, he had been drinking beer and using cocaine, according to the police. He made sexual advances to Charisse. When she refused him, he killed her and her daughter and tried to kill her son. The crime was mentioned in passing in a 1991 *New York Times* report about a U.S. Supreme Court decision to allow victim impact statements before prisoners were sentenced. No additional details were given (Case 834).

Sudden Attack

The "sudden attack" category includes people who cannot control their rage. Over one-fifth of the perpetrators (22.6 percent) told police or newspapers of their anger, most of them directing it at the child, a few claiming that they were angry at everything (Table 1.32). Sometimes the rage was directed at the world in general, but more often these perpetrators simply "lost it" and struck out over something that the child (or someone else) did. The "something" in the cases in this category was often very ordinary — a small child's prolonged crying, wetting or soiling clothes, or unwillingness to go to sleep. Of course, babies cry, toddlers soil diapers and wet clothes, and little children create messes. Some adults, particularly males, cannot deal with these annoyances and respond by losing control and killing the child. In 1981, for example, an 18-month-old boy was thrown from a fifth-floor window by his uncle, whose only explanation was that the baby "bothered him" (Case 149). Perhaps the trigger is the refusal of the child to obey a command, or the child interrupts some adult activity — one blocked the perpetrator's television screen, as mentioned in one of the cases above. Sometimes drug or alcohol use weakens the perpetrator's control over his or her own anger.

In the first example of a sudden attack, Byron Halsey, a 24-year-old factory worker, killed the two children he was caring for in 1985 while their mother, his girlfriend, worked. He raped and strangled the 7-year-old girl and killed her 9-year-old brother by pounding nails into the child's head with a brick. The children, who showed no other signs of abuse or neglect, were honor students and had enrolled themselves in Sunday School at the Salvation Army Center next to the roominghouse where they lived. The perpetrator lived with their mother, and, although he may have been slightly retarded, nothing suggested that he was dangerous. He had a history of problems with alcohol, however, and a series of "minor legal infractions" on his record, none of them violent. The only indication of possible danger was reported after the crime by the manager of the roominghouse, who said that when Halsey was drinking, "he was not someone you would want to be around. He had a temper." The newspaper articles did not indicate whether he had been drinking at the time of the killings, and there was no later information on the outcome of the case. Since the children showed no signs of previous abuse or neglect, the "sudden attack" category seems appropriate (Case 320).

In 1986, Harry Shamoon, an unemployed Iranian immigrant living in Queens, New York City, was caring for his two sons after his wife left him to return to her native Germany. She had been the main financial support of the family, which added to his stress. He was playing chess with his older son, Simone (6), but his younger son, Julian (4), kept interrupting the game and would not obey his father. Enraged, Harry ordered him to kneel on the floor and then beat him to death with his hands and a broomstick (Case 347). This sort of case differs from the ones described in Chapter 4 in that the murder seemed to be the result of a sudden loss of control triggered by some event rather than being the culmination of a period of worry with no specific single cause.

In a case that was particularly upsetting to people in the community, Kenneth Seguin (35), a computer executive in Holliston, Massachusetts, killed his wife and children. He was an "involved father," according to one of the men who had a child in the same soccer league as Kenneth's 7-year-old son Danny. Kenneth devoted weekends to the children and helped coach soccer. He seemed like "anyone else in town," the friend said; his own son had asked his mother, "Mommy, would Daddy ever do that to us?" He added, "This kind of thing scares people. You ask yourself, would something in my life make me crazy enough to snap like that?"

One April evening in 1992, Kenneth took his two children for a drive. He gave them sleeping pills and, when they were unconscious, slit their throats. He sank their bodies in a pond about ten miles away. He went home and lay beside his sleeping wife for two or three hours, then arose and killed her with one ax blow to the head. He dumped her body in a nearby river and slashed his own wrists; he would have died there if two fishermen had not happened by. During the trial, the defense argued that Kenneth was having a psychotic episode. The jury believed that although he was mentally impaired, he understood the wrongfulness of his actions, and so they convicted him. His lawyer said that he would appeal because the jury members were prejudiced and biased about mental illness. There were no further articles by the end of 1993 (Case 747). This case was not included in the "insane" category because the psychotic episode defense was not accepted by the jury. One of the continuing problems of the criminal justice system is the definition of insanity. Seguin's jury agreed that he was "mentally impaired" — whatever that meant — but not legally insane. His friend, quoted above, thought that he had "snapped," which suggests a sudden attack either of rage or insanity. Although Seguin went about his killings deliberately and took time to accomplish them all, the case is classified as a sudden attack because there apparently was no warning of any trouble.

Mass murders (discussed separately in Chapter 2) cross into the category of "sudden attack." Examples are given in both chapters to illustrate the difficulty in trying to understand cases using single categories. Child murders are not easy to understand or to categorize. To clarify the complexity of the problems involved in understanding the whole topic, the best strategy is to use examples in different places, as seems appropriate. The first, from Prospect, Connecticut, in 1977, is not only an example of sudden attack as well as of mass murder but also of murder to cover up sexual molestation by someone not a serial killer. The implication in the newspaper articles was that the sexual molestation, for which there was no other indication than the confession of the killer, had occurred just prior to the murders.

The people involved in this case are not the ones we usually think of in connection with abuse and child murder. Prospect is a small community of fewer than 8,000 people about fifteen miles west of New Haven. There, some time after four o'clock in the morning of July 22, 1977, firefighters found numerous bodies in a burning house. Nine were counted when they were all finally removed from the burned-out building later in the afternoon. Frederick Jr. (12), Sharon (10), Debbie (9), Paul (8), Rod (6), Holly (5), Mary Lou (4), with their mother, Cheryl Beaudoin (29), and Jennifer Santoro (6), a niece who was staying overnight, all died. It was clear that the deaths were not accidental — some of the victims were bound, and some died of head injuries rather than of smoke inhalation. Investigators found blood and bloody fingerprints in a bathtub. The family dog was chained, unharmed, to a tree outside the house.

Fred Beaudoin Sr., the husband of Cheryl and father of all the children except Jennifer, was notified at the Pratt & Whitney aircraft factory where he worked the midnight shift. According to the newspaper accounts, the Beaudoins had lived in their $40,000 ranch-style, red-shingled house for eleven years. The neighborhood was one of $35,000-to-$45,000 homes (at 1977 prices) owned primarily by technical workers in nearby industrial plants. Beaudoin had been a machinist at the aircraft plant for twelve years and had grown up in a home nearby. Neighbors said that the family was quiet, with well-behaved children. Fred Jr., the oldest boy, delivered newspapers and consequently was the best known of the children.

One neighbor, who had been a friend of the family since she moved to the area nine years earlier, said that the whole family was very close and had planned to go camping together in Maine in two weeks. Beaudoin had just bought a small camper for the trip. Cheryl Beaudoin was a full-time homemaker who baby-sat for an acquaintance who was a programmer for a data-processing firm. That woman usually brought her children to the Beaudoin house at 7:30 in the morning and picked them up after work. Neighbors had called her that morning to tell her about the fire.

Since the fire started while Beaudoin was at work, he was not a suspect. The police did not take long to identify one. Early the next morning they arrested Lorne Acquin (27), referred to as a "roofer," and charged him with nine counts of arson. Lorne, Beaudoin's foster brother, had grown up with him and now lived off and on with Beaudoin's family, sleeping in a basement room. Beaudoin's mother — Lorne's foster mother — said that Lorne had been "troubled" ever since a fire (in which no one was killed) destroyed their home fourteen years earlier. According to her, he began stealing after that and was arrested once for a shooting. Police stated, however, that Lorne had a long record of larceny and burglary arrests and "had served at least two sentences in state correctional institutions."

Lorne's foster sister had difficulty in believing in his guilt. "You should have seen him with those kids. He'd sit and play with them for hours," she told reporters. Others, however, had less trouble believing that Lorne was guilty. People who knew him said that he had a "hot temper," was quick to fight, and had been arrested for a shooting in a tavern. In fact, on the night the fire broke out, he had had a fight in a bar shortly after the blaze in the Beaudoin house began.

The defense tried to show that the fight occurred at the same time as the murders, but witnesses from the tavern and a clock damaged in the fire confirmed that the house fire started an hour or more before the brawl in the tavern took place. Lorne Acquin confessed to the crime and admitted that he had set the house on fire to cover up the fact that he had sexually molested one of the children. This act of molestation seems to have been the triggering event that set off his killing fury; as noted, some of the victims died of head injuries, some were bound. This case was not simply one of arson. After the deaths, Lorne attempted to cover up the crimes by burning the house. The jury convicted him despite the defense's charges of police ineptitude and misbehavior and attempts to exclude the confession as "coerced" (Case 4).

The Beaudoins were quiet people who had lived in their small community for years: a working husband, a boy with a paper route, a mother who stayed home with the children and sometimes took care of a friend's child. A grandmother of the murdered children had fostered the convicted killer from the time he was 9 years old, and his foster brother, the children's father, gave him shelter when he was homeless. The children knew their killer, played with him, and had even gone berry picking with him on the day before they were killed. This picture of the family is almost idyllic. On the other hand, the convicted killer, born on an Indian reservation in Canada and fostered at least from the age of 9, had a troubled past involving crime and violence.

The next case involves farmers living in rural Missouri. The Buckners ran a small dairy farm in Elkland, a community of about 250 people with one gas station, two stores, and two churches, not far from Springfield. The family members were hard workers, with little money and no phone, but they were well respected. In 1987 the oldest boy, Kirk (14), had just started high school in nearby Marshfield. People in town liked him. He never complained of poverty, never skimped his work, and always "looked you in the eye and talked sense," as Elkland residents told reporters. Yet his uncle, Jim Schnick (36), married to Kirk's Aunt Julie (20), his father's sister, accused Kirk of wiping out his own family and trying to destroy Jim's, too. According to Jim, after Kirk killed his parents and siblings, he had driven to the Schnick home and killed Julie. He would have killed everyone, but Jim, though injured, grabbed a knife and fought back, killing Kirk. Jim's 8-year-old son called police, who found Kirk dead, with a gun in his hand, and Jim wounded. They rushed Jim to the hospital and began to piece the crime together.

At the Buckner house they found Michael (2), Dennis (8), Tim (6), and their mother, Jeanette (37). The body of the father, Steven (35), was found at a nearby cemetery. They were all shot dead. According to the first reconstruction of the crime, based on what Jim said, Kirk had killed his brothers. Then, as his mother raced to the house in response to the clamor, he had shot her. Next, he killed his father, placed the body in their pickup truck, drove to the cemetery, and dropped off the body there on the way to his aunt's house. Poverty was suggested by the police as Kirk's motive. The Buckner house was shabby and poorly kept. Since Kirk had just started high school, the sheriff speculated that the new experience had exposed him to a better life-style that made him unhappy and resentful at being poor and having to work so hard on the farm.

Even though he presented this scenario, the sheriff was uneasy about it. Townspeople were even more upset. Many of them knew Kirk and could not believe that he was responsible for the killings. Moreover, the brothers-in-law, Jim and Steve, had been quarreling lately (the police refused to reveal what about). When the sheriff looked more closely at the case against Kirk, it unraveled: Kirk was lefthanded, but the gun was found in his right hand; moreover, he weighed 90 pounds, and his father a hefty 280. Could Kirk have maneuvered his father's body into the pickup and then unloaded it at the cemetery? Furthermore, Jim was not nearly as badly wounded as he had pretended to be; the hospital was ready to release him, but he did not want to leave. Jim was arrested and confessed, although at the trial the defense said that the confession was "forced." He was tried only for the murder of his wife and two of the Buckner children. His motive was never revealed in the newspaper articles, but his murderous behavior apparently came as a complete surprise to everyone, and so the case is included here. He was convicted; the jury recommended the death penalty, and the judge agreed. The townspeople were in shock, even though they were the ones who had revealed the trouble between the brothers-in-law. According to the news articles, they had believed that Jim was a "good man" who went to church and always helped people out when they were in need. For the first time, the townspeople began to lock their doors (Case 365).

Desire for revenge can trigger a killing rage. In 1978 in Rockford, Illinois, Simon Nelson (whose age was not given in the newspaper articles) shot, stabbed, beat, and slit the throats of his six children, who ranged in age from

3 to 12. His wife had left him and gone to Milwaukee. There, she phoned him to say that she planned to divorce him. After the call he killed the children "to get even" and then went to Milwaukee to demand that she return. When they argued, he began to beat her. Police were called, and when Nelson was being questioned, he told them to "check the children." A psychiatrist testified that he was sane when he killed the children. He was convicted and sentenced to six concurrent terms of one hundred to two hundred years. Since the first news report in the *New York Times* appeared on January 8, 1978, it is possible that the killings took place in December 1977. None of the articles gave the precise date (Case 50).

Marital strife often places the children of the marriage at risk, as shown by examples in earlier chapters. Sometimes these murders come without any warning while in other cases they occur after threats or previous violence, but when life appears relatively tranquil, the violence is unexpected. In the case of the Greens, in 1985, Donald (27), who worked at odd jobs, had been separated from his wife, Josephine (23), for a few months. She had taken their daughters, Shaquoia (5) and Ebony (3), to live with her sister, Evelyn Lloyd, in a housing project in the Bronx, New York City. There was documented hostility between Josephine and her husband. Early in September, they had had a fight and he slashed her, but she had refused to sign a complaint. She talked about getting a protection order against him but never did so. On September 18 she gave him permission to take his daughters home to spend the night, and he brought them back the next morning before ten o'clock. Evelyn was in her bedroom at the time. She heard no argument, no raised voices — but suddenly three shots rang out. She ran to the room where the shots were fired and saw Donald put a gun to his head and fire once more. Josephine, Shaquoia, and Ebony all died at the scene. Donald died about an hour later at Lincoln Hospital (Case 307).

Another case of a sudden attack stemming from a broken marriage was that of Edward Brenta (41), a construction worker in the borough of Queens, New York City. He and his wife, Judy (37), had separated after fifteen years of marriage. According to the news article, he was "very, very depressed." On Sunday, December 20, 1987, he telephoned his wife, offering to take one of their daughters to Radio City Music Hall and then on Monday to pick up Judy and drive her to work. She agreed, and the Music Hall visit went off without incident. Then on Monday, after he drove off with Judy in the car, the couple began to argue. Friends later told reporters that they were always fighting. He shot her less than a block away from their home. After he killed her, he drove around the block and entered the apartment, where he shot and killed both his daughters — Marie (11), in her bedroom, and Carmell (15), in the kitchen. He poured kerosene around the kitchen and started a fire. Afterward, he went into the living room, sat down, and shot himself (Case 363).

Sometimes the marital breakup does not inspire an immediate response, but it may be part of a combination of stresses that causes an individual to snap. In March 1979, Walter Grudzinski (43) showed no reported signs of serious mental imbalance. He was upset, however, because his wife had divorced him and gone to Florida some months earlier. Moreover, the profits of his small garden-supply and gift shop in Elwood, Long Island, New York, were down. His distress over these matters apparently sent no warning signals to his acquaintances. Then on March 10, 1979, in late evening, he quarreled bitterly with his business partner, Paul Gebel. Walter had a permit for a gun that he kept in the store; as the quarrel escalated, he snatched it up and pointed it at Paul, who ran out the door. Walter shot at the other people in the store — Paul's stepson, John, and three of John's friends. He killed John, wounded the others, and then ran out of the store and jumped in his car. According to the newspaper, the survivors' first thought was that he was going after Paul, but instead he drove home, shot and killed his 15-year-old daughter, and critically wounded his 12-year-old son, Edward, who died four days later. After he shot his children, he killed himself. The newspaper offered no explanation for Walter's behavior other than the quarrel with his partner, which seems to have been the trigger for his actions (Case 78).

If adults can feel overwhelmed by the pressure of caring for more than one small child at a time, the pressure on adolescents can be especially severe. In 1989 a 12-year-old girl, Arva Betts, in Fort Lauderdale, Florida, was caring for her 15-month-old half sister, Tiffany Caesar, and 2-year-old half brother, Andrew Caesar. She said that when she caught Andrew about to drink bug spray, she took it away from him and he started yelling. She hit and choked him and then put him, still alive, to bed. Next, Tiffany broke a figurine. Arva started to choke her, too, and then realized what she was doing and stopped, but in the morning she found Andrew dead and covered him with a blanket. She did not tell her mother, Sally Butterfield. Arva had no history of violent behavior and no criminal record. She told investigators that she had been overwhelmed by the responsibility of daily baby-sitting, but her confession was ruled inadmissable. A psychiatrist testified that Arva's mother had told her that she must not reveal to anyone that she had been abused by her mother's lover. Arva was tried as an adult and her mother investigated for neglect. There was no further information (Case 428).

Sometimes there is no warning because the victim is left with people whom the parents do not know well or who have no stake in the child's well-being. In early November 1981, in Omaha, Nebraska, Carrie Farfolla left her 2-year-old son, Dustin, and his 9-month-old sister, Jessica, with Christine Contreras (31), a woman whom Carrie did not even know. Carrie had told a friend that she did not like kids and wanted to put hers up for adoption. The friend recommended Christine. Carrie said that she would leave the children with her for a week or so to see how it worked out. Meanwhile, Carrie's friend found a couple willing to adopt Jessica, leaving Dustin with Christine, who said that she wanted to adopt him. On February 22, 1982, Dustin wet his pants and Christine slapped him, knocking him across the room, where he struck his head on the sink. She took him to the hospital, but he was dead on arrival (Case 823).

It is difficult to classify this perpetrator because Christine was not the mother of the victim, or a relative, or a friend, or legally a foster parent, and she could not be called a baby-sitter under the circumstances. "Parafoster" seems to be the most logical category. This case also illustrates some of the difficulty faced by any government agency charged with protecting children. Carrie, Dustin's mother, continued to get money from AFDC (Aid for Dependent Children) for Dustin and Jessica. There is no indication that the agency administering that program knew anything of Carrie's plans to give up her children or to involve Christine. Indeed, Christine claimed that she did not even know the mother's name when she was arrested after Dustin's death. Police learned who the mother was after news of the death had been published, and Carrie called her "common-law husband," who called social workers, who then called police.

In another case, in Queens, New York City, in 1990, careful investigative work absolved a dog of the crime of murder. Its owner, Jason Radtke (19), said that the dog ate 6-day-old Anthony Radtke. The German shepherd was X-rayed and baby parts were seen in the stomach, but the investigators felt impelled to look more closely. The dog was killed and the parts autopsied. The medical examiner reported that the dog had not dismembered the infant and that the father's story that the dog ate the child alive was not true. Jason ultimately confessed that the crying baby woke him; when he took the baby from the crib and began to walk him, the baby suddenly peed on him, so he threw the infant to the floor, killing him. Then Jason dismembered the body with a razor and left it "in a position to be consumed" by the dog to cover up the crime. Although he later recanted, saying that the confession was co-erced, his wife, who had pretended to be asleep during the murder and butch-ery, cooperated with the police to verify the original confession. With the medical evidence clear, Jason was charged with intentional murder and mur-der resulting from depraved indifference (Case 645). Jason's 11-month-old stepdaughter Kayla slept unharmed through the whole incident.

Summary

There is no possible way to eliminate the specific incidents that trigger rage. They are, for the most part, too common, too ordinary in human interac-tion. There are several possible approaches, however, to reduce the frequency with which child deaths occur as a result of adult rage. One is to continue to emphasize the danger of shaking infants. Organizations concerned with child abuse already employ posters and slogans, but the information needs to reach a broader audience. Another is to increase education about techniques that people can use to control their rage. And we need to prepare people in con-tact with small children to have more realistic expectations of what small children are likely to do and how vulnerable they are. The cases described in this chapter show that such education is essential.

In our society there is no approved way for a child to express anger — anything that he may do to show anger is met with disapproval. As a result, children pick up their ideas of how to react to anger from their peers or from the mixed messages that we adults send in our behavior in person, on televi-sion, in films, and in newspapers. We have to start teaching ways of express-ing anger other than violent ones to our children much earlier than we do now.

If the newspaper reports on all the cases classified as violent abuse gave more information, it is probable that most or all of them could be classified either as sudden attacks or as the culmination of sustained abuse. The assess-ment of risk to children must be improved if we are to reduce the number of deaths. Such an assessment will be more difficult to make directly with the sudden attack cases, since there has been no previous involvement with agencies charged with protecting children. Consequently, instead of direct intervention with the family or the child, the only effective approach will be the general education of the public, particularly young parents or couples about to start families. Moreover, the dangers of uncontrolled rage need to be presented to everyone. Currently, "road rage" — a different aspect of the same problem that is involved in a substantial amount of child abuse and child killing, the inappropriate expression of anger — is being mentioned as a growing problem. The use of television and other mass communications media has tremendous power to influence public behavior. With the proven ability of the media to manipulate consumer behavior, surely we can develop messages for parents on how to channel expressions of anger in less dangerous and destructive ways.

CHAPTER 6

Death after Sustained Abuse: Killing without Remorse

The most difficult cases to write about are the ones whose perpetrators seem to lack any empathy for their victims. In Table 1.19 they make up the 13 percent categorized under "sustained abuse," but their number should be significantly higher. Many of the cases counted under "violent abuse" had insufficient information to place them in either the "sudden attack" or "sustained abuse" category. Both categories are consequently lower than they would be if more information had been available.

People who are sustained abusers seldom express any remorse for the suffering that they cause children. A recent article in the *Lexington Herald-Leader* reported on a study in a British hospital where researchers secretly filmed parents whose children were hospitalized for injuries from abuse. An appalling thirty-one of thirty-three parents who were filmed further injured or attempted to kill the hospitalized children when they thought that they were alone. As soon as a nurse or doctor entered the room, they pretended to be affectionate with the children (*Lexington Herald-Leader*, October 28, 1997). These sustained abusers also rarely commit suicide, unlike other child killers.

The children whom sustained abusers kill have sometimes been tormented for years. The litany of injuries inflicted by these perpetrators almost always includes one or more of the following: broken ribs (in different stages of healing); extensive bruises (also in different stages of healing); spiral fracture of limbs (most likely a leg), which indicates that the limb was twisted until the bone snapped; cigarette burns, especially around the eyes or genitals; lacerated internal organs, particularly the liver; and skull fractures.

The victim in one of the worst cases in our records was a 3-year-old boy, nicknamed Baby Lollipop by police because of the T-shirt he wore. His body was found on November 2, 1990, abandoned in Miami Beach, Florida. His skin was almost entirely covered with black and blue bruises, his bones were broken, and his body was shriveled by malnutrition. According to the newspaper, he had been beaten with a bat, broomsticks, and belts, his eyes were poked, and plates had been smashed over his head; the tops of two front teeth were missing, and he had scars from lit cigarette burns. The abuse had been going on for so long that his left arm was fixed at an obtuse angle and his left leg was bigger than the right one. His mother, who had at least three additional but unabused children, was addicted to cocaine, while his father was a drug dealer who had died before Baby Lollipop (whose real name was Lazaro Figuero) was born. The mother's partner in the killing was another woman with whom the mother and children were living (Case 827). There was no information on the final outcome of the case.

Another child who endured a miserable existence before she was killed was Randi Anderson, who was born on May 26, 1985, to crack addicts on welfare. Despite this history and the fact that her parents were reported to Social Services five times between 1985 and 1989 for neglect and violence in the home, she stayed with her six brothers and sisters until March 1989 when she was finally removed and sent to a kin foster home with her father's sister, Sandra Priester. Sandra told case workers that she was having trouble with Randi and was not sure that she was the right person to care for her. By this time, two months short of her fourth birthday, Randi was a very difficult child to handle—she scrawled on the wall with lipstick, stole items, broke toys deliberately, defecated on the floor, and hoarded food. According to Child Welfare workers she badly needed counseling but never received any. During the fifteen months she spent with Sandra, Randi had several different case workers, one of whom was dealing with forty-four cases, well above the recommended number.

Randi and her sister were finally removed from Sandra's care on June 15, 1990. Randi was again given to a kin foster, another aunt, Sophilla Murray, who was already looking after two of Randi's little brothers. Randi lived with Sophilla for less than five months before she was killed in November 1990 by Sophilla's son, Robert, a 20 year old who took care of the children while his mother worked as a telephone operator. Robert said that Randi "got on my nerves." Her thigh bone was broken in two, her liver lacerated, her body battered. Robert was sentenced to one and one-third to four years. His mother drew the same sentence after she pleaded guilty to attempted murder because she did not get medical attention for Randi. Case workers said that since Sophilla was already caring for two foster children, adding Randi may have been too much to ask of her and her son (Case 832).

Our files only have twenty-four cases of children who were killed in foster homes. The next case, like the previous ones, indicates how a failure to supervise the situation properly can be fatal. In October 1993 the *Arizona Republic* reported the death of China Marie Davis, a 2-year-old girl who lived in a foster home in Maricopa County. Her foster mother, Dorothy Jane Livingston (47), was charged with fourteen counts of child abuse, and first-degree murder. Dorothy had taken China Marie into her home on December 1, 1992. She twice had asked Child Protective Services to remove the girl, and employees had twice talked her into keeping the child. China Marie's parents had lost custody because of drug abuse, but they had complained to Child Protective Services that their daughter was being abused at the foster home and asked that she be taken out of it. In the hospital, detectives found scratches on her upper right shoulder, head, and face as well as bruises on her chest, stomach, ribs, groin, and the tops of both feet. The indictment against the foster mother mentioned fractures or breaks in China Marie's collarbone, both arms, both wrists, her left hand, both thighs, a rib, and her spine. The injuries had occurred between December 1, 1992, and October 31, 1993, when China Marie died in the hospital. Several of the broken bones had never been treated. The police investigation indicated that eleven years before Dorothy became a licensed foster mother, two children whom she had been baby-sitting were injured. Dorothy pleaded not guilty and said that the injuries occurred at the house of Alice Colter, an unlicensed baby-sitter with whom China Marie was left at times. Alice denied the allegation, and the newspapers did not report any charge against her. Two Child Protective Services employees, a supervisor and a case worker, were fired for mishandling the case. There was no additional report before the end of 1993 (Case 756).

Returned Children

Children who are placed in foster homes may sometimes be at risk if supervision is poor, but those who are taken away from their parents by Social Services and then returned should be considered as extremely high-risk cases. Children are not usually removed unless there is already strong evidence for severe abuse. Richard Gelles, an expert in the field, suggests that great caution should be used before returning such children to their homes, and he believes that in many cases they should not be returned at all (Gelles, 1996). We agree. Our records have twenty-three victims, almost all of whom were killed within the first year after their return and many within the first few weeks (Table 1.26). One example is the case of a 19-year-old unemployed single mother who in 1982 poured boiling water over her 6-month-old son. He had been returned to her a month earlier by the Department of Social Services. The reason for his original removal was not mentioned in the news article, probably because confidentiality laws did not permit the department to release it. The mother had two other children, a 3-year-old boy and an 18-month-old girl, who were unharmed (Case 522).

Another case of a returned child dying is that of Shawn Nicely. Renee Nicely (20), Shawn's mother, came from a broken home and had been abused as a child. The public tends to assume that all abused children grow up to be abusers, but Gelles argues that only about 30 percent do (1996:77). Renee had been sent to live with an aunt where she met Allen Bass, a young man her own age. She had five children by him, but because she lived on welfare, she did not share her apartment with him. He continued to reside with his mother most of the time. In July 1982 their 3-year-old son Shawn died of a beating, but it was difficult to determine who actually did the killing. Shawn's 5-year-old brother said that "they [his parents] hated" the boy; he added that Allen had stepped on Shawn's back and then hit him on the head with a broom. According to the prosecutor, Shawn had suffered "no less than a dozen . . . hateful beatings" in his last few months of life. It was claimed that when the boy played on a small wooden horse, Allen repeatedly pushed him into a door frame so he hit his head. Allen also gave Shawn beer until the boy was too drunk to stand up. Allen's lawyer, on the other hand, said that Renee killed the child unintentionally in a psychotic rage triggered by an abortion that she had undergone the day before and that Allen had slept through the whole thing. The lawyer contended that Shawn's brother lied to protect his mother and to put the blame on his father. The prosecution was concealing evidence that Allen had a "good relationship" with the children, the defense claimed.

Some witnesses also blamed Renee. They said that she was repeatedly a child abuser, that once she had dropped Shawn on his head on the pavement. Moreover, Renee had told friends that the boy was not hers; she thought that she had been given the wrong baby when he was returned to her at the age of 3 months (she had left him in the hospital and he had lived with a foster mother for that time). Allen's mother had legal custody of all the children, and, according to one news report, it was she who told Renee that she had been given the wrong child. A neighbor took in Shawn for a time and wanted to adopt him, but Renee balked at the last moment and took him back. The neighbor said that Shawn did not want to go with his mother, but she could not protest because she had no legal right to him. At the trials, Allen and Renee each was found guilty, she of murder, he of aggravated manslaughter. He was sentenced to twenty years, five short of the maximum, while she was sentenced to life plus twenty-five years with no eligibility for parole until she reached the age of forty-two. Both accused the other of the killing. Both said that they would appeal, but no additional information had appeared in the *New York Times* by 1993 (Case 205).

Not all children are killed soon after their return. Her 8-to-9-year-old children seem to have posed particular problems for Shulamis Riegler (33), who, in 1986, pleaded guilty to assault of her oldest son, then either 8 or 9. She was put on probation for five years, and he and his two siblings were turned over to foster homes through Ohel Children's Home, the only orthodox Jewish organization in Brooklyn that places children in foster or adoptive homes. The children were returned to Shulamis in 1989, for reasons that no agency will discuss because of legal confidentiality constraints. At the time of the 1986 incident, Yaakov, another son, mildly retarded but teachable, was about 4 years old; he was killed in 1990, when he was 8. Other children in the home, including Yaakov's two older brothers, 12 and 10, and a 15-month-old toddler, were apparently not being abused. Shulamis's husband, Moses, was charged with child endangerment because he had not done enough to keep

Yaakov from being abused. He and the older boys were at synagogue for Yom Kippur observances when Yaakov was killed. If it were not for the earlier incident when Yaakov's older brother was assaulted, the retardation might be regarded as a main cause of the abuse. School officials, however, did not indicate that the retardation made Yaakov a difficult child.

Several organizations had reported that they believed that Yaakov was being abused before he was killed, but no action was taken. Yaakov died of head injuries, but in addition he showed a "pattern of broken bones and other injuries" in various stages of healing, including a broken leg fractured shortly before he was hospitalized for the final time. His mother admitted twisting his leg so hard that she heard a bone crack. On the day of the beating that killed him, she said that he was sick, vomiting, and had diarrhea. She was fasting because of Yom Kippur but she was also six months pregnant and did not feel well. Since her other children and her husband were at synagogue, she repeatedly had to clean up Yaakov. Finally, she lost control, she said, and lashed out, striking him several times so hard that his head hit the wall and he lost consciousness. Nurses and doctors at the hospital were unable to save him. Shulamis pleaded guilty to manslaughter and received a seven and one-half-to-fifteen-year sentence (Case 647).

Another example of a reunited parent killing a child is Lance Corporal Kenneth Cook, a 22-year-old Marine stationed at Camp Pendleton, California, in August 1993. In this case, however, it was the parent who returned, not the child, so the victim is not counted in Table 1.26. Kenneth had recently returned from assignment in the Pacific where he had been since July 1992. His daughter, Tiffani, was 13 months old, having been born just about the time he left. According to the news article, he "apparently felt the child had rejected him" and had been battering her for weeks. On August 8 he grew furious at her crying, punched her in the abdomen, and picked her up by the head and "squeezed it in his hand while whipping her body back and forth." To make it look as if she had fallen out of her crib, he took the crib apart and left her on the floor. She died during the night. He was charged with murder. His wife was charged with child endangerment because she had left Tiffani and Tiffani's 2-year-old brother, Nate, in Kenneth's care. The *New York Times* had no later information on this case (Case 778).

One of the earliest cases recorded in our files is an example of a returned child who was subsequently killed. On June 24, 1977, Rubin Almeyda, a

3-month-old boy, was dead on arrival at Columbia Presbyterian Hospital in Manhattan, New York City. He had been taken from his parents, Ralph Almeyda and Lourdes Delgado, in March, a week or so after he was born because, according to one news article, the Bureau of Child Welfare did not think that the couple could make a decent home for him. Lourdes was in a wheelchair and they were homeless at the time. A psychiatrist had said that Lourdes was paranoid and self-destructive, a threat to the baby. In April, at a hearing over whether to return Rubin or leave him in a foster home, the presiding judge decided that he should be sent back to his parents, who now had an apartment. Thus, Rubin was returned to them on May 2, but he was dead on June 24. A homemaker helper reported, only seventy-two hours before he died, that Lourdes and Ralph seemed to be "capable and good parents." However, Ralph's mother, who was never called to testify in the hearing that determined Rubin's fate, said that she might have convinced the judge not to return the child. She had evicted the couple from her home because her son had been abusing *her* for years.

Between May 2 and June 24, Rubin had been horribly treated—every rib had been broken twice or more, his buttocks and feet were burned, his skull was fractured. Lourdes said that Ralph put the baby into a hot, empty pot on the stove. Rubin's body was first buried in Potter's Field when Lourdes said that she could not be bothered with funeral arrangements and Ralph was in prison. The St. Vincent de Paul Society ultimately buried Rubin in a plot that they owned. One newspaper article mentioned that warnings such as the abuse of Rubin's mother, her possible testimony, and the Almeydas' refusal to admit a visiting nurse—all of which were known, or should have been, to people in the Bureau of Child Welfare—were "dissipated" in various ways. The article also indicated that in the advocacy competition between lawyers, no one spoke for the child or his safety. Ralph was sentenced to fifteen years to life but there was no information about Lourdes, who had not been charged. Indeed, one article reported that she wanted to "work with kids" (Case 2).

Although the information is sketchy, it appears that 5-year-old Adam Mann may be another example of a child whose fate was sealed when he was returned to an abusive home. Adam died on March 5, 1990, of massive head, chest, and abdominal injuries; his liver was split in two by the final beating. At one time or another, nearly every bone in his body had been broken. His mother and father were originally charged with murder but pleaded guilty to lesser charges. Michelle Mann, Adam's mother, was unmarried, in her twenties. Adam's father, Rufus Chisham, did not live with the family but, according to an upstairs neighbor, "came and went all the time." Michelle had at least five children including Adam, who lived with her in public housing. Neighbors said that she was a "good mother," did not work, and stayed home with the kids. Adam had three brothers, ages 7, 8, and 10, who also bore the marks of abuse: scars, burn marks, and welts. His sister, 8 months old, showed no signs of abuse. The maltreatment of the older boys was long-standing. They had been photographed in 1983, before Adam was born, for a television documentary on child abuse. Its producer, Carole Langer, said that they showed signs then of having been beaten. When the program aired in 1985, an update reported that the children were in foster homes.

Confidentiality laws, the *New York Times* article stated, prevented the newspaper from getting any additional information. Reporters did discover, however, that Rufus had been in prison for six months for robbery and assault, but they did not say when. He was charged in 1985 with beating his child, but, according to the *Times*, the outcome "could not be learned." In January 1990, two months before Adam was killed, Rufus was arrested and charged with assault, presumably of the children, although the newspaper article did not specify the victim, but he failed to show up for the court appearance. After Adam's death, Rufus was charged with first-degree assault that was later upgraded to second-degree murder; there was no information in the newspaper on the outcome of that charge. Michelle pleaded guilty to assault. The news article said that she would be paroled and that Child Welfare authorities planned to reunite the family (Case 640). This case is a stereotypical example of the problem that Richard Gelles raises with family reunification programs in *The Book of David*. He does not believe that children should ever be returned to a home when the evidence of abuse is persistent and clear. We agree.

In this next case, the child was killed after being returned to his father, but the return was not ordered by a court. In fact, Andrea Murray, the mother, had legal custody. Two-year-old Datwan Murray was beaten to death in June 1993 in Brooklyn. His father, Christopher Willis (28), was charged with murder and also with possession of illegal firearms and controlled substances. Andrea had allowed Datwan's father to take him on a visit on March 13 but he never returned the child. For reasons unknown to the police, Andrea did not report the situation. Wanda Brown, who was Christopher's girlfriend, found Datwan naked and unconscious in bed and took him to the hospital, where he died the same day. Details of the abuse were not given, although police told the newspaper that there was evidence that the toddler had been abused since March: "We believe the abuse took place almost continuously during that time," Captain Plackenmeyer said. Police found thousands of vials of crack, six handguns, and $80,000 in cash at Christopher's home. According to the news article, Christopher was not just a street-corner pusher but an upper-level drug dealer (Case 797).

Home, Sweet Home

Not all the victims of sustained abuse have been previously removed from the home. Apple Miranda, 2 months old, was living with her mother and father in Manhattan. Her father, David (20), wanted to be a rap singer but was unemployed. Although her mother, Eurize Miranda, worked, the couple was having difficulty making ends meet on her salary and had applied for welfare. Their building manager said that they had not paid rent for several months. One Thursday morning in October 1992, David called Eurize at work to report that the baby had stopped breathing. She came home as soon as possible and took Apple to the nearest hospital, where the child was pronounced dead eighteen minutes later. The specific cause of death was a brain hemorrhage, but the medical examiner said that the brain hemorrhage was only the final problem, compounded by a series of earlier injuries, including broken ribs.

Friends of David said that he always played gently with the baby and could not have been the one who broke her ribs, but neighbors told conflicting stories. David was charged with second-degree murder, although his defense lawyer argued that Eurize had injured the child "inadvertently" in the morning and left for work unaware that anything was wrong. Eurize was not charged and there was no additional report (Case 729).

Another example of a child who was never taken from the home is that of 5-year-old Amy Shipley of Crown Point, Indiana. In 1990, Amy vomited and choked on pepper-laced milk. Gloria Shipley, her stepmother, said that she began putting pepper in the little girl's food to discourage her when she started to mimic an older sister's habit of gorging: "I didn't believe the pepper was going to hurt her in any way." However, at the hospital before she died, Amy was found to be malnourished, dehydrated, and covered with bruises. The

autopsy showed that she had been weakened by beatings and starvation before she had choked on the milk. Gary Shipley was a surgeon, and his wife
was a former pediatrics nurse, so ignorance of the effect of the pepper seemed
unlikely. Gloria, Gary's second wife, the stepmother to his three daughters,
had her nursing license suspended in 1988 because she failed to complete a
drug-rehabilitation course. At the same time, Gary was placed on probation
for ten years by the Indiana licensing board because of allegations that he
improperly prescribed medicine for relatives. In 1989 the couple were investigated in Vincennes for abusing Danielle (8), but no indictments were handed
down. At the trial after Amy's death, Danielle testified that the children were
forced to take cold showers and ice baths and eat food laced with pepper. The
Shipleys denied most of the allegations and said that they only spanked their
children to control "wildly deviant behavior." Jury members apparently were
not convinced by the defense's claim that the death was an accident. The
Shipleys were convicted and sentenced to sixty-five years — fifty for murder
and fifteen for child neglect — to be served consecutively (Case 648).

In another case, Kristie Bruen, age 4, was beaten to death on October 8,
1980, in the White Plains, New York, apartment where she lived with her
mother and her mother's lover. Both adults were convicted of the beating.
Neighbors testified that the two had beaten, kicked, whipped, starved, and
imprisoned the little girl. When Kristie was brought to Peekskill Community Hospital, workers counted over two hundred bruises on her small body;
moreover, she had lost over 40 percent of her blood. The defense said that
the autopsy photos should not have been allowed as evidence because they
were so prejudicial. Kristie's mother, Jana Lee Bruen (26), and her boyfriend,
Wesley Fisher (32), were convicted on July 31, 1981. She was sentenced to
eight and one-half to twenty-five years; he was given twelve and one-half to
twenty-five (Case 102).

In still another case, Jeffrey Harden (5 months old) died of burns in New
York City on January 17, 1992. Jeffrey Phillips, Doris Harden's boyfriend,
said that he had accidentally caused the fatal burns to the baby's groin, buttocks, and legs because he wiped him with a cloth that he had not realized was
soaked with cleaning fluid. The medical examiner had a different explanation: the burns were caused by immersion in scalding water. The baby also had
three broken ribs. Doris, a crack addict who had refused treatment, had served

three years in prison for holding down a 7-year-old girl while another woman sexually assaulted the child with a toilet plunger. At the time of the news article, no one had been charged and the case was still under investigation. There was no followup article in the *New York Times* (Case 724). This case was classified as a death caused by the mother's boyfriend, but since the investigation had not been completed it is possible that the mother herself was responsible. Cases were usually classified according to the individual charged and only changed to another classification if later articles warranted it.

The next case provides an example of some of the frustrations faced by Social Services and legal personnel because of a lack of consensus in the society about what to do to protect children. In June 1981, Jeremy Fourthman, 6 months old, died in New Port Ritchey, Florida, of an infection complicated by malnutrition, dehydration, and severe sunburn. His mother and father were both charged. After Jackie, Jeremy's mother, pleaded guilty to third-degree murder and aggravated child abuse, the judge ordered both parents to refrain from having any more children for fifteen years. Jackie was 20; the father, James Burchell, was 29. He appealed, and the Second District Court ruled that the prohibition was unconstitutional; she never appealed the decision. Probation officers allowed Jackie to leave Florida for Indiana, but then she left Indiana without permission and her probation officer obtained an arrest warrant. In June or July 1983 she gave birth to a son in Phoenix, Arizona, and allowed an aunt to adopt the boy. The newspaper article did not name the father of this child, nor did it specify whether the "aunt" was hers, the child's, or the father's. When Jackie applied for money from AFDC (Aid for Dependent Children), she was apprehended. She was placed in jail in Pasco County because neither she nor her family could post the $10,000 bond required. A shipyard owner who heard about the case posted the bond because, according to the newspaper, he could not see how the state could decide when someone "can breed and when you can't. That's Big Brother." Jackie took a bus back to Indiana. In March 1985 she was sentenced to three years for giving birth outside the state (Case 148). This case raises a host of issues that indicate some of the complications involved in protecting children in a society as highly mobile as ours. Even though this particular case occurred more than a decade ago, its concerns are still current. These issues are discussed at greater length in the final chapter of this volume.

The case of Jeremy's parents involved Florida, Indiana, and Arizona and created multiple problems for Child Welfare personnel. The next case also indicates some of the difficulties caused by events that occur in more than one state. Gary Dale Elliott Jr. (1 month old) died in April 1986 in a Brownsville, Texas, hospital of a brain hemorrhage from a fractured skull while he and his family were visiting South Padre Island. The doctor who supervised the autopsy said that the infant had suffered two skull fractures about ten days before the final hemorrhage. Greg, Gary's twin brother, had not accompanied the family because when Gary died in Texas, Greg was still hospitalized in Des Moines, Iowa, with a skull fracture and a broken arm. The parents were extradited to Texas for separate trials concerning Gary's death: Gary's father's trial was set for December 7, and his mother's about a month later. A newspaper article dated October 30, 1987, in the *Omaha World-Herald* stated that her attorney planned to argue that Iowa had jurisdiction since the injury took place there, but Iowa was not planning any prosecution since the couple was extradited to Texas. There was no follow-up in the Omaha paper (Case 564).

Apparently, in this case, both children were injured in Iowa about the same time. Greg was hospitalized but Gary went out of state with his parents and died in Texas. Greg seems to have recovered. The problem of jurisdiction is one that arises in other cases as well when an injury or crime occurs in one state and the death or disposal of the victim occurs in another. The issue is seldom discussed in research on child abuse or child fatalities. Moreover, there is little legislation to deal with the problem as it affects children.

The case of Michael Saad (3 months old) also had a special legal dimension. On Christmas Eve in 1980 his father, Thomas Saad, brought him to a hospital in Wichita, Kansas, in critical condition with multiple head injuries, which Thomas said were the result of a fall. Michael was placed on life-support systems. According to one article in the *New York Times*, Kansas law can declare an individual legally dead if three conditions are met: 1) the individual cannot breathe on his own; 2) the heart does not beat for a substantial amount of time without aid; and 3) there is an absence of spontaneous brain function. Michael met these conditions, but his father obtained a court order to keep hospital personnel from turning off the life support. If the child died, Thomas would be charged with murder, but his lawyer argued that he was "protecting his son," who was still alive. A January 5, 1981, article in the *Times* reported that a judge said that Michael was dead and should be taken off life support. He was, and his heart stopped immediately. An autopsy showed that in addition to his severe head injuries, both arms and several ribs had been broken "possibly at an earlier date." There was no follow-up on the outcome of the case against the father (Case 121).

The Cortez case is an example of sustained abuse that indicates the difficulties that legislation and official regulations can create for law officers and family members concerned about the welfare of a child. Jessica Cortez's death became a central issue in questions of confidentiality law and family preservation efforts. Child Welfare services came in for considerable criticism and the accusation that New York confidentiality laws were used to shield inefficiency and to avoid accountability. Jessica, age 5, died in December 1988 from a severe beating: she had bruises over her whole body, face, and head, her left arm was broken, she had a two-inch ulcerated scar on her lip, and her genital region was bruised. Neighbors had called police when they heard screams. Police found another child, Jennifer, 1 year old, apparently unharmed, who was turned over to Child Welfare officials. On the day after Jessica died, detectives returned to the apartment and found 9-year-old Nicholas, badly beaten but alive, in a closet; he was taken to the hospital. Abigail Cortez (25), Jessica's mother, and Adrien Lopez (25), Abigail's lover, both unemployed and living in a public housing project, were charged with second-degree murder.

The family of Jessica's biological father, Carlos Cortez, who had separated from his wife two years before Jessica's death, claimed that the Child Welfare staff had known for at least six years that Abigail beat her children savagely. Child Welfare first denied any investigation of child abuse, but, confronted with the claims of Jessica's paternal relatives, they agreed to make a more thorough search of the records. Ana Maria Barrios, Carlos's mother, had kept Jessica for two weeks in 1986 but was forced to return her to Abigail and Adrian. Carlos's mother and sister said that both Special Services for Children and the Bureau of Child Welfare were aware of the problems because they had intervened in the custody battle. The relatives complained that the court that returned Jessica to her mother had not been shown the documented history of neglect from a 1983 case in which the state was awarded custody of two other children. In the 1986 investigation, however, the social workers characterized Abigail as a "good mother"; since their report was favorable to the mother and not to the father, Abigail was given custody.

Numerous news articles on the case referred to bureaucratic bickering, charges and countercharges about mishandling the case, abuse of confidentiality laws to cover up inefficiency, and overall difficulties with the services that are supposed to protect children. According to one article, neighbors and relatives said that Abigail's boyfriend, not Abigail, was the abuser of Jessica and her siblings. However, in December 1988, the mother was indicted. She tried to use a "battered female" defense, which had been used successfully in an earlier case, but it was not accepted because Abigail herself showed no signs of abuse. In January 1989, Abigail and Adrian both pleaded not guilty. At Adrian's trial in October, he pleaded guilty in a plea bargain; the prosecution agreed to a sentence of twenty-two years to life, to spare Nicholas the trauma of testifying. Abigail was tried in November for murder, manslaughter, and endangering and pleaded guilty to manslaughter in the case of Jessica and first-degree assault of Nicholas. According to the newspaper, Adrian had actually killed Jessica. Abigail was convicted because she failed to stop Adrian from beating the children, failed to call police, and failed to get medical attention for Nicholas. In February 1990 she was sentenced to five to fifteen years. The article reporting the sentence alleged that social workers had frequent contact with the family before Jessica's death "but at critical stages failed to keep aware of the children's well-being" (Case 402).

In 1981, near Owensboro, Kentucky, there was another case of sustained abuse. One night, Wayne Maglinger pulled up behind a police cruiser and flashed his lights to attract the officer's attention. When Officer Wethington approached the car, he saw a baby lying on the seat. Wayne said that he had been feeding her when she suddenly started choking. At the trial, however, the officer testified that Wayne had been heading away from the hospital when he signaled the patrol car. Although Wayne said that the baby was choking, at the hospital no food particles were found in her throat. Melissa Maglinger, 4 months old, died, and Wayne was charged with murder. Ultimately, he and Melissa's mother, Theresa, pleaded guilty to lesser charges — he to first-degree manslaughter, she to criminal facilitation of assault. The trial was moved from Owensboro to Elizabethtown because of pretrial publicity.

Before Wayne was tried, the Daviess County coroner, who was also the child's great-uncle, was found guilty of official misconduct for failure to report child abuse before Melissa's death. During her brief four months of life, Melissa had had her skull fractured and thirteen ribs were broken. The state medical examiner said that she died of suffocation caused by compression of her chest. When the Jefferson County coroner reviewed the autopsy report, he concluded that she died from multiple injuries inflicted by someone. Two examples of parental behavior should have alerted authorities to the danger to the child. First, Melissa had been hospitalized with bronchitis two months before she died, but Wayne never visited her while she was in the hospital. And second, Theresa had taped a pacifier to the baby's mouth; a nurse removed it and admonished Theresa, but fifteen minutes later the pacifier was taped there again. Wayne was sentenced to two twenty-year sentences, while Theresa received one two-year sentence. The judge decided that the pair needed punishment, not treatment (Case 515).

Another case illustrates the complexities that are discovered through case reviews of child killings. In 1980, James Greene's daughter, Tamika, was born in New York City. Tamika's mother left James shortly after the birth because, according to the newspaper account, James beat her. The mother left Tamika in the Bronx with Connie R. Greene, James's mother, because she believed that Connie could take better care of Tamika than she could. In 1983, James proposed to Wanda Pruitt, then 17, who already had a son, Levalle. James did not tell her that he was already married, or that he changed her boy's name from Levalle Pruitt to James William Greene, or that in March 1984 he took out two $10,000 life insurance policies, one on Tamika and one on Levalle, naming himself the father and principal beneficiary of both. One day in April, James volunteered to give Levalle his bottle and put him to bed. He told Wanda to stay out of the room or the boy would not go to sleep. One news article said that Wanda left the apartment without knowing that James had suffocated Levalle with a plastic bag. Levalle died in a Harlem hospital the next day; the death was thought to be accidental. A later article reported that Wanda went into the bedroom an hour after James left and found Levalle dead, suffocated by a plastic bag, but when James told her that it was an accident, she believed him. A month later James got the insurance money and stopped seeing Wanda.

The complexities multiply. In June 1985, James, who was living with a 13-year-old girl at the time, took Tamika from his mother. Connie visited them and saw bruises on the child, but James would not let her take Tamika back. While Tamika was living with James, she was whipped with an electric cord, forced to eat until she threw up, and finally poisoned; she died of an overdose of Tylenol and Benedryl. James Greene applied for the proceeds from the life insurance policy, but investigations began after Tamika's death and he was indicted on two counts of murder and welfare fraud. He was convicted of both charges and in November 1987 was sentenced to fifty-nine years to life (Case 479). The simple statistics of this case reveal little or nothing about James's relationship with Wanda or his 13-year-old mistress, or the involvement of his mother. Only a case review of Levalle's death might have uncovered the danger to Tamika. Since the death was regarded as accidental, however, with no automatic child death-review panel, no investigation was made and Tamika lost whatever chance she may have had.

Another case, with a slightly older child, is unusual because of the complex household involved; it was reported in the *Lexington Herald-Leader* in 1992. In the town of Beauty, Martin County, Kentucky, Sherman Newsome, age 2, was stomped on and died of a broken vertebra and a liver injury. William McNeely (23), the boyfriend of Rebecca Newsome, Sherman's mother, was charged with the child's death. Long-term abuse was suspected. Witnesses had seen William punching the boy, who also had a broken collarbone. The complications in this case arose from the fact that William apparently was living with his wife and six children along with Rebecca in Rebecca's rented house. There were no additional details in the news article, but the dynamics of the interpersonal relationships in such a household give rise to considerable speculation (Case 895).

Summary

Persistent abusers use a variety of excuses to explain the injuries suffered by their victims, particularly any milder ones that the children endure before they are finally killed. Perpetrators claim that the child was clumsy, fell downstairs, bumped against a lighted cigarette, accidently turned on the hot water in the bathtub, or some similar excuse. Since children can be or do all of these things, it is often difficult for hospital or Social Service authorities to be certain that abuse has occurred. The perpetrators also may claim that they were only disciplining the child for misbehaving. How can a case worker or law officer distinguish between the perpetrators who really did not know any better and those who sadistically were inflicting as much pain as possible without killing their victims? It may be even more difficult to prove that distinction in a court of law, especially if the perpetrator can afford a good defense team.

The sustained abuse cases are often the most tragic. People who grow up in loving, "normal" households find it difficult to believe the horrors that take place in families where severe physical abuse is a constant factor. Ironically, the ideological commitment to the preservation of families is unintentionally responsible for a great deal of suffering. Children in families of the sort represented by the examples in this chapter should be removed from the home and never returned. They would have had a better chance of developing into happy and productive adults in almost any other type of domestic arrangement. Those children who were killed in foster homes might have been spared if state supervision had been carried out more effectively or if family rights had been terminated earlier; they could have been adopted before so much damage was done. Tragedies similar to the ones described above will continue to occur as long as the desire to preserve the family outweighs the rights and safety of the child.

CHAPTER 7

Wrong Place/Wrong Time and Bad Decisions: Unintended Victims

A number of children in our files were killed by a combination of misfortune, bad decisions, or by simply being in the wrong place at the wrong time. The perpetrators rarely intended to kill the children; probably in some cases, they were not even aware of their victims' existence. In other cases, however, they did intend the murder, but they killed the children to keep themselves from being identified to the police. In other words, the victim was killed simply because he was a witness. The perpetrators in the first group of cases simply made bad decisions that were often compounded with bad luck. These people, some 5.9 percent of the perpetrators, were generally thoughtless or irresponsible, sometimes making poor decisions out of ignorance about the physical frailty of children or without foreseeing the consequences of their actions. Such people deliberately left children in cars for one reason or another (the parents of one child did not want to wake him [Case 497]) or simply forgot them, fed them inadequately, disciplined them by giving them cupfuls of salt or poured pepper down their throats, left them in bathtubs, or locked them unattended in rooms for hours. In June 1996 one child was killed when her parents allowed her to ride on a mattress fastened to the roof of their car and she fell off. This case happened too late to be included in our sample, but it can be easily classified in the "bad decisions" category. These perpetrators usually claim, perhaps quite honestly, that they had not intended to harm the child.

Bad Decisions

A child's safety is directly tied to family life-style. Good intentions, financial stability, and close family ties cannot shield a child from the consequences of bad decisions. Involvement of any kind in the drug culture is a bad decision that increases the risk to children both in the family and in their neighborhood, as later cases in this chapter demonstrate. Drug use by parents can in itself lead to problems for their children, even when the parents stay out of conflicts. In 1992 a 34-year-old father was convicted of involuntary manslaughter because he physically abused and gave methamphetamine to his 5-month-old daughter, who died as a result; the child's mother also used drugs. In this incident the administration of the drug may have been the physical abuse mentioned (Case 861). In a number of states the use of drugs while pregnant, or giving drugs to children, is classified as physical abuse. The practice of giving alcohol to infants to quiet them or lull them to sleep has a long history, however. The extension of this practice to other drugs is an easy step. While some people might say that the father in Case 861 was deliberately trying to harm his baby by giving her drugs, there are plenty of statements in the literature on drug use that suggest that users who enjoy drugs merely want others to share in their pleasure.

Drug use can also cause parents to ignore the existence of children or forget to take care of their needs. In 1993 police responding to a 911 call in Yonkers, New York, saw Rebecca Groom in front of her apartment, frantic, screaming, "My baby's dead!" Her neighbors were not sympathetic, and one of them even punched her in the face when word of the death spread. Thirteen-month-old Saleem had starved to death, apparently forgotten by his mother who was high on drugs. When the police found him, he had been dead for several days. While neighbors said that several children had been taken away from Rebecca because of neglect, the police were not able to confirm it, probably because of the strict New York confidentiality laws (Case 784). Although Rebecca could be considered a sustained abuser, newspaper reports indicated that Saleem died from neglect—he was simply ignored by a mother under the influence of drugs.

Another example of the consequences of the bad decision by a parent to take drugs comes from Philadelphia. On Christmas Eve 1990 the starved, dehydrated bodies of 7-month-old twins, Tanika and Tanisha Miller, were found. Tanisha weighed only 5.8 pounds, Taneka, 7.6. They and five other children ranging from ages 2 to 8 lived with their mother, Marcelette Miller, in a two-story row house littered with empty liquor bottles and crack vials. Marcelette at first said that the babies were fed at 1:00 A.M. on December 24 and found dead later that morning, but under further questioning she admitted that forty-eight hours had elapsed between the time when she remembered to feed them and the time when she found them dead. At first she was charged with endangering the welfare of her children and reckless endangerment and released, but on January 22, 1991, she was rearrested on homicide counts that were added to the original charges. At that point she admitted using drugs. She told police that she might have smoked ten caps of crack between feeding the babies and finding them dead. An official from the medical examiner's office said that the infants had been dead for fifteen to twenty hours before the police were notified. At a preliminary hearing on February 11, a Municipal Court judge ordered her held for trial on charges of third-degree murder and involuntary homicide. Her five other children had been placed in foster homes when the twins' bodies were discovered. The *New York Times* did not report on whether she was convicted (Case 639).

Drug use can also result in violence against children. These cases were placed in the "violent abuse" category rather than the "bad decisions" one because the violent abusers were actively trying to harm the child, whereas the latter group is limited to people who did not intend to hurt, let alone kill, their victims. The choice of categories for classification makes it difficult for us to compare statistics from our files with public ones on child abuse. While physical abuse and neglect are reported together in the public statistics, caregivers who simply neglect a child usually do not mean them any harm. Abuse and neglect are therefore separated in this study. Most neglect cases fall into the "bad decisions" category. No matter how long neglect continues or how often it occurs, it should not be combined with physical abuse because the conscious state of mind of the perpetrator is often decidedly different.

There are a few other life situations that may place children at risk, often to the dismay of the parents who apparently had their child's welfare in mind. In 1982, Faith Hirschy, a 9-month-old girl in Evansville, Indiana, died of pneumonia and carotenemia (a jaundice-like disease) because for six months she had been fed on a diet consisting exclusively of carrot juice, bananas, and avocados. The short news article gave no information as to why the parents chose this combination. Both the mother and father were charged with reckless homicide and child neglect, but since the *New York Times* did not have any later report on the case, the outcome and evidence at the trial were not available (Case 528). Fortunately, parents who impose unusual diets on their children are more likely to change the regimen when the children do not thrive than to persist until a child dies. (An exception is when the diet is designed to rid the child of demons or evil spirits; cases of this type are described in Chapter 4.)

Families do not have to be involved in illegal activities or strange diet fads for their life-style to endanger their children. Members of a number of religions, such as Christian Scientists, who believe that "knowing the truth" about illness is more effective than medical treatment, or Jehovah's Witnesses, who reject blood transfusions, may put children at risk. We have eight such cases where children died. Seven of them involved Christian Scientists, overrepresented here because of the activities of Rita Swan of Sioux City, Iowa. She was a Christian Scientist until her infant son died; afterward she blamed the church for his death and began a campaign to have Christian Scientists prosecuted when their children died (Case 486, source #6). The *New York Times* in 1990 featured a key case. Robyn Twitchell, a 2-year-old boy, died in April 1986 in Boston of a bowel obstruction. The Twitchells had three other children who were well and healthy with no evidence of abuse. Robyn's 34-year-old parents, charged with and convicted of his death, each faced a twenty-year prison sentence. The prosecution, however, recommended probation. The Twitchells were sentenced to ten years' probation on the condition that they take the children for regular medical checkups and seek professional medical help if the children became really ill. According to one article, this case was the fourth conviction of Christian Scientists in the past fifteen months. None had gone to jail. The inquest report on Robyn's death stated that three officials of the Christian Science Church had contributed to his death by discouraging Robyn's parents from resorting to physicians. The officials were never charged, nor was the inquest report mentioned until 1990. In 1993 the original conviction of the Twitchells for involuntary manslaughter for withholding care was overturned by the Massachusetts Supreme Court (Case 486).

Jehovah's Witnesses and Christian Scientists, whose members are often in conflict with federal or state governments, are the best-known examples of religious groups that reject some or all aspects of medical treatment. It becomes a difficult issue when a citizen's right to pursue his religious beliefs runs counter to laws concerning child welfare. Legal cases involving parents who leave the country to avoid court orders about cancer treatment, parents who reject blood transfusions for minor children, parents who refuse to send children to school (such as the Amish and Hutterites), and similar cases occasionally appear in the news today.

Religious sects that encourage their members to refuse medical care are not the only ones in which religious beliefs can lead to the death of a child. The case of John Yarbrough (12) is an example. He was beaten to death on July 4, 1983, for refusing to do his chores at a religious compound called the House of Judah. It was run by William Lewis Sr. who was, according to the *New York Times*, a self-styled prophet of Black Israelite Jews who cited the Bible as the authority for strict discipline of adults and children alike. All the children in the compound had no choice but to work or be brutally beaten. The sect had "no connection with Judaism." Ethel Yarbrough (33), John's mother, was charged with manslaughter and bound over to stand trial. William Lewis Sr. and several of his deputies, including William Lewis Jr., were booked on charges of child cruelty. The charges against William Lewis Jr. and one other deputy were dropped, but William Lewis Sr. and five others were ultimately convicted of child cruelty and also of holding John in involuntary servitude from 1981 until his death. The last article in the *Times* was in September 1984. All the individuals charged were free on bond pending sentencing, but no date had been set at the time of the article and there was no additional report in the *Times* (Case 261). To include this case with others in the "sustained abuse" chapter would obscure the role that religious beliefs played in the behavior that caused the child's death. The bad decision of the victim's mother to ally herself with members of the sect and then to continue with them despite the brutal treatment accorded her son places this case in this category.

A number of other cases in our files were the result of poor decisions combined with bad luck. For example, Raymundo and Luz Elena Cruz enjoyed parties. One cold January evening in 1979 they planned to go to one in the Bronx, New York City. Mr. Cruz (27) left on Saturday afternoon and his wife,

Luz (24), joined him two hours later. Their four children—Luz Elena (6), named after her mother; Mari Luz (5), Maria (2), and Raymundo (1), named after his father—were too young to take to the party so, to keep them safe, the parents locked them in a bedroom with the door bolted. The bad luck was that Mari Luz was fascinated by the steam radiator valve; according to Luz Elena, the only survivor, she was playing with it when it broke, allowing scalding steam to pour into the room. The parents arrived home about 1:30 Sunday morning to find Luz Elena screaming and the other three children dead. Neighbors called police, who arrived about twenty minutes later and found the room still "like a steam bath." The parents were arrested later that morning and were charged with manslaughter, negligent homicide, and endangering the welfare of children. Luz Elena was placed in the custody of her grandmother. There was only one article on this case in the *New York Times*, and the result of the trial was not given (Case 70). In this incident, it is reasonable to assume that the Cruzes had no intention of killing their children.

A similar poor decision cost Sherry Rendle (23) four of her six children: Kimora (8), Bobby (3), Dehaven (2), and Contessa (6 months). In 1984 she left them at home in Albany, Georgia, with her son Aurallio (9) while she went to a nearby bar. A fire started in a bedroom, and when the firefighters arrived about midnight, the house was engulfed in flames. Aurallio and his younger brother Adrian (5) escaped, but the rest of the children died. Sherry was charged with cruelty to children (Case 290). Leaving children alone, locked in a house or a room, is a poor decision, no matter what the circumstances. The risk is always there.

There are other types of poor decisions. Adults sometimes think that drunken children are amusing, so it is possible that Anthony Jimerson (21) thought it would be funny to get Raymond Griffin (5) drunk. During a party at Patricia Griffin's house in Dallas, Texas, one Friday night in February 1990, Anthony gave Raymond ten ounces of whiskey and told him to "drink it like a man." Raymond did so, but at 3:00 A.M. he started having convulsions. Either no one remembered Raymond's drinking feat or understood the danger that alcohol poses to a child. For whatever reason, an ambulance was not summoned until 2:45 in the afternoon. Hospital authorities said that Raymond's blood alcohol level was still .55, more than five times the legal limit in Texas for drunkenness. According to hospital personnel, they might have saved Raymond had he been brought in earlier. Now, however, he was in a coma and suffered irreversible brain damage. He died on February 28 after being removed from life-support systems (Case 629).

Often perpetrators in the "bad decisions" category do not realize that their actions will prove fatal. To avoid hitting a child, they try an innovative alternative. Elizabeth Jewell (26) killed her 5-month-old son by pouring pepper in his mouth to punish him for crying, according to the prosecution. Her version was that she put pepper on his fingers and tongue to keep him from sucking his thumb. Whichever was correct, she used too much pepper and he died. She was convicted on March 12, 1987 (Case 374). Similarly, in 1989, Katrina Buchanan (22), who was angry over her 2-year-old son Tyrell's disobedience, poured pepper into his mouth, thus making it impossible for him to breathe. He died on October 25 in St. John's Episcopal Hospital, Brooklyn. She was arrested on the next day (Case 430).

Salt can also be a problem, as Beth Riggs found out in 1988. She force-fed salt to her 4-year-old daughter, Heather, in Salem, Virginia, on May 16 to punish her for stealing sugar. She said that she did not know the amount would be fatal, but the Roanoke County Circuit Court imposed a twelve-year sentence anyway (Case 419). Other people fed salt to children with fatal results, but for religious rather than disciplinary reasons: they believed that salt discourages demons. Examples of these cases are found in Chapter 4.

On several occasions, animals caused or were accused of causing a child's death. One unusual incident of poor judgement involved a ten-foot python, a family pet weighing eighty-five pounds, which killed an 11-month-old boy in 1984 in Ottumwa, Iowa. The father was charged with negligence because the python had "apparently" escaped from its enclosure, found the baby, and, according to the autopsy report, "bit and suffocated" him (Case 284). A number of cases involved dogs. In one distressing example of irresponsibility, Christopher Johnson, only 12 days old, died in Louisville, Kentucky, on November 3, 1979, of kidney failure and blood poisoning. His legs had been chewed off at the knees by the family dachshund three days earlier. The dog belonged to Christopher's uncle, who was in Japan. Christopher's mother was asleep in another room when the attack occurred, and the baby was discovered by his 16-year-old aunt when she came home from school. At an inquest held partly because neighbors were blaming the mother for killing the child and trying to put the body down a garbage disposal unit (there was none in the house), the evidence made the dog's guilt clear to a jury and they ruled the death accidental (Case 498).

The cases described so far in this chapter illustrate the fatal consequences of carelessness, indifference, irresponsibility, ignorance, and stupidity. The best approach to reduce the child deaths that result from ignorance and stupidity is education. Carelessness, however, is a character trait that both family members and teachers rail against with varying success. When people are persuaded to be more careful (by using restraints in cars, for example), child deaths (from auto accidents) decrease. Irresponsibility and indifference have been fought for centuries by religions, philosophers, and governments without much success, so deaths resulting from these factors will be difficult to reduce.

Wrong Place/Wrong Time

The second set of child fatalities discussed in this chapter again deals with cases where most perpetrators do not intend to kill the child. The victim is simply in the wrong place at the wrong time. Table 1.18 lists the number of children in our files killed under these circumstances. As far as can be told from the news articles, the victims usually do not have the remotest connection to the perpetrators. For example, 7-year-old Christine Ayala was playing on a fire escape in the Bronx, New York City, in August 1985. A quarrel broke out between Sergio Maurice (31) and DelRoy Campbell (24) on the sidewalk beneath her. Shots were fired, and Christine was killed by a stray bullet. The two men were each charged with murder. The newspaper did not mention the reason for the quarrel, and no indication was given that the men either knew Christine or were aware that she was playing on the fire escape when they began their gunfight (Case 301). There were no further articles on the outcome of the case.

In Brooklyn one evening in July 1978, Mario Arroyo, an 11-year-old boy, was shot in the head by a 23-year-old gas station attendant, Recet Ahmedoff, a Bulgarian immigrant. Recet was drinking in a tavern to celebrate his birthday. To add to the celebration, he said, he went into the street and fired a gun into the air. Mario happened to be crossing the street when he was hit in the head and killed. Recet was found guilty of second-degree manslaughter and sentenced to a five-year term (Case 40). Again in Brooklyn, in May 1983,

Edgar Gonzales, whose age was not given, was waiting for a bus with his mother and grandmother. Two members of the gang known as the Filthy Mad Dogs were sitting in a Jeep parked at the intersection. The Filthy Mad Dogs were warring with the gang members of La Familia, who fired six or ten shots at them. The only person hit was the child. Seven people were ultimately charged and three members of the La Familia gang—all males, one age 17, one 18, and one 21—were found guilty of second-degree murder. No news article mentioned the sentence given (Case 238).

Shaniqua Brown, a 10-year-old girl, was killed in 1990 by a stray bullet, also in Brooklyn. An 8 year old was wounded. Both children were simply bystanders. The two men charged with the shooting, ages 21 and 22, were arguing with a clerk in a jewelry store; one beat the clerk, and, as they left, both men fired at him. The girls were walking by the store when they were hit. Although there were lots of witnesses, police had difficulty in getting any testimony because, according to the news article, "no one wants to get involved." The store owner contended that his employees had called police "at least twice" about the argument, but there was no response until after the shooting. One article said that since Shaniqua's death, at least five more children under age 16 had been killed by stray bullets, with another five or more wounded. By the end of 1993, there had been no additional articles about the trial of the two men charged (Case 617).

Our files have twenty-seven cases of children killed by stray bullets, snipers, or drive-by shootings. In many of these incidents, the perpetrator was never identified in the newspaper articles, so we have no way of knowing whether he deliberately intended to kill the child victim or someone in the child's family, or was simply shooting at random. Occasionally, in other cases, when killers were identified, it appears that they did intend to kill someone but made an error. For example, on one night in December 1987, Ricardo Reynolds, high on crack, fired a shotgun through the peephole of a door in the building where he lived. He killed 12-year-old Aaron Upshur, who had gone to answer the door. Ricardo apparently thought that he was firing into the door of the Upshurs' neighbor, with whom he had been arguing (Case 391). In 1988, Laurie Dann, evidently looking for the children of her former in-laws, shot up a classroom in Winnetka, Illinois, and killed Nicholas Corwin, a stranger to her. The children whom she sought had gone on a field trip (Case 403). This case is discussed in more detail in Chapters 2 and 4.

In another case, Louis Giambi (47) was hired in 1982 to kill Larry Augustin, who lived in Pine Hill, New Jersey. Augustin was scheduled to testify against another man in an assault case. Giambi broke into the wrong house and killed William Stuart, his wife Catherine, and his 3-year-old daughter Sandra as they were watching television. Another daughter was asleep in her bedroom and was not harmed. Giambi was convicted and sentenced to three life terms plus sixteen and one-half years on other charges (Case 216).

In September 1984 in Los Angeles, survivors and neighbors said that two men broke into a house, shooting rifles as they entered. A 6-year-old boy and his 12-year-old cousin were killed along with their grandmother and her daughter. The people in the house were all related to a retired football player, so the newspaper gave the case more space than it otherwise might have done. Two gang members, Tiequon Cox (18) and Horace Burns (20), were subsequently tried and convicted of first-degree murder. According to the newspaper, they wanted revenge on a cocaine dealer. They found the right house number but were on the wrong block (Case 271).

Not all the cases where something went wrong involve guns. In 1989 in Brooklyn, Alfredo Acosta was at home with his girlfriend's son Daniel (4 months old). Daniel's mother, Diane (27), was not there. At seven that evening, Warren Nogueras (22) broke in, yelling that he was Daniel's father and that he wanted his son. He grabbed the boy and dashed out the door, with Alfredo racing after him with a three-foot metal pipe. As they fought, Alfredo hit Warren on the head with the pipe but inadvertently hit Daniel, too. Daniel died in the hospital. Warren, also injured, was arrested and charged with burglary. Alfredo had not been charged at the time of the news article, but his case was before the grand jury in Brooklyn. He denied being the father of the child. Diane agreed but said that Warren was not the father, either. She claimed to have a court order against Warren to keep him away from her and her baby, but the police said that there was no record of it (Case 443).

Our files have thirteen cases that were originally indexed in the *New York Times* as murder or manslaughter, but no one was ever charged and the people involved all claimed that the deaths were accidental. Seven were shootings. Of these, one was particularly tragic. In March 1983 a 24-year-old police officer answering a call in Stanton, California, entered a darkened apartment. He saw what he thought was an intruder pointing a gun at him. He fired and killed a 5-year-old boy who was sitting in the dark, clutching his toy gun.

The police officer was hospitalized briefly for depression and subsequently retired from the force because he feared that he could no longer function effectively. The news article did not mention why the little boy was alone in the apartment or who had called police. No one was charged and there were no later articles in the *Times* (Case 249). This incident might also be included in the section on bad decisions.

Six other cases listed originally as murder or manslaughter but which were probably accidents did not involve shootings: two children fell out of windows (Cases 81 and 663), one child drowned in a neighbor's pool (Case 524), one fell several feet off a hay bale (Case 546), one boy apparently died from sniffing the fuel fumes from an oil tank on a farm (Case 526), and a 4-year-old girl was walking on the sidewalk with her grandmother when a bottle dropped from a fifteen-story building, fell on her head, and killed her (Case 435). Although all these cases were indexed in the *New York Times* as murder or manslaughter, there was no report in the newspaper articles of anyone being charged. With the exception of the girl who was killed by a falling bottle, the cases indicated a lack of supervision, which would place them among the child abuse and neglect statistics in many states.

Some cases are difficult to classify, both due to unusual circumstances and because they fit more than one category. A dog was the killer in one such incident. In 1987 in San Jose, California, Michael Berry (39) was growing marijuana. To guard his 243 plants, he kept three pit bulls. When a dog was on guard, Michael restrained it with a heavy collar that was hooked to a strong chain, padlocked to an auto axle sunk in the ground. One June day his neighbor's 3-year-old son, James Soto, was left alone on the Soto patio and apparently wandered too near the fifty-three-pound dog. When the parents came out of the house, the child was being "torn apart." Berry had not fenced his yard, and police charged him with murder on the grounds that he did not adequately restrain his dog, even though he knew that it was dangerous. The Humane Society personnel who were boarding Berry's dogs during the trial were said by the newspaper to be unhappy that the dogs were to be killed when they were no longer needed for evidence because they were all "sweethearts." Berry was acquitted of murder but convicted of manslaughter and sentenced to three years and eight months in prison. The family was awarded $3.5 million in a civil suit (Case 384). In other cases where dogs killed children, often no one was charged. Clearly, both Berry and James's parents made several bad decisions. But by wandering into the yard when the dog was on guard, James was also in the wrong place at the wrong time.

Our files also have cases of children who died in arson fires that were set by people who were trying to harm someone else. For example, on a night in March 1977 in Jersey City, New Jersey, three men started a fire at the base of a stairwell in a twelve-family building. Six young children died, along with some older children and adults. One of the men charged with the crime, Luis Barrios (20), an unemployed mechanic, had been quarreling with a resident of the building who was unrelated to the people killed. Barrios was charged with buying the gasoline used in the fire, but the judge declared a mistrial in his case because the jury could not agree. One of his companions was found guilty of striking the match that started the fire. A third man had not yet gone to trial at the time of the last article in the *New York Times*. There were no reports on the outcome of the last trial, the sentence for the men found guilty, or on any retrial of Barrios (Case 21).

In another case, in Queens, New York City, in June 1991, Carter Ward (35) was charged with murder and arson. He allegedly set fire to a building in which his former girlfriend lived with a male companion. They occupied a first-floor apartment and were rescued. However, Louis Contreras (10) and his older brother, Gustavo (17), who lived in an apartment on the second floor, were not so fortunate and died in the fire (Case 665). There was no additional information.

A suspicious fire in Jersey City, New Jersey, in March 1989 killed Michael Tagliarinni (12), his older brother and sister, his mother, and his father, who lived on the third floor of a three-story building. Neighbors said that the senior Tagliarinni was ill and had trouble seeing or hearing. The children all attended schools for the mentally handicapped. The fire had been deliberately set on the second floor in a vacant apartment whose tenants had been evicted three weeks earlier for nonpayment of rent. At the time of the news article, no one had been arrested. There were no later articles in the *New York Times* (Case 465). In all these cases the perpetrators were apparently indifferent to the fate of the victims and may not even have been aware of their existence.

In still another arson case, the perpetrator knew the victim but was probably after her parents, if indeed she meant to kill anyone. Anne Marie O'Brien (18), the daughter of a high-school vice principal in New Milford, New Jersey, had never been in trouble with the law, but apparently she was arguing with her family over friends whom she was seeing after her high-school graduation. In November 1982, about 3:30 A.M., she poured gasoline around the ground-floor recreation room of their split-level home, set it on fire, and then she hitchhiked to a friend's house in Jersey City. The rest of the family — her mother, father, maternal grandmother, four brothers, and two sisters — were asleep upstairs. All escaped with minor burns except for her 9-year-old brother Kevin, who was killed, and her mother, who fractured a vertebra when she jumped from a second-floor window. No additional details were given in the *New York Times* story (Case 206).

Some of the children in our records were killed during the commission of another crime or when one of their close relatives was the target. For example, in February 1982 the body of 2-year-old Johnny Castro, who had been shot, was found in Miami, Florida. It had been lovingly prepared for burial: bathed, clothed, wrapped in sheets, and decorated with roses. The police thought that the boy's father, Jesus Castro (44), from Colombia, had attended to the body. Over the telephone (the only contact the police ever had with him), the senior Castro told them that he had refused to carry out certain orders given him by a drug supplier who had hired him. That marked him for death, he said. On February 6, while he was in his car with Johnny asleep on his shoulder, a van drove up and its occupants opened fire. Johnny was killed; his father was not. According to police, drug or gang killers sometimes target a child to "send a message" to the adults who love him, but it is also possible that the assassins were aiming at the senior Castro. In any case, Castro understood the message. He informed police that he planned to go after the killers. He expected to be killed, he said, but he would "take a few of them with him." There was no *New York Times* follow-up (Case 179).

That same year, in New York City, Orlando Galvez was driving with his wife, his son Damien (4 months old), and his daughter Dorothy (18 months old), possibly heading for a late-night meeting with someone, when he stopped his car on the shoulder of a parkway about two miles from home. Another car pulled up nearby, and one man got out while the driver stayed inside the vehicle. Despite passing traffic, the man fired a sawed-off shotgun and a 9-mm automatic into the window on the driver's side of the Galvez car, killing everyone inside. He got back into his car and the two men drove away. During the investigation, police found nearly $1 million in cash and $10 million in cocaine in the Galvezes' $1,000-per-month luxury apartment. The Galvez husband and wife, who were Colombian, had so many false identity papers and forged documents in the apartment that police were not sure if the official identifications that they gave to the press were correct, even though they obtained them from passports. Along with the money and the cocaine, there were drug paraphernalia throughout the apartment. The police suggestion that the killings were drug related was hardly wild speculation (Case 188). This incident is also an example of the danger in assuming that all unemployed persons are poor.

In most of the cases the weapons are common: guns, knives, or the well-known "blunt instrument." The man who used a crossbow is unique, however. In 1992, Christopher Hightower, a former commodities dealer, killed Ernest Brendel, a business associate, with a crossbow. He strangled Brendel's wife and killed their 8-year-old daughter, whose body was destroyed by quicklime so that the cause of death was impossible to determine. Hightower claimed that Asian drug dealers forced him to watch while they killed the Brendels, but the jury rejected that defense and convicted him in 1993 (Case 723). Again, the 8 year old was apparently killed only because she was a witness to the murder of her parents.

Although alcohol and other drugs are often implicated as causal factors in crime, almost any source of contention can lead to violence. In the case of 5-year-old Lekia Williams, her father apparently owed money to some neighbors in the same building in Brooklyn. Shortly after midnight on an October evening in 1979, according to the girl's mother, the two men, William Meachem (27) and Mario Herrera (26), "pushed their way" into the apartment. The father was not at home. Frustrated, Meachem and Herrera shot both Lekia and her mother. At the time of the news article, Diane, Lekia's mother, was in the hospital in fair condition with two bullet wounds in her head, but Lekia had died. There was no later article in the *New York Times* (Case 95).

Sometimes a marital dispute, instead of being confined to the arguing spouses and their children, spills over to other relatives and causes the death of additional children. On September 20, 1980, Danny Crump, a housepainter by trade, was charged with killing several people. Witnesses said that they saw him put a box on the hood of a car in the garage of his former wife's parents, and someone (not identified) from the house was seen carrying the box inside. Ten minutes later a violent explosion blew out the walls, collapsing the roof. Nine people were inside: five of them were killed instantly, one died on the way to the hospital, two were in critical condition at the time the news article was written, and one escaped with facial cuts. Crump's former wife, Diane Post (about 20), was one of those killed, and their son Randy (4 months old), who ordinarily would solely have been at risk in this case of bitterly estranged parents, was in critical condition. Diane's whole family was decimated: her father, her mother, and two brothers, including 10-year-old James, were killed.

The only fault of James, if it may be called that, was that he was related to Diane. As her younger brother, he was unlikely to have been directly involved in the marital conflict between Diane and Danny, but he was in the wrong place at the wrong time. Diane had filed for divorce six months after she had married Crump, and the divorce was final only a month before the killings. After a bitter dispute, Diane had gained custody of Randy. Crump himself claimed that he had been shot in July by someone while he and Diane were separated, but police did not have enough evidence to charge anyone with that shooting. It is possible that Crump suspected someone in Diane's family. The police believed that the bombing was prompted by revenge, but Crump denied ever having made the bomb (Case 104).

This case, like the previous one, could have been placed with mass murders in Chapter 2, but since the child victims were not directly involved in the marital dispute between the perpetrator and his wife, the "wrong place/wrong time" category seems appropriate. In Farwell, Michigan, the Gaffneys were having a family reunion. George and his wife Vaudrey had welcomed home Helen Gaffney (29), George's daughter by his first marriage, along with her three children, Angela (10), Tom (8), and Amy (7). Garnetta Haggart (23), Helen's half-sister, who was George and Vaudrey's daughter, was also there; she had come back from Florida over the weekend to appear in court for the final decree of divorce from her husband, Robert Lee Haggart (31), a livestock auctioneer. Late in the afternoon on February 16, 1982, the day before Garnetta was to appear in court, Robert showed up at the house. Helen, Robert's sister-in-law, and her children were in the cab of their pickup truck, where he shot them. Robert's mother-in-law and his estranged wife were inside the house in the dining area; his father-in-law was in the basement. Robert killed them all and then fled. Since Garnetta was not outside the house by the car when Robert killed his sister-in-law and her children, he had to search for her inside. Robert shot Garnetta and her mother; then he had to look for his father-in-law. Robert was either eliminating witnesses or he may have wanted to kill as many of the family as he could find (Case 187).

Criminals who are interrupted while they are committing a crime and who want to eliminate witnesses sometimes become killers. In 1980, when the Gilligans returned home in Evansville, Indiana, they evidently surprised a burglar. The bodies of Patrick and Theresa Gilligan (both 30) and their two children, Lisa (5) and Gregory (4), still had on their coats, and the motor of the family car in the driveway was still running. The bodies were discovered by a state trooper who was checking on a vacationing friend's house next door and investigated the empty, running car. Inside the house, guns looted from Gilligan's gun cabinet may have been used to shoot everyone but Gilligan himself, who was beaten to death, apparently with a barbell. The 24-year-old man subsequently arrested for the crime was caught climbing into the attic of another house. At the time, there was an arrest warrant out for him for still another crime (Case 109).

Also in 1980, in New York City, Housing Authority police officers were called when neighbors heard shots around 6 P.M. In a sixth-floor apartment of a thirteen-story high-rise housing development, police found Vidal Lopez (56), his "common-law wife" Jesus Reyes (56), and her granddaughter, Doreen Ortiz (11), all shot to death. Police, led to him by "forensic tests," arrested Larry Pounds (32) the next day. He had killed the family during an attempted robbery, police said. A second person was being sought. There was no additional article in the *New York Times* (Case 118).

Another example comes from Queens, New York City, in 1992. During a robbery at a house in Queens Village, two young girls, Tawana Sharp (5) and her sister, Desiree Bernard (2), were shot to death. Their mother, Joan Bernard (38), was shot, then jumped from a third-floor attic window, and was in critical condition at the time of the news article. Her 17-year-old daughter, Nathalie Hayes, who escaped uninjured, was placed in protective custody. At the time of the crime, George Desmond Bernard, whom the *New York Times* identified as the father of both of the dead girls, was serving seven years in a Tucson prison for money laundering. The police eventually arrested four people.

As the investigation unfolded, it appeared that the children's baby-sitter, Claude Millery (19), who lived next door, had come to the house asking to use the phone, and Joan Bernard let her in. Claude's husband, Ismael Ramos (25), and another man, later identified as Vincent Williams (25), entered the house with her and ransacked it, stealing jewelry, clothes, and about $40,000, and then tried to kill everyone. Police theorized that the trio were trying to eliminate witnesses who could identify them. Claude later claimed that she did not know they would harm the children. The couple — she from Haiti, Ismael from Puerto Rico — were eventually arrested in his uncle's apartment in the Bronx. Vincent Williams, along with Donald Sealy (23), another friend of Ismael's, who was apparently suspected of also being involved in the robbery, were arrested at their homes in Cambria Heights, a quiet middle-class neighborhood. Both men were described by neighbors as "quiet, respectful, hard working." Claude was convicted of second-degree murder and robbery and was sentenced to twenty-five years to life. Ismael, on parole after serving three years on an arson and weapons charge, pleaded guilty and was sentenced to 126 years to life. Williams was on trial for murder at the time of the last article *Times* in 1993, but there was no mention of Sealy (Case 746).

Still another example is from Rising Sun near Greenwood, Mississippi. In November 1990, Henry Curtis Jackson (26) killed four of his nephews and nieces, ranging in age from 2 to 5, and badly wounded three other people, including his sister, Regina (23). According to one news article, Henry had gone to his mother's house for drug money while his mother was at church. He demanded the money from his sister, who refused to give it to him. Henry then attacked her and the six other people in the house, who were all children. Henry fled; after eluding capture for three days, he turned himself in to his uncle. He claimed that "he just went nuts," although he swore that he was not on drugs at the time.

Henry worked in a food plant less than a mile from his home in West Point, where he had lived about five years. In 1986 he had been ordered to receive psychiatric treatment after he pleaded guilty to an armed burglary in Leflore County. He was placed on five years' probation that was due to end on March 14, 1991. None of this information appeared in a later article in the *Memphis Commercial Appeal* that reported on the grand jury hearing. In that article, Sheriff Banks told the grand jury that Henry had stabbed his sister when she refused to give him the combination to a safe containing money belonging to a relative — money needed to pay some bills that Henry and his wife had accumulated. When he stabbed his sister, the children "jumped on him" and he started to stab them, too. According to the sheriff, the robbery was planned because Henry had parked about two blocks away and cut the phone lines before he went into the house. He planned to steal the safe since he did not know the combination. He had not expected his sister to be home, Henry said. If all the family had been at church, he would simply have stolen the safe and left (Case 632).

Summary

The examples in this chapter are children who were unfortunate in being victims of bad decisions or for being in the wrong place at the wrong time. The dynamics of their relationship to their parents, their caregivers, or to each other are not always relevant in understanding the reasons why they were killed. Even Henry Jackson, who killed relatives, did so because they were at home instead of in church, where he expected them to be. As long as people in the United States resort to violence as the first, best, or only solution to problems, these unhappy cases will continue to provide newspaper headlines. All of the social ills that lead to violence are responsible, and this aspect of the crisis will not disappear until we find better solutions in dealing with tensions and discord. Social service agencies and legislation cannot do much, but more effort toward teaching methods of conflict resolution to children and adults might help reduce the readiness to resort to force. A major change in attitude throughout our society is required.

CHAPTER 8

Research Problems and Causal Explanations: A Discussion of Key Factors

Many people ask whether the crisis of child fatalities is getting worse. As violence in society becomes more pervasive, the number of inadvertent deaths of children also rises, as suggested in Chapter 7, but the evidence for an increase in the intentional killing of children is not strong. Averaging the *New York Times* reports from the decades of the 1970s, 1980s, and 1990s does suggest some change, but caution is necessary in interpreting the figures. The decade of the 1970s in our files includes only the years from 1977 to 1979, when the reports from these three years in the *Times* averaged 32.7 cases per year. However, the *Times* endured a strike in 1978 which lasted for several months and lowered the number of cases reported in that year to 22. Without that major deviation in 1978, the average for the decade would be higher.

In the 1980s the average was 40.8 cases per year, while the decade of the 1990s includes only four years, 1990 to 1993, with an average of 41. Although both the 1980s and 1990s show an obvious increase over the 1970s, it is not clear whether the lower figure reflects the strike or the higher figures result from better reporting, or whether there was a real increase in incidents. The similarity between the 1980s and 1990s leads to the suspicion that cases of children murdered by caretakers, relatives, friends, and neighbors have tended to hold relatively constant from one decade to the next.

When the *Chicago Tribune* kept a complete count of the deaths by violence in the Chicago area, it recorded 37 cases of children age 12 or under in 1992. Of course, this count pertained only to Chicago, whereas the *New York Times* included cases from across the United States. A comparison of newspapers from Nebraska and Kentucky showed that the *New York Times*, like the *Chicago Tribune*, was more thorough about reporting cases that occurred in its metropolitan area. Even though the *Times* does include cases from the rest of the United States, there was none listed from Chicago in 1992.

Serial killers add another complication since most of them killed at least some of their victims in different years or even in different decades. Each of their crimes was counted separately, although all were placed under a single identification number in our files. For example, the Atlanta child murder cases, most of which occurred in 1980 and 1981, were all placed under the same identification number as the first murder in 1979.

Fluctuations in the total count may also reflect the increase or decrease in random violence correlated with the general level of violence in the society combined with fluctuations in public concern. The latter especially tends to be reflected in newspaper reports. In addition, if the rate remains relatively constant, there would still be an inevitable increase in the number because of the population increase.

It is difficult to confirm or refute any hypothesis about the rate of child killings because published statistics are so different. A National Center on Child Abuse Prevention Research study does indicate an increase in the rate of child maltreatment fatalities from 1985 to 1992: the rate rose from 1.3 per 100,000 children (under 18) to 1.94 per 100,000 in 1992. This rise parallels an increase reported by the National Center on Health Statistics in the homicide rate for children under the age of one, which rose from 5.3 per 100,000 in 1985 to 8.2 per 100,000 in 1988 (McCurdy and Daro, 1993:18). Again, these figures must be read with some caution. Child abuse statistics always include neglect, which is interpreted differently in different states. As we know, some "neglect" deaths are cited as accidents in the vital statistics, and homicide statistics do not include all the deaths found in the child abuse and neglect statistics. The ages of the victims either of homicide or fatal child abuse that are reported in published statistics are not usually limited to children 12 and under; for example, the *Chicago Tribune* used 14 as their upper limit. National statistics tend to use 18, since legally anyone under that age is still a child, but some states use other upper-age limits for their records. Fatal child abuse by definition does not include murders by neighbors, acquaintances, and family members who are not caretakers of their victims, with the result that statistics of the death of children by misadventure are simply not comparable with one another or with the ones in this volume.

In the same report by Karen McCurdy and Deborah Daro, the rate of increase between 1991 and 1992 was less than 1.0 percent. Of the states that reported for the survey, fifteen had an increase, but nineteen showed a decline and two showed no change between 1991 and 1992. Until there is some comparability between the definitions and reporting by different organizations, it will be difficult to determine overall increases or decreases in the murder rate of children.

To give us some perspective, the rate of child killing may be less in the United States today than it was in England in the late 1860s. In a nineteenth-century work on infanticide that documents the killing of children in England in the 1800s, William Ryan reported 1,103 inquests in London on the suspicious deaths of children under age 2 in a single year (1862:61). He also gave detailed figures not only from England but also from other parts of Europe (1862:45–176). A study of that section of his book is a good antidote for the assumption that the United States today is particularly afflicted with child murderers. One writer went so far as to suggest that the high infant mortality rate of the time was not entirely due to disease or natural causes but was substantially inflated by the murders of children (Granville, quoted in Ryan, 1862:24). Contributing to this toll in England was the "burial club," a form of insurance that provided burial money. It was possible to enroll a child in several such clubs. In one reported case, the amount received by one father when his child died was more than a laborer's annual wages — an amount that was as much of a temptation then as it would be now. We have cases in our files of people who killed children for a much smaller payoff. Enrollment in a burial club was, according to one writer, the equivalent of a death sentence for the enrolled child (Ryan, 1862:22–24, 43).

The problem of murdered children is not unique to the nineteenth or twentieth century. The classic Greek myth of Jason and Medea, in which Medea kills their two children as revenge after Jason abandons her, reminds us that the murder of children is hardly new. The Greek and Roman custom of exposing—that is, killing—deformed infants is also known to readers of ancient history. Moreover, the folk tales about wicked stepmothers who tried to kill their stepchildren are familiar to anyone who has heard the story of Snow White or Hansel and Gretel. In addition, prohibitions against sacrificing children to the gods appear in both Jewish and Christian texts. China, India, Japan, and innumerable smaller societies throughout history have practiced infanticide, sometimes out of economic necessity, sometimes for cultural reasons.

Although child murder is not unique to this century or this country, some features associated with it differ over time or space while others do not. Today in the United States, members of mainstream religious groups do not ritually sacrifice children. The occasional scare stories about satanic baby sacrifices turn out to be false upon examination. There are people in our records, however, who have killed children to exorcise demons—either their own or those suspected of dwelling in the child. Furthermore, poverty, strongly associated with infanticide in England, according to Ryan, is still associated with it today. Effective solutions sometimes seem as far away as ever.

Research Problems

One of the reasons why it has not been easy to find ways to decrease the number of children who are killed is that barriers hinder anyone who attempts research in the area. Finding adequate statistics is a problem, as are establishing definitions, gaining access to confidential records, and forming correct and accurate diagnoses of the cause of death. Add to these the unreliability of witnesses and the lack of cooperation between different branches of government. Variations in the law from one state to another also can cause problems because they make it difficult or impossible to correlate information between states. Even uniform crime reports are only useful when there is agreement on what constitutes a particular crime.

Daly and Wilson describe the difficulties encountered in attempting to use statistical data. For example, they state that "census bureaus in the United States, Canada, and elsewhere have never attempted to distinguish natural parents from substitutes"; thus, official statistics are lacking on how many children live in each of the various household arrangements (1988:88–89). Newspaper articles usually indicate in-laws, but we, too, had problems with "uncles" and "aunts" who were not always identified as maternal or paternal relatives. The specific relationship makes a big difference in evolutionary selection thinking. We also found that a man who fathered children by the woman with whom he lived was not always identified as the biological father when he was not married to the mother. Conversely, a man was sometimes identified as the father of a victim even when the length of time that the couple had known each other would make that impossible. This problem makes less reliable any statements about the greater frequency with which stepfathers (legal or not) kill children as compared to biological fathers.

Fatal child abuse statistics are almost always reported as deaths by "abuse and neglect." The number included under "neglect" is not usually distinguished from the rest, although it may represent as much as 45 percent of the total deaths. If one adds 20 percent for medical neglect (that is, failure to get medical help in time, errors by medical or hospital personnel), emotional maltreatment, and so on, the figure rises to 65 percent, with only 22 percent of the reported cases attributed to physical abuse (Gelles, 1996:45). Neglect, other than medical neglect, includes "failure to supervise" — for example, a child who drowns at a picnic, very young children who are left alone, children who are not adequately dressed for the weather (whose death from a respiratory disease would be classed as "natural" in vital statistics but not necessarily in child abuse records), children who are not properly fed, and children whose homes are below standard in repair, facilities, or cleanliness. The definition of "neglect" varies from state to state. We found neglect to be a much less serious factor in the death of children than violent behavior on someone's part. The deaths by neglect counted in the fatal child abuse statistics are more apt to be counted as accidents or death from natural causes in vital statistics.

The statistics and much of the literature that refers to fatal child abuse include only deaths at the hands of a caregiver. We have a number of cases where the killer was not the victim's caregiver, so these would not be reflected in the child abuse statistics at all. In order to determine patterns in the deaths of children, it is important to include all known killers.

There is a tendency to expand any definition used for a social problem. "Child abuse" is an obvious example. For a variety of reasons the definition of physical child abuse as originally posed by C. Henry Kempe and his colleagues for battered children — "deliberate acts of physical violence that produce diagnosable injuries" (1962:17) — has been almost forgotten. The term "child abuse" now includes behavior that many people do not consider abuse at all. For example, while some people think that slapping and spanking, regardless of how lightly done, constitutes abuse, others do not. Emotional and psychological mistreatment are also included in child abuse now, rather than physical abuse alone, which was the original limitation. With so many different types of behavior now under the rubric of child abuse, prevention has become more difficult. The addition of sexual abuse further complicates the issue.

Sexual abuse, like physical abuse, is defined differently in distinct ethnic or racial groups. In one study the same questions about whether specific behaviors should be considered examples of sexual abuse were asked of Caucasians, Hispanics, Afro-Americans, and Asians. People in the different groups gave opposing answers, with Asians varying most from the others (Berrick and Gilbert, 1991:112–13, 152). Although there is consensus about some examples of physical or sexual abuse, both the law and the attitudes of case workers have moved into a gray area where not everyone agrees. Thus, hostility and resentment are directed toward case workers and law officers from clients behaving in what they regard as a "normal" fashion, only to find themselves in danger of losing their children. Since there are occasions when it is essential to remove children from a home for their safety, it is important to clarify definitions on the basis of a wider consensus about which behavior is abusive and which is not.

The fuzziness of the definition of child abuse is one of the reasons that I chose to study fatalities. At least all of the cases had a grimly similar outcome: a dead child. But having a tangible, unmistakable victim did not solve the definition problem. Was the death a homicide, or not? Police tend to classify deaths differently from social service agencies, or even from the courts. Many of our cases initially classified as murder became manslaughter in the courts, and incidents defined as fatal child abuse by welfare agencies were classified as accidents by police. One example was the case of two children who drowned at a picnic; they were among the "fatal child abuse" cases listed in Kentucky statistics, but the cause was "failure to supervise." There was no indication that this case was ever defined as anything but an accident by any other agency. However, states vary in what they call negligence and what they call abuse. Some behavior, such as substance abuse during pregnancy, or a drunk-driving accident in which a child is killed, may be regarded as abuse, negligence, or accident by police, child protective services, or the courts, depending on the state and the agency.

In addition to the difficulty of defining behavior as homicide or abuse, there are problems with attempts to classify the perpetrators into categories already existing in the criminology and justice literature. For example, the definitions of mass murderers and serial killers are not clear, with the choice of a numerical lower limit posing problems. How many victims must an individual kill to qualify as a mass murderer or serial killer? Should victims wounded but not killed be included in the total? Should people who try but fail to kill large numbers of people be counted as mass murderers? We counted only dead victims in establishing our lower limit. But what about Laurie Dann, whose case is discussed in Chapter 2; should she be considered a mass murderer, or not? For our purposes, we did not think so, but to understand the social and psychological dynamics that drive a mass murderer, it might be well to include those who try but fail along with all those who succeed. The reasons for failure may provide a key to understanding the successes. It also may be useful to examine closely the psychological state and attitudes of the recent young killers who have shot schoolmates. Do their motivations differ from adult mass murderers? And, if so, how?

It is interesting to note that many of the reference works on mass killers do not include women, particularly women who only kill children. Most of the material written about mass murderers concentrates on people such as those who enter a tavern, a restaurant, or workplace and open fire. The few writers who do discuss female mass murderers usually concentrate on women who shoot up playgrounds or school classrooms, regardless of the number or age of their victims. Do the women who kill several children, most of them their own, differ from other mass murderers? If so, how? We do not know enough about these people.

Using the lower limit of three victims, and including those injured as well as killed, Holmes and Holmes developed a typology grouping multiple killers into five categories: Disciple, Family Annihilator, Pseudocommandos, Disgruntled Employees, and Set-and-Run Killers. The Family Annihilator is the only one where perpetrators specifically seek out children, but children may be killed by any of the others. Our files therefore have perpetrators who could fit into other categories, and several who could fit into more than one. Since all of our killers killed children age 12 and under, the Disgruntled Employees category had the fewest members.

In their definition of the Family Annihilator, based on a 1986 article by Park Dietz, Holmes and Holmes state that the perpetrator "is one who kills an entire family at one time. . . . The murderer is the senior male in the family" (1992:53–62). The killer sometimes commits suicide, but sometimes does not. The description in both the Dietz and the Holmes and Holmes articles could fit people in our records who killed only two individuals, a child and the spouse. Does a Family Annihilator who kills only two victims differ from one who kills three or more? Again, if so, how?

One problem with classifying Family Annihilators relates to the definition of "family," an issue that Holmes and Holmes do not discuss. Perpetrators in our files who killed four or more victims often killed members of their extended family along with their spouses and children. They also killed in-laws, more distant relatives, and even people outside the family or household who were in some way involved in their lives (see the Simmons and Banks cases, described in Chapter 2). Legislators and social scientists have been wrestling with the problem of what constitutes a family for decades. It so far has proved impossible to devise one definition that suits everyone or that covers all or even most situations in which people actually live. As long as the definition of family remains ambiguous, categories such as Family Annihilator will exclude some cases that observers think should be included.

Also, why limit a Family Annihilator to the senior male? We have women and juveniles in our records who fit the category. The women may have no partners, but they kill all the children and themselves, thus effectively annihilating a family. Also, in one of the cases that Holmes and Holmes give as an example, the killer is a juvenile, not the senior male, at least not until after the killings. Rick Brom, who used an ax to kill his family, was a 16-year-old high-school student at the time of the crime (Case 398). Two of the other three cases mentioned as examples by Holmes and Holmes as Family Annihilators are also in our records. Only one includes among his victims all the members of the standard popular definition of a family: a spouse and offspring. However, in that case, Simmons not only killed his wife, children, grandchildren, sons-in-law, and daughters-in-law but also some people whom he had worked for or with, who were not part of his family. If Banks, the third

Family Annihilator mentioned by Holmes and Holmes, killed his "family," it was a peculiar one, consisting of several women to whom he was not married, his children, some stepchildren, and a neighbor. Banks did not kill his parents or his wife, who lived in another state. Family Annihilator may be a useful category, but the definition needs to be refined.

The problem of the definition of serial killers is discussed at length in Chapter 2. While Holmes and Holmes include serial killers in the category of mass murderers, Elliott Leyton limits the term "mass murders" to "killings in one explosive burst" (Leyton, 1988:4). Both Leyton and Holmes and Holmes agree, however, that serial killers are different from the people who kill in a sudden outburst. We defined a serial killer as an individual who killed more than one victim with the deaths separated by a period of time, from days to months or years. This definition is essentially the same as that of Eric Hickey (1991:8), who labels all murderers who kill more than one victim over time "serial killers," a definition similar to that given by Philip Jenkins, as detailed in Chapter 2. That definition, however, is rejected by Stephen Giannangelo, who focuses only on the individual who "kills because he wants to," "for the implicit thrill, satisfaction, or satiation of the act," whose victims are strangers, and whose crime is not motivated by profit "or any other tangible motivation that might render incidental the killing aspect of the crime." Giannangelo's serial killers are all motivated by the "ultimate control of another human being and the accompanying catharsis" (1996:5).

Using Giannangelo's definition would rule out most of the serial killers, especially the women, discussed in Chapter 2. Some of the female serial killers in our files killed at least five victims, but only one of the female mass murderers killed that many children. Although women do kill multiple victims, they do not kill as many at a time as men do. We do not know whether men or women who kill only one child differ from those who kill one victim at a time or from the people who kill their victims in bunches. Which definitions are most useful? We have chosen to distinguish serial from mass killers, but to use a broad definition of serial killer. Eliminating all but what appears to be a subcategory of serial killers from study hinders our understanding of the phenomenon.

Another problem in definition is the term "child." When does a child become an adult? For individuals under age 14, the issue of how responsible they are or whether they are fully aware of the consequences of their actions is usually raised. When a very young child, age 6 or 7, for example, kills some-one, law enforcement personnel, child advocates, social workers, and members of the general public argue vehemently over how to handle him. When a legally defined "child" acts in what seems to be a deliberate manner in committing a crime, some adults, particularly those outside the perpetrator's family, think that he should be treated as an adult. Other people have problems with judging a child's behavior by adult standards, no matter how deliberate the crime. Ultimately, when does a person stop being a child?

The age at which a person is no longer a child and can make his own decisions also enters the picture in discussions of religious practices. Chapter 7 includes an example of bad decisions where parents refused to get medical help for children who subsequently died. There have been highly publicized cases involving Jehovah's Witnesses' refusals to allow blood transfusions. In at least one case more than a decade ago, a 12-year-old boy agreed with his parents in wanting to reject a transfusion, but his position was ignored on the grounds that he was too young to reason. In the United States, many of our laws support our belief that a person is not an adult until age 18. In other societies, however, children are permitted to decide serious issues, even life or death matters, at a much younger age. For example, in the mountains of Peru, an anthropologist tried to persuade the father of a seriously ill 5-year-old boy to allow him to be taken to a hospital in another town. While the father agreed that the boy was so ill that he might die and that the hospital staff could probably save him, he said that the decision was the boy's to make. The child refused to go, and the father honored his choice. In another example, in the United States but among Native Americans on a reservation in the northeast, a 7-year-old boy from a poor family had earned several hundred dollars one summer, traveling with a singing and dancing group. The anthropologist working with the child's family asked the mother what she had done with the money. The mother looked baffled: "I don't know what he did with it, it was his money." Again, members of the dominant majority in the United States would not allow a child that age to make a decision about such an important resource.

Members of our society have not come to any clear consensus about the appropriate decision-making age in different situations. Although 18 is usually regarded as the age when one is legally considered an adult, even a superficial look at our behavior and the laws in different states raises questions.

Most states do not allow consumption of alcohol until age 21, although until recently most states set the age at 18. Moreover, the age of consent for marriage varies widely, not only from state to state but within states according to the gender of the individual; girls may be allowed to marry without parental permission at an earlier age than boys. The age at which sexual intercourse is legally considered rape, regardless of the partner's consent, also varies. Other examples abound. While automobile insurance for young men is extremely expensive for those under age 25 with some companies, age 35 with others, it is usually less expensive for young women. Children over 12 pay adult fares on most buses, trains, or planes. Further, there are age limits for buying cigarettes, seeing movies or videos, getting a driver's license, signing contracts, and voting, but again these age limits may vary from one state or locality to another. Recently a couple were fined for their teenaged son's illegal activities. It raised a storm of controversy. At what age must a person take responsibility for his actions?

At the other end of the age continuum, the problem is equally difficult. Is abortion a form of child murder? If human life begins at the moment of conception, then abortion is a way of killing a human. Some states accept this definition, while others do not legally recognize a zygote, an embryo, or even a fetus as a human person. The federal law that permits abortion during the very early stages of pregnancy is not equally permissive about the later months. The issue is a sensitive one and there is no national consensus on the matter. Yet the whole topic of child killings — both the question of the victim and the perpetrator — to some extent revolves around the definition of "child."

In this study, to avoid the ambiguity of the teen years, the term "child" refers to individuals age 12 and under, as stated earlier. Legally, individuals of that age are rarely, if ever, defined as adults, whether they kill someone or are themselves victims. Our data base does not include ordinary cases of abortion since they were not indexed under either murder or manslaughter in the *New York Times*. There are a few cases, however, when a fetus was included because the mother-to-be was either murdered or injured and the perpetrator was also charged with killing the fetus. In our data base, people who were accused of killing a fetus and who came to trial were usually found not guilty by a jury.

States are trying to cope with the problem of protecting both children and religious freedom when the two appear to be in conflict. The definition of "adult" is obviously crucial to this process. One news article on the pros-ecution of Christian Scientists whose children had died pointed out that forty states have exemptions to murder charges where religious beliefs are involved. Prosecutors have circumvented those exemptions by charging manslaughter instead of murder. The American Academy of Pediatrics is trying to elimi-nate the exemptions, but at the time of the article (*New York Times*, August 6, 1990) it had succeeded only in South Dakota. In 1997 the Committee on Bio-ethics of the American Academy of Pediatrics again published a call for "the end of religious exemption laws" (1997:279–81). According to an article by Marilyn Elias in *USA Today* in 1997, there were forty-six states that allowed exemptions from prosecution for neglect to parents who failed to seek medi-cal care for sick children on religious grounds (February 11, 1997). This is an emotional issue, and parents have gone to jail or fled the country to avoid violating their religious convictions. The situation is volatile, and there is no consistent national policy.

In this volume, we have used a cut-off for the age of victims (but not per-petrators) of 12, not based on whether older children were no longer "chil-dren" but on newspaper practices and the behavior of the youngsters themselves. We did not expect, and did not find, that many of our victims were engaging in high-risk activities, but some were. For example, a 7 year old (who is not in our files because the event took place after our closing date of 1993) recently tried to pilot a plane across the continent but was killed in the attempt. States and localities also vary in defining the age of children in research on child abuse and fatalities — some use 18, others use 14, still others use different ages. Psychologists have made a number of studies of juveniles who kill, using under 18 as the definition of "juvenile" (Benedek and Cornell, 1989:29–36). We have followed this practice in the discussion of juvenile kill-ers in Chapter 3. This lack of agreement within the United States makes com-parisons difficult between one set of data and another.

Access to confidential records is another perennial problem. All states have regulations that keep the records of child protective agencies confidential, in part to shield people who are being served from scorn or gossip by neighbors or the news media. The type and level of confidentiality vary from one state to another, according to the laws of the particular state, but all of them create barriers for anyone attempting a case review of the deaths of children. Case workers and psychologists insist that this confidentiality is essential to increase the willingness of families to turn to child protective agencies for help and to insulate innocent family members from negative publicity. However, these laws continue to apply even after a child has been killed. Critics protest that in cases of child deaths, the confidentiality laws protect only lazy and neglectful public officials, especially those in social service agencies. Even police investigators may have to obtain court orders to learn whether a suspect in a child murder has had any previous contact with the family services offered by the state.

There is no easy answer, but some of the information provided here may help legislators decide where the limits should be placed to allow for both accountability and the protection of family members from harassment. According to Richard Gelles, whose field is child abuse and domestic violence, "nearly half the children killed by their parents or caretakers had been reported as an abused child and his family had been served by the state child welfare system" (1996:8). Our figures of previous involvement are not so high (see Tables 1.34 and 1.35), but that may be precisely because of the confidentiality laws. Even newspaper reporters cannot gain access to the records available to well-known researchers with special mandates from a state or national government. In fact, we found a number of editorials and articles that complained about reporters being unable to get any information from social service agencies. When I was part of a state work group reviewing policies concerning at-risk children, I had to sign a confidentiality document, but the work group had all the necessary access to the records. At the start of this research many years ago, I attempted to obtain names of dead children from child protective agencies in Kentucky so that I could follow through in local newspapers. I offered then to sign a confidentiality statement, but my request was refused since I was not working for the agency. The research on which this book is based is thus both more extensive and less detailed than it would have been had confidentiality laws not raised so many barriers. To find the kind of information I was interested in, newspapers were the best alternative.

Another type of problem — one of diagnosis — surfaces in sudden infant death syndrome, or SIDS. The causes of SIDS are unclear. It is difficult or impossible to detect without an autopsy, and even an autopsy does not always reveal the answer if the coroner is not skilled in detecting subtle signs of deliberate asphyxiation. It is frighteningly easy to smother a baby. Indeed, no one knows how many murders of infants have gone undetected or how many people have been blamed for a death of which they were innocent. We have cases in our files of murders almost accidently discovered or else found out only after another child had been killed by the same person. For example, when Ella Rose Fletcher was hospitalized and died in January 1992, doctors diagnosed an epileptic seizure. When her brother Tommy was hospitalized with a drug overdose not long afterward, state police had Ella Rose's body exhumed. An autopsy showed that she had died of an overdose of an antidepressant and had also been sexually molested. A $5,000 life insurance policy had been taken out on both Tommy and Ella Rose (Case 734).

The dilemma facing investigating officers or medical personnel is obvious. Families already suffering real pain from the devastating loss of a baby from SIDS may face the additional trauma of an accusation of murder. If a family is poor, or if its members belong to a particular ethnic group associated with violence, live in a high crime area, or have been in trouble with the law, they may be deemed guilty by authorities or by news media personnel on very slight evidence. Conversely, the death of a child of a well-to-do family of the "right" ethnic background, living in a "good" neighborhood, may not be investigated closely on the assumption that the death must be natural if there are no obvious injuries. These differences in treatment are both the cause and the consequence of blatant or subtle stereotyping and prejudice.

Problems of diagnosis also occur in cases of emotional instability. Psychiatric diagnosis is not an exact science, and physicians, social workers, and lay people vary in their competency. A number of cases mentioned in these pages occurred because appropriate intervention did not take place in time. Renee Green's case in Chapter 4 is an example of an inaccurate psychiatric evaluation made in an overcrowded facility. Psychological diagnosis is a problem in the prevention of cases, in jury trials after a killing, and in the assessment of risk to a child. Frequently, when the behavior of the mother, father, or juvenile appears normal, the danger does not become apparent to anyone until it is too late.

A number of these problems are not limited to the murders of children, of course. Problems of definition, access to records, and diagnosis are difficulties faced by the investigators or researchers of any homicide. Another problem, related to all crimes but particularly difficult in child killings, is the reliability of witnesses. Are witnesses reliable, especially when they too are accused of killing a child? Are children, especially very young ones, able to describe a situation accurately? And what about cases of remembered sexual molestation? Sometimes recovered memories are created rather than recalled, and there is considerable legal and psychological controversy over distinguishing between real and fictional memories. Case workers, police investigators, and psychologists have all been accused of creating memories of events that never occurred in children, retarded adults, or anyone who can be easily influenced or intimidated. In the interest of self-preservation, child killers sometimes try to cast doubt on the charges against them by raising the real specter of false accusations. These false accusations of abuse, especially sexual abuse, are often made during bitter custody battles in divorce cases. Since sexual abuse typically occurs in private, such charges are often extremely difficult to either prove or disprove.

Some individuals, even without any prodding or coercion, confess to crimes that they did not commit. Law officers and psychologists are also familiar with this type. But is the confession genuine, or does it stem from a person's own psychological problems or result from the undue influence of someone in authority? In October 1983, Ottis Toole (36), in the Florida State Prison at Raiford, confessed in a sworn, signed statement that he had killed Adam Walsh (6) in July 1981, luring him away from a toy store while his mother was shopping nearby. The boy's head was discovered in a canal near a turnpike west of Vero Beach, about one hundred miles from where he had disappeared; Toole said that he buried the rest of the body in a marsh about seventy-five yards off the turnpike. The body was never found, however. Toole also confessed to thirty to forty murders with Henry Lucas, who was in jail in Texas and charged with another killing. Police initially linked the two men with sixty-nine murders in nine states. In November 1993, however, Toole recanted and denied ever making a confession. Toole, who is now dead, went on to confess and recant several more times (Shiflett, 1997:55). Did he really kill Adam Walsh, or was he confessing to the crime from some motive of his own? The case is still officially unsolved (Case 171). Emotionally unstable or passive and unsophisticated individuals are known to confess to crimes that they never committed (Douglas and Olshaker, 1997:300, 304, 330–31).

Accusations of child abuse may come from individuals who have a grudge against those whom they denounce: neighbors, former friends, alienated family members. Many of such reports turn out to be unsubstantiated. However,

Gelles emphasizes that reported cases of abuse that cannot be substantiated are not necessarily false (1996:41). First, he points out that "perpetrators must be caretakers or in a caretaker position" for a report to be investigated (1996:40). And second, the dividing line between substantiated and unsubstantiated reports of abuse is not always clear. Children often shield parents, or they may be too young to explain what happened to them. If the initial report accused the mother of abuse, but the investigation reveals that someone else was responsible, the report may be classified as unsubstantiated. One cannot assume, however, if a case is not opened or if it is closed by the Child Welfare Department, that the report was false.

Another difficulty lies in the investigation of a case of child murder itself. Gelles acknowledges that regardless of confidentiality laws, someone has to report, investigate, and determine the level of risk faced by a child if he continues to live in the home: the "unwillingness of private physicians and other mandated reporters to report abuse and neglect" is "one of the most serious fissures of the child welfare system" (1996:29). Persons who fail to report cases are rarely punished or even reprimanded, although in most states failure to report suspected abuse is against the law. Our data do not provide much information on this problem, although the work group on which I served in Kentucky found similar situations. We only have one case in our files where a judge was reprimanded for not reporting abuse (it involved a relative). The work group's published report points out failures of judges to hear cases or to punish parents who fail to comply with court orders. It refers to lawyers for social service agencies who were reluctant to bring cases for family termination before judges, and physicians who were reluctant to state probable abuse as the cause of injuries. Case workers also were reluctant to push law enforcement personnel to bring cases to trial or to charge noncompliant parents. Furthermore, psychological centers charged with evaluating individuals to assess the risk that they posed to a child were sometimes so ambiguous, ambivalent, or dilatory in their reports that case workers could not use the information. All of these examples of reluctance place children in peril (Policy Review Work Group, 1995:80–83).

Evidence that a child has been killed may be subtle. Even when an autopsy is performed, medical personnel — due in part to the fact that not all coroners are properly trained to detect evidence of an induced death in the case of a child — may be unwilling to attribute the cause of death to abuse. In an investigation of several child deaths, doctors were so unwilling to attribute nonfatal injuries to abuse that the case worker could not persuade the court to permit removal of a child from the home (Policy Review Work Group, 1995:80–81). Particularly in small communities, doctors and coroners may be reluctant to believe that people whom they know could be guilty of fatal abuse and thus may give them the benefit of the doubt. Moreover, this is another area where unconscious or conscious ethnic or socioeconomic biases can affect the outcome.

The degree of denial present, not only in medical personnel but also in neighbors, co-workers, acquaintances, and, most often, close relatives, complicates the investigation. It also is a major obstacle in obtaining convictions. Everyone involved in cases of child murder is aware of the number of people who are "sure" that the accused "could not have done such a thing," even in the face of overwhelming evidence.

Some of the cases in our files were exposed because police intervened to insist on an autopsy or a closer investigation. Unfortunately, it is not always possible to rely on the integrity of the police. Detectives have been convicted of planting evidence when they were sure that they had the guilty party. For example, on December 22, 1989, a gunman robbed and killed the Harris family in Ellis Hollow, New York. The youngest child, Mark (11), was in our sample group. The killer set fire to the house and stole the Harrises' van, which was abandoned at a shopping plaza near Ithaca. On the same day that the bodies were found, the Harris credit cards were used by a man and woman to buy clothing, electronics, and diamonds at malls in Syracuse and Auburn, New York. Suspicion centered on Anthony Turner, also known as Michael Kinge. In February 1990 his mother's house was staked out, and police tried to arrest him when he came home. He had told friends that he would shoot it out because he was not going back to jail. According to one newspaper article, when troopers entered the house, Michael held a shotgun pointed at his chin. He turned the gun toward the officers and fired one shot. The troopers returned his fire and killed him. His mother, Shirley Kinge, was also arrested, tried, convicted of arson and burglary, and sentenced to thirty years in prison.

In 1992, however, the chief investigator, Trooper David Harding, was jailed after admitting that Shirley's fingerprints, supposedly found on a gasoline can at the Harris home, had actually been taken from her own house. Shirley received a new trial in which she pleaded guilty to using the stolen credit cards, a misdemeanor. Since she had already served two years, she was released. Harding pleaded guilty to falsifying evidence and admitted that he had faked evidence to obtain a confession or to make an airtight case in two other crimes when the police were sure that they had the guilty party. A forensic specialist, Robert Lishansky, also involved in the Kinge case, confessed that he had helped his partner, Harding. Before the inquiry was over, five investigators were implicated and three admitted fabricating evidence; more than two dozen cases were involved. Lishansky is serving six to twelve years for fabricating evidence in twenty-one cases (Case 437).

Causal Explanations

There are no easy answers or single explanations that will fit all cases of child killings. People's lives are filled with problems, and they do not always know how to deal with them. Only a few institutions even try to teach coping skills, and there is little flexibility in laws or in social service agencies. The frequency with which neighbors, friends, and relatives call brutal killers "nice people," "good parents," and "loving fathers" (or mothers) reveals the depth of denial indulged in by most of us about the relationships between parents and children as well as the difficulty of predicting home behavior from any observation of public behavior. Indeed, the old saying, "street angel, house devil," may be accurate after all.

One of the advantages of using newspaper data is that the killings are presented in a context that allows for the discovery of unsuspected factors. Some cases in particular reveal how closely the crimes are tied to issues that plague American society. For example, our files include cases where racism and prejudice clearly played major roles. David Rice, an unemployed drifter, spurred on by survivalist and hate literature, killed a family because he erroneously believed that they were Jewish (Case 469). Survivalist leanings were also involved in the case of the serial killers Leonard Lake and Charles Ng (Case 283). We also have a record of a young man who was accused of deliberately hitting a young Peruvian boy with his car after making racist remarks to his passengers (Case 233), and the possible influence of racial hatred in the Banks case is detailed in Chapter 2. There is no way of knowing from our data how many other cases were inspired by some form of ethnic, religious, or racial rage, but such attitudes in our society obviously can lead to violence. Elliott Leyton, in *Hunting Humans*, blames race and class oppression for all mass and serial killings. While our data do not support that hypothesis, it is clear that tensions in the society as a whole are reflected in many child killings.

There are several modern approaches to the study of child fatalities. One of these approaches, the focus of the book *Homicide*, seeks to determine underlying causes of all homicidal behavior, placing the murders of children in this broader context. Daly and Wilson begin their book by asking, "Why do people kill one another?" They mention a number of popular theories to account for murder: 1) violent people who were abused in childhood; 2) envy engendered by social inequities; 3) penalties not severe enough to serve as a deterrent; 4) psychoses induced by substance abuse, hormone imbalance, or brain tumors; 5) modern weapons so lethal that they allow people to bypass natural inhibitions; and 6) violence on television that encourages violent behavior (1988:1–2).

While recognizing that any or all of these factors may play a role in a specific homicide case, Daly and Wilson also suggest the use of "selection thinking" or evolutionary psychology as a major approach to an explanation. Selection thinking suggests that "the evolved motivational mechanisms of all creatures, including ourselves, have been designed to expend the organism's very life in the pursuit of genetic posterity" (1988:5). The term "genetic posterity" refers to offspring who can pass on the genes of the parents to the next generation. Daly and Wilson caution that evolutionary psychology is not a theory of motivation. Fitness — that is, the degree to which an individual produces numerous healthy offspring able to pass along his genes — is not a "goal" directly, but "it is used to explain why certain goals have come to control behavior at all" (1988:7). Specifically related to the study of child killings by mothers, they say that "selection thinking leads us . . . to a set of detailed predictions about variations in the strength of maternal love as a function of the mother's age, the child's age, and several other variables" (1988:8).

Daly and Wilson examined all homicides in Detroit in 1972. Our figures are not directly comparable since our data cover a longer time (1977 to 1993) and a wider area (the United States) and record only homicides where the victims included at least one child age 12 or under. When Daly and Wilson focused on perpetrators, they set age 14 as the younger limit because they found that to be the age when people begin to kill one another. Our data along with specialized studies of juvenile killers agree that people start to kill one another more frequently from age 14 onward, but there are enough examples of younger killers (see Chapter 3) to convince us that they should not be left out. We included all killers regardless of age or gender.

The term "selection thinking" is another name for a sociobiological approach. Daly and Wilson use selection thinking because they believe that it provides new ways of looking at old problems as well as suggests both new questions and alternative solutions, but they use it cautiously. They are careful to qualify their suggestions. They point out that specific behavior, such as the killing of a rival male, need not be more useful now to increase someone's chances of having more children than a rival if that type of behavior was useful in the past (1988:12). Behavior selected as useful by evolution is necessarily based on past advantages rather than current ones. They argue that in the past, a violent reaction by a male toward a rival resulted in the violently jealous male having more offspring than a less aggressive one, thus increasing the frequency of whatever gene led to or allowed the violent behavior, if genes are involved. We do not know whether the jealous male did have more offspring. An alternative hypothesis suggests that males in a society might have allied to kill or drive out the violently aggressive male — in which case genes encouraging in-group cooperation may have been passed along more frequently than those encouraging in-group violence.

One general hypothesis suggested by Daly and Wilson is that "natural selection has shaped psychological mechanisms of interpersonal 'value' such that Ego will ordinarily tend to value other individuals in rough proportion to their expected contribution to Ego's inclusive fitness" (1988:32). "Inclusive fitness" is a term with a broader reference than the term "fitness" alone. An individual shares genes with brothers and sisters as well as with a mother and a father. Behavior that allows any of these people to pass along their genes increases a person's inclusive fitness. The hypothesis of Daly and Wilson simply suggests that the more a person is likely to improve an individual's chances to have his genes passed along to the next generation, the more the individual is likely to value that person. Applying this hypothesis to homicide leads to the expectation that conflicts between individuals "will tend to be increasingly severe and dangerous the more distantly related are the participants" (1988:34). If this hypothesis is correct, then one would expect a person to kill nonrelatives before a relative. Thus, in terms of child murders, a stepchild would be killed before a biological child, or a stranger's child before the child of a relative.

Our cases do not strongly support this hypothesis. When children are killed, relatives are usually the killers, and the closer the relatives the more likely they are to be the killers (Tables 1.20, 1.21, and 1.31). The size of the population from which the categories are drawn is factored in by Daly and Wilson to reduce the significance of parent killers—that is, there are many more biological parents of children than there are stepparents, adopted parents, foster parents, or mothers' lovers—so the killings by nonrelatives, though numerically less frequent, are actually disproportionately high. Table 1.20, however, shows that the number of victims of biological parents is over four times the number of victims of friends, acquaintances, neighbors, and nonbiological in-laws, although the population size of that category must be much larger than the population of biological parents of victims—each of whom could only have two.

Using concepts of evolutionary psychology, Daly and Wilson argue that stepparents or mothers' lovers are much more likely than fathers to kill children. Our data do not support this conclusion (Tables 1.20–1.22, 1.29, and 1.30). Regardless of the way in which the relationships are calculated, fathers lead the list, parents' lovers (almost all mothers' lovers) are next, then stepparents, then adoptive parents, and, finally, foster parents. The last two are very close in percentage. All the males in these groups, except the fathers, are usually unrelated to the victim (with the exception of a few perpetrators who were part of kin foster families). Genetically there is no difference between them. If past evolutionary selection pressure is operative, they should all kill children at an equal rate. The size of the potential perpetrator population should be the only cause of variation if the rates are equal. Unfortunately, there is insufficient information available to compare adequately these four groups in the general population. The U.S. Census figures combine stepfathers and live-in male lovers in one category. While they distinguish them from adoptive parents, they do not separate out foster parents (*Statistical Abstracts: 1995*, Table 77). By combining all the "stepparents" in the census data, they amount to a larger proportion of the general population than combining paramours and all step relatives in the study's perpetrator population. Since not all of the step relatives acted in a parental role to their victims (there were some stepsiblings and stepcousins who killed children), our data base indicates that the killing rate is not so high for them as their number in the general population would suggest. Adoptive parents, according to the U.S. Census figures, also are a larger proportion of the general population than they are in this study's data base.

In terms of evolutionary psychology it makes sense to combine legal stepfathers and lovers in the same category. However, based on our data, men who married the mother of a child killed their stepchildren less frequently than a mother's lover did. Both legal stepfathers and mothers' lovers killed these unrelated children more often than did either adoptive fathers or foster fathers, although the males in those relationships are equally unrelated to the child. Socially, however, there are differences. For one, marriage, adoption, and fostering all suggest a greater commitment by the male. With adopted and foster parents, however, the mothers as well as the fathers are unrelated to the child. (There are exceptions, with kin fosters or when relatives adopt children.) In sociobiological terms, one would expect them to kill children more frequently than mothers' lovers or stepfathers do because neither parent is related to the child. While the foster and adoptive fathers are both making a commitment to the child, the stepfathers and mothers' lovers are making their commitment, at whatever level, to the mother. Thus, the child may be merely a condition for living with her and may be perceived as being in the way of a better relationship with the mother. On the other hand, since foster and adoptive parents expect from the start to raise a biologically unrelated child, their expectations about their connection to the child may be more realistic from the beginning.

Another complication in using statistics rather than case reviews is that "mother's lover" might well be the child's father, depending on how long the relationship has lasted. Statistics do not make it clear, nor do all the newspaper articles. Frequently, however, the newspaper story does give enough information about the length of the relationship between the mother and her lover to suggest the probability that he is the father of the victim. In such cases we have classified him as the father and listed the relationship as stable.

In addition to the general hypothesis about nonrelatives being the most likely victims of homicide, Daly and Wilson specifically applied selection thinking to the murder of children. They quote from Richard Alexander's *Darwinism and Human Affairs*, which listed three cost-benefit questions that could affect parental behaviors. First, is the child really mine? Second, what is the child's potential to pass along parental genes? And third, what alternative uses might a parent make of the resources that will have to be spent on the offspring? (Alexander, 1979:109, cited in Daly and Wilson, 1988:44). The basis for these questions is the concept that natural selection will favor those parents who best promote their own fitness – that is, their ability to pass along their genes.

Daly and Wilson used Alexander's questions to formulate three "issues" which they then reviewed crossculturally by using the Human Relations Area Files, a collection of coded information on several hundred societies worldwide. First, "Is the infant the putative parent's own?" which is the same as Alexander's first question. Second, "What is the infant's quality?" which again is essentially the same as Alexander's second question. And third, "Are present circumstances favorable for child rearing?" This issue modifies Alexander's third cost-benefit question from possible alternative uses of resources to one of general circumstances favoring (or not favoring) child rearing.

Our data base shows that the first issue – whether the child is really the parent's offspring – may well be a factor in some cases. Men may doubt the fidelity of their wives during a separation or when a divorce is pending or contemplated. It is possible that a man unmarried to the mother of his child has more doubts about the child's paternity than a legal husband does. If so, it could account for why mothers' lovers' killing rate is higher than that of stepfathers. When paternity is questioned, children are at risk, as a number of our cases demonstrate. Unfortunately, we have no data on how many male killers actually doubted that they were the father of the child whom they killed. We do have a few cases, however, where a male killed his own child and spared his stepchild. One example is Jason Radtke, whose case was described in Chapter 5 (Case 645) and which does not support the Daly and Wilson hypothesis. On the other hand, we also have cases where the male perpetrator specifically questioned his wife's fidelity, as in the example of Ramon Salcido (Case 457), described in Chapter 2. Salcido, however, killed adults and children related to his wife (but not to him) as well as some of his own offspring. This case supports the Daly and Wilson hypothesis but adds victims who do not fit.

A number of perpetrators gave revenge rather than concern with infidelity as a motive. These perpetrators were almost all males who claimed that they wanted revenge because the woman had left them or wanted to leave them. Could this abandonment cause the father to suspect that the child might not be his? Is the blow to the man's ego and pride enough reason for him to kill without considering the parentage issue? Daly and Wilson suggest that evolutionary selection pressure might have favored the male who protected his family with violence. Is the revenge behavior part of this pattern? Newspaper articles do not give sufficient information to answer these questions, nor do statistics. To answer these questions accurately, one would have to interview the perpetrator intensively. Unlike Medea, there are no women in this study who claimed revenge as a reason for killing their children.

The second issue, the question of the condition of the child — whether the child is healthy enough to effectively pass along the genes inherited from the father and mother — would equally underlie murderous behavior for men or for women. Table 1.32, which gives the rationale of 403 perpetrators, has only 3.2 percent who claimed mercy killing in order to spare the child from suffering. These cases support the Daly and Wilson belief that children may be killed because of perceived genetic inferiority. The McKay case (Case 250), described in Chapter 4, involved a deformed infant; in two others, also in Chapter 4, the child was retarded (Case 520) or had a genetic disorder (Case 213). Perpetrators did not always claim mercy killing, however; some who were raising a retarded or disabled child simply were no longer able to cope or were angry. Are these explanations evidence that evolutionary selection pressure was at work? Again, we lack information to give a definitive answer.

There were not many cases of children killed because of these problems. A few murdered children had been maimed earlier by physical abuse, as was the case of Baby Lollipop (Case 827, described in Chapter 6). In the few cases where the child's lack of quality fits the Daly and Wilson hypothesis, the perpetrators often mentioned the problem either in their statements to the police, during a trial, or in a suicide note. The numbers are too few to make statistical analysis useful, but it appears that women were slightly more likely than men to claim that they were sparing the child from pain. Is this due merely to the cultural expectation that women should take more interest than men in a child's welfare? A female perpetrator trying to escape punishment for killing a child by claiming concern for its welfare might be more credible than a male perpetrator in the same situation.

Most children who were killed were not handicapped, or at least no disability was mentioned in the news articles. In several cases the child was said to be intelligent, active, or hardworking, none of which indicates a lack of potential for passing along parental genes. Our data suggest that while children with disabilities may be at slightly greater risk than normal children, this factor is not a major one in child murders, so the data do not give strong support to the Daly and Wilson hypothesis.

The third issue raised by Alexander — the alternative uses of the resources for raising a child — was modified by Daly and Wilson to include the question of the availability of social and economic support. Daly and Wilson have two other hypotheses concerning infanticide that can be compared with our data. They point out that in Canada, statistics for the years from 1977 to 1983 indicate that single women had only 12 percent of the babies born but were responsible for over one-half of the 64 recorded infanticides (1988:63). They found that even when maternal age groups are considered separately, single women are more likely to dispose of a new baby than married women of the same age. Their hypothesis is that single women lack social and economic resources, and infanticide increases as these resources decrease. Our data tend to support the hypothesis for infanticide. It has been pointed out in previous chapters that almost all of the newborns were killed by mothers who gave birth unattended. While they were not all single mothers, the fact that they were alone when they gave birth indicates a lack of social support.

The proportion of mothers who kill children is much higher than people in our society expect. The figure for females with collaborators who kill children, however, may be misleading because of our society's attitude toward mothers. If a child's mother is present at the time of the crime, she is usually charged with some level of murder or as an accessory. If she did not try to stop the male killer, she may be charged with the same level of crime as the male even when she claims that she did not interfere because she was afraid of him. A number of examples illustrate this point. Teresa Slone (18) was convicted of complicity in the killing of her daughter, Rebecca, in Kentucky in 1983. The 14 month old was beaten to death by Timothy Terry, Teresa's boyfriend. Timothy also beat Teresa, but those beatings were not regarded as a valid reason for Teresa's failure to intervene for Rebecca (Case 856). Ann Marie Epps (2) of Avondale, Arizona, died after she was beaten with fists, a coat hanger, and electrical cord on November 20, 1984, by John Samaniego (20), her mother's boyfriend, who beat the toddler because she soiled her pants and would not stop crying. The prosecutor said that Rosie (20), Ann Marie's mother, participated in the abuse and failed to call for medical help. John pleaded guilty to two counts of child abuse; Rosie was charged with second-degree murder (Case 828). In 1990, Christopher Wohlers (2) died in Austin, Texas, on January 3. His stepfather, Gerald Christopher Zuliani (23), was accused of beating him and slamming him into a bathroom wall. His mother was also charged with murder for failing to protect the boy, although she claimed that she, too, was frequently abused and was afraid for herself and her older child, a 4-year-old girl (Case 654). An exception is the Lisa Steinberg case in New York City in 1987 (Case 385). Charges against Hedda Nussbaum, Lisa's adopted mother, were dropped; she testified against her lover and convinced the court that she had been so terrorized by him that she was unable to defend her daughter. Hedda escaped punishment even though the adoption was informal and never legalized.

When a woman is the killer, men are not usually charged with the same level of crime as are mothers when the man is the killer, although one could assume that a man would be able to stop a violent woman more easily than the reverse. Frequently, men are not charged at all when the woman is a killer, or they are charged with a lesser offense as happened with the Riegler family mentioned in Chapter 6. Mrs. Riegler pleaded guilty to manslaughter after being charged with second-degree murder. Her husband was charged with child endangerment.

In our data, unfortunately, we have family status for only 34 cases of homicidal mothers, not all of whom killed infants. Fifteen of the homicidal mothers were single (44 percent), which supports the Daly and Wilson hypothesis. Only one of the 34 was in her original relationship; nine had remarried, and the remaining nine were widowed, divorced, estranged, or separated from their husbands — that is, twenty-four of the women who killed their own children were not married at the time of the crime. These data support the hypothesis that a lack of social or economic support can be associated with most cases of child killing by mothers, not just with infanticide. Our data indicate that children of any age in a broken home are at higher risk than children in a home with both biological parents. Several of the hypotheses suggested by Daly and Wilson might apply to this situation: lack of economic resources, lack of emotional support, and questions of paternity.

Concern about how to support the children was given as a rationale in some cases when older children were the victims of either women or men, although it was more frequently mentioned in cases where mothers killed the children. Several women and female juveniles claimed that they were not only overburdened with child care but also lacked emotional as well as financial support. This lack upholds the Daly and Wilson hypothesis in general, not only in application to infants.

The number of perpetrators who gave this rationale for murder was so small that they are included in the category of "other" (Table 1.32). Most of the men left with the care of children claimed that revenge on the wife was their motivation for killing the children. Women were more likely to express fear that children would be taken away from them, plead insanity, or cite an inability to cope. Any of these reasons could indicate the lack of social or economic support suggested by Daly and Wilson, but, once again, much more detail than is given in newspaper articles is necessary to determine the significance of this factor in child murders.

Daly and Wilson hypothesize that women are less likely to kill babies when they are farther along in their fertile years—that is, infanticide should decrease as maternal age rises (1988:52, 53, 62, 63). In their figures, the probability of infanticide decreases with age in both single and married groups. Also, the older the child, the less likely he is to be killed (Table 1.1). Daly and Wilson suggest that the decrease is related to the increased parental investment that would be written off if the child were killed.

Clearly, one factor that may decrease the rate of infanticide by older mothers may simply be that fewer babies are born anyway as women age. Most homicidal mothers are in their peak child-bearing years; there was only one newborn killed by a woman over the age of 31. These figures support the Daly and Wilson hypothesis. All but one of the children killed by the women over 30 (there were 69 victims) was an older child, although, of course, the children of women over 30 tend to be older. These older women have fewer children under age 3, who are shown to be at highest risk in all studies. Very few of the women under 20 have any children over 3 years of age. In other words, the relationship between the ages of maternal perpetrators and child victims may only be one of availability of targets rather than the result of evolutionary selection pressure.

Older mothers were more likely to have multiple victims, but they were also more likely to have more targets. All age groups had more victims than killers, but the over-40 group had the highest average. Both the 30-to-34-year-old and over-40 groups supported another hypothesis of Daly and Wilson—that older mothers were likely to be desperate and to commit suicide (1988:78). Neither the 30 to 34 year olds nor the over-40 group killed newborns (with the one exception mentioned above), and both groups showed a high rate of suicide.

While Daly and Wilson's hypothesis about the age of the mother and its relationship to the killing of the child has been examined, they also hypothesize that the older the child, the less likely it is to be killed—a prediction that all studies, including this one, support. Their explanation is based on the increasing value of the child to the parents both in terms of the amount of time and resources invested and the child's increasing potential for passing along the parental genes as he grows beyond the hazards of childhood toward reproductive maturity (1988:73–75). Daly and Wilson also predict that the proportion of children killed by nonrelatives will increase with the age of the child while the proportion killed by parents decreases. Certainly, some of any increase could be due to the increased contact that nonrelatives have with the child as he gets older. Table 1.33, however, supports the Daly and Wilson hypothesis. After age 3, the percentage of victims killed by nonrelatives outnumbers those killed by parents, and from age 7 onward the proportion killed by nonrelatives exceeds that killed by parents and other biological kin combined. The proportion of victims killed by biological kin other than parents remains virtually constant after age 3, although the proportion killed by biological parents decreases. The reasons are not known, but the parental decrease may be due to the evolutionary selection factors suggested by Daly and Wilson.

Table 1.1 as well as Table 1.33 indicate age 3 as a major dividing line. Why are children 3 and under so much more likely to be killed than older children? Besides the Daly and Wilson hypothesis of the increasing value of the child to parents, followed by a slow decline in the number of victims killed by parents, our study of the newspaper reports of child murders suggests that cultural factors also need to be considered. For example, ignorance of the kinds of fragility specific to very small children may be important. As noted earlier, an act that will kill an infant or toddler, such as shaking, may not harm a 12 year old. In our society, with its small two-generation families, many young people, especially males, do not have experience in taking care of small children. Schools recently have attempted to lower the frequency of teenagers having babies by giving realistic dolls to high-school students to take care of for a week or two. The program has been fairly successful, which would not be the case if teenagers were already familiar with the problems of taking care of babies.

Our culture places an unusual emphasis on cleanliness. Advertisements trumpet the value of products that reduce body odor or leave clothes both clean and fragrant. However, vomit, urine, and feces are part of the messes that a small child creates, and many people, especially males, in our relatively sanitary society never have to deal directly with such unpleasantness. A large number of perpetrators in our files have a low tolerance for stress and react violently when angered or upset The combination of an unexpected event (vomiting, defecation, urination) that provokes extreme disgust with a tendency to react with violence may be the trigger in a number of cases.

Summary

A thorough examination of the implications of applying evolutionary psychology's concepts to the problem of child murders would take another volume and much more case review research. The factors are too interrelated and complex for statistics alone to give more than suggestions for additional research, as this brief overview indicates. One point is clear, however. The whole question of why children are killed cannot be resolved by depending on only one factor. While psychology may provide answers as to why individual A becomes a perpetrator while individual B does not, for law enforcement personnel, legislators, and social case workers the situations and circumstances that raise the risk for the child are the only factors subject to evaluation and intervention.

The difficulties in understanding and reducing child deaths result from a combination of at least two factors: the barriers to thorough investigation, and the variety of circumstances in which such deaths take place. The barriers to investigation include psychological or cultural factors, such as our beliefs about the "instinctive" love of parents, especially mothers, for their children; and institutional factors, such as laws, division of responsibility between government agencies, and the conventions governing crime reports. The circumstances in which deaths take place are so varied that single explanations — even broad ones such as evolutionary selection thinking — are not sufficiently precise to enable us to translate their hypotheses into courses of action. It seems to be dodging the issue to insist that more research is necessary, but for a topic as complex as this one, we still have surprisingly little information. The final chapter will offer some suggestions, based on the data from this research, as to where we should go from here.

CHAPTER 9

Recommendations: Where Do We Go from Here?

It is essential to point out that the social work literature is rich with information about available resources, legislation, and problems — information developed over the years by researchers, organizations, and social workers who deal directly with families. Consequently, although this chapter organizes some of the recommendations that result from analysis of our data base, it does not spell out details of how suggestions should be implemented. There are already agencies in place and knowledgeable people in positions of authority who are able to use the information presented here in the most effective way possible.

After sifting through our case files in a search for discernible patterns and significant exceptions, one conclusion is inescapable: the problem of people killing children cannot be eliminated entirely. There are too many different reasons why children die. Even the most confirmed optimist must recognize that factors leading to the loss of innocents will always be present, and the most that we can do is try to minimize their effects. The analysis of cases between 1977 and 1993 does reveal patterns, however, and some of these patterns can be modified if people will act carefully, intelligently, and energetically. The recommendations that emerge from a study of the cases are not all easy ones; none alone will solve the problem, nor are they all necessarily new. Some of these recommendations are more easily implemented or have already been instituted in some states, so they are not listed in order of priority or importance — with the exception of the first one.

Be Willing to Terminate Parental Rights

The termination of parental rights — that is, the process of taking a child out of the home and legally freeing it for adoption — is currently a difficult and cumbersome process in almost all states. This issue cuts to the heart of American tradition, touching on the values and cherished beliefs that we hold dear: the sanctity of the family, the role of the state, and the right of privacy, to name only a few. However, this study reveals cases of children who were killed after they were returned to an abusive home or who were not removed from such a home even after complaints were made and investigations took place. Richard Gelles, one of the most respected names in research on child abuse and family violence, has recently come to a similar conclusion. In *The Book of David*, he calls attention to the failure of child welfare agencies to protect the lives of children and asks for more effective legislation to prevent deaths, especially those of children already brought to the attention of such agencies. Gelles blames this failure primarily on the societal demands to preserve and reunite the family. Legislators are reluctant to make termination of parental rights easy. Many believe that a child is safer with its biological parents than in an adoptive or foster home. The realization that the victims in almost 50 percent of the cases in our sample were killed by one or both biological parents, however, should give any legislator pause.

Our figures of children killed by someone in a family previously served by child welfare agencies are not nearly so high as those of Gelles. We have only 58 victims out of 554 where there was enough information to say with confidence that although their families had been involved with social services, the children were not removed from the home. In some of these situations, an older sibling was abused so badly that family rights over that child were terminated, or that child was removed from the home, yet the child in our data base was not removed and was later killed. The Riegler case in Chapter 6 is an example. We also have 23 cases of children removed from abusive homes by child welfare agencies, then returned and killed. It is noteworthy that except for two of those children whose time at home before their murder was not known, all returned children in our files were killed within less than a year after being sent home, and most died within a few weeks (Table 1.26).

Certain types of abuse are indicative of an increased likelihood that the abuser will eventually kill a child. Bites, spiral limb fractures, skull fractures, cigarette burns (especially around the eyes and genitals), and broken ribs are warnings of the fatal consequences that can result if the child is left in the home. Any of these signs should prompt serious consideration of immediate and permanent removal of a child. Previous severe abuse of a sibling, especially when it has led to termination of parental rights, is also a danger signal that should make case workers and judges more willing to remove a child. Attempts to reunite such a family should proceed only if there is strong evidence of a valid change in attitude and behavior on the part of the people in the home; and even then, only if careful monitoring for the immediate future is available.

Laws in most states require that child welfare services must make a "reasonable effort" to keep the family together, but "reasonable effort" is never defined. State agency personnel therefore may go to extreme lengths to preserve a dysfunctional family because in their experience, judges are more apt to side with the family if there is the least ambiguity in the evidence of maltreatment. Yet termination of parental rights so that a child may be adopted into a nurturing home can be an essential part of ensuring the safety and normal development of that child.

The case mentioned in the Introduction is an example of a child killed after she was returned to parents by a judge, despite child protective agency recommendations that she remain in foster care. The judge ruled that under the law he had no choice but to return her to her home. At the time of this writing, some states and the federal government are considering bills that would make it easier for parental rights to be terminated. Although there are a number of strong advocates for such laws, based on evidence similar to what is presented here, these laws predictably will have a difficult time passing because the forces for family preservation are also strong. The widespread feeling that somehow biological parents are the best ones to raise a child, regardless of evidence to the contrary, makes passage of a bill favoring easier termination of parental rights anything but certain. Yet the priorities legally given to biological parents may be seriously misguided. The physical act of giving birth or siring a child does not guarantee, or even indicate, one's parenting abilities (Gelles, 1996:9), nor does genetic relationship ensure loving care and patient instruction.

Whoever makes a decision about removing a child has a tremendous responsibility. Even in states that take a more liberal stance on terminating parental rights, decisionmakers most often opt for preserving the family — the cost of which is too often paid by a child. A recent example in Kentucky (not in our files, both because it occurred after 1993 and because the children were not killed) is a case in point. The children were removed from the mother's care time after time, and neglect was documented over and over again, but the children were always returned to the mother in order to keep the family together. The children were so accustomed to this routine that on the most recent occasion the oldest girl herself called the social agency to report the neglect (*Kentucky Post*, October 6, 1995).

The suggestion that orphanages might be a better solution than foster families is currently being discussed at state and national levels. Unfortunately, orphanages have a poor public image. People do not realize, however, that for a child to be separated from his siblings and moved from one foster home to another is not much of an improvement over a dysfunctional biological family. The stability of an orphanage, followed by an early adoption — possible only if parental rights are terminated in a timely manner — provides a more secure childhood than one filled with uncertainty, pain, and terror in an abusive family.

Improve Instruments and Training to Identify Potential Risks to Children

One difficulty for child welfare case workers is assessing the risk to the child and then convincing authorities that the risks are real. Instruments have been developed by various investigators, including psychologists, to profile or identify potential abusers. One example is the Child Abuse Potential Inventory (Milner, 1994), and a review of the various instruments can be found in Ammerman and Hersen (1992). One problem with these instruments is that even if they identify potential abusers with reasonable accuracy, they may not identify potential killers because not all abusers are killers, although a number of killers also abuse (Gelles, 1996:77). Another problem is that existing instruments are misused, as, for example, in employing a physical child abuse scale to assess the risk of sexual abuse (Milner, 1994:548). Better training in the use and interpretation of risk assessment documents and forms is clearly needed.

On many current risk assessment documents used by case workers, the items listed are all counted as equally important. For example, the fact that a parent has previously fractured a child's skull is given equal weight with alcohol or substance abuse and with the condition of the home. These factors are not as strongly related to fatal abuse as is earlier violent behavior. In our data base, we found that people with a history of violence or crime killed disproportionately more victims than people without such a history (Table 1.35). Other researchers agree (Gelles, 1996:73). Information in this study may assist individuals and organizations such as Psychtec, Inc., who develop the forms, to improve their tests.

Another area where improved assessment and interpretation is essential is that of mental or emotional disturbance. A number of cases described in Chapter 4 illustrate the need. The emotional state of individuals in a child's home is a significant component in risk assessment. Few case workers are trained in the recognition of danger signals.

If an abusive home is to be made safe for the child, then the abuser must change his or her attitudes and behavior. But not every abusive person is willing to change. Serious problems arise when case workers do not recognize this fact and encourage people to take parenting programs or other therapy in the expectation that the abusive behavior will cease. To have any success at all, the abusers first have to acknowledge that they have a problem and want to change. If they do not, their attendance at programs will be wasted effort, and their compliance may be merely to keep authorities at bay. Scarce resources are wasted on people who have no intention of changing. The case workers and anyone else in regular contact with the family, such as doctors or teachers, need to be trained in recognizing abusers who are not likely to respond to recommended programs and therefore distinguish between them and the ones who will benefit from such programs.

Many large universities offer degrees in Social Work, and this university training usually provides information on the variety of organizations nationally available for assistance. In addition, states that employ social workers have training programs to teach their case workers the various local laws, guidelines, facilities, and procedures. The general training also informs new social workers about the kinds of tests that are designed to help them distinguish between families who can benefit from existing assistance programs and families in which children are in such danger that they should be removed at once.

However, the training may not provide extensive information on the types of difficulties that the case workers are likely to encounter in family abuse investigations.

Support, Nurture, and Encourage the Maintenance of the Family

After calling for greater ease in granting the termination of parental rights, this recommendation calls for encouraging the maintenance of the family. The reason for the apparent contradiction is that the option of maintaining a family or removing a child from it depends on the rest of its members. To state the obvious, a family consists of more than simply two adults and one or more children. In the issue of child murders, relations between the adults in the household as well as those between each adult and each child are important. Our records indicate that a broken home is a major component in high risk to the child and is at least as significant as the past behavior of the adults (a factor regarded by Gelles as the most significant one). Only 26 percent of the homes in our sample were intact with both biological parents, whereas 63.6 to 81.5 percent of the children age 18 and under in the general population in 1990 were living with both biological parents (U.S. Bureau of the Census, 1995:64). Since our victim sample consists of children age 12 and under, the discrepancy can be assumed to be even greater: the younger the child, the more likely are the parents to still be together.

A healthy two-biological parent family is good for children, but a healthy family is not an isolated one. In our current society, the stress placed on two adults trying to raise children is enormous. The American family has almost always been larger than the household. Uncles, aunts, grandparents, and other relatives have helped to raise children in the past, and they still do to an extent that may be unrecognized by the general public. Leaving a child at a day care center or hiring a full-time nanny—solutions that are viewed with alarm by many people—is expensive and difficult to arrange.

In the American household of the past, for economic and social reasons there were frequently relatives (grandparents, unmarried parental siblings, cousins) living in one home. In a less mobile society, even when parents and children lived alone, they frequently had close relatives nearby who could help with child care and recognize abuse or intervene in a dangerous situation. Most people in these large households learned how to get along with others, how to be patient and tolerant, how and when to be assertive, and how and when to be conciliatory. Today, with smaller households, children and adults may have to learn those skills outside the family. Through counseling, therapy, education, and practice, young people need to be encouraged and taught how to settle conflicts without violence and how to maintain relationships in a family setting. If children and adults learn how to become better partners, friends, neighbors, relatives, parents, or spouses, family rights may not need to be terminated as often as they should be now.

Improve Counseling for Unwed Pregnant Teenagers

Programs to prevent teenaged pregnancy are important, since pregnancy among young people in the United States is said to be the highest in the industrialized world. Programs aimed at reducing pregnancy have been introduced into a number of high schools around the country, but however effective they are at reducing sexual activity and consequent pregnancy among teenagers, some females are bound to be sexually active and some will get pregnant. The children of unwed teenaged females are at high risk almost automatically because of the common lack of social and economic support. Daly and Wilson's figures indicate that in Canada young single mothers are the most likely women to commit infanticide. In our figures, women who have a child while they are teenagers are likely later to live with a male who is not the child's father, which also increases the risk to the child. Programs offered in schools and by private agencies are essential in reducing this risk, although counseling abstinence is less likely to work than advice on how to avoid pregnancy and on how to parent. In fact, information on the requirements and responsibilities of parenthood may be the best approach to encourage abstinence. Programs requiring high-school males and females to care for a realistic doll, even for only a week, have convinced most participants that parenthood should be postponed.

Once pregnant, however, the teenager needs education in the options available to her. Encouraging abortion may not be in favor politically, but these girls should be made aware of their legal rights. They also need to be well informed about the advantages of giving their child up for adoption as well as about whatever financial, emotional, or social resources are available to them in their community. Infanticidal mothers in our data base, however, often concealed their pregnancy from their parents and even denied it to themselves—in some cases, up to the time of delivery. Teenagers frequently are too afraid of the negative reaction of their parents or other adults to confide in them. This fear may translate into hostility toward the newborn baby — hostility that may grow because of the confining effect that caring for the infant has on their lives. These statements can be documented in any of the material that discusses the problems of teenage pregnancy. Many organizations already exist to help protect the child from the consequences of his young mother's actions, but they need more funds, both public and private, and more public awareness of their existence.

Judges have occasionally tried to control undesirable pregnancies by forbidding a male or a female (or both) to have a child. Such an order rarely works, as evidenced by Case 148 in Chapter 6. There are also some serious questions as to whether such an order is either ethical or permissible under the U.S. Constitution. Control over one's body is the same issue in prohibiting pregnancy as it is in the question of abortion, and it needs as much discussion and research.

Clarify and Simplify Definitions

To demonstrate both the complexity and the necessity for this recommendation, let us suppose that you, the reader, ask ten people two questions: 1) Is it abuse to hit a child on the buttocks with the flat of the open hand? And 2) how many victims does someone have to kill in one incident to be labeled a mass murderer? Do not poll personal friends, who may share your opinions. Instead, ask two people from white-collar and two people from blue-collar occupations, someone from a generation above and someone from a generation below your own, and four people from different ethnic groups. The chances are very good that there will be no unanimity on the answer to either of the questions.

These differing opinions, often strongly held, indicate that attempts to reach a consensus in definition will be difficult. Chemists have no problem in defining sodium, for example, because its characteristics are unchanging, but doctors and nutritionists cannot reach a consensus on how much salt should or should not be in one's diet. The problems of defining terms for social behavior run into the same difficulty. Perhaps some commercial or government organization could sponsor panels of social scientists, lawyers, practitioners in social work, and others who routinely use terms such as sexual abuse, child abuse, and serial killers to come up with legal definitions that all can agree on. At present, when laws are written using these terms without specifying exactly what is meant, people who are responsible for interpreting or enforcing the laws have to use their own judgment, and complications arise.

Devote Additional Research to the Creation of Safe, Nurturing Environments for Children

This recommendation has three parts. First, what is a safe and nurturing environment? People from different segments of society have different opinions. For example, does a safe environment require indoor plumbing? Central heating? Electricity? A house that is clean and tidy? A vegetarian diet? A total lack of violence? How much risk is acceptable?

Second, once there is a consensus as to what constitutes a "safe, nurturing environment," how can one be created? What factors do safe, nurturing homes for children have in common? Again, everyone has a different opinion on the best way to bring up children. Clergymen, newspaper advice columnists, psychologists, friends, relatives, and experts from Dr. Spock to Dr. Seuss all bombard parents with contradictory ideas about how best to allow a child to develop and how to discourage unacceptable behavior. Those people involved in child protection, child development, and child care need to examine which ideas have worked to produce happy, productive citizens who also make good parents.

Third, children can be very provoking, so what inhibitions keep most people from killing children? And what happens to break down these inhibitions? It is easy to see the dysfunctional elements in a person's life when he becomes a killer, but how many people with similar life histories never became killers? It is a cliché that child abusers become abusers in their turn, yet research reveals that only about 30 percent of them grow up to become abusive as adult caretakers (Gelles, 1996:77). What is the difference between the child raised in an environment that was neither safe nor nurturing who becomes a sustained abuser or killer and the child raised in a similar environment who does not? To create a safe, nurturing environment, adult behavior will have to change in some cases. How can this be done, and who will do it? Will a safe, nurturing environment teach children how to be good parents in their turn? If we can narrow down the crucial factors, treatment and prevention of child murders will be easier, although there are still a lot of unanswered questions.

Use Case Review in Addition to Statistical Analysis to Learn More about Patterns of Killing

However useful statistics may be for determining demographic information, statistics alone fail to uncover patterns of behavior. We must hypothesize that a particular pattern exists before we can use statistics to demonstrate its distribution and frequency. Case review is a slower process than the use of statistics, but it is much more effective in uncovering patterns. Once patterns have been determined, statistics can be used to verify them, or to learn how they are distributed within a society. The data in this study, which is based on a case review method, have made it possible to identify a number of patterns that call for additional research on how they are related to child murders. For example, the involvement of perpetrators who are not caretakers of the child, the use of different methods by mothers' lovers or by fathers for killing a child, and the different circumstances of the killing that are related to the age and gender of the child murdered all need exploration by additional research.

Case review shows up connections between factors that statistics alone do not easily reveal. An exploration of the problem by case review can also uncover unexpected relationships and unanticipated factors that are involved in the crime. Statistics give only a superficial sketch of the parameters of the problem while case review, though time consuming, reveals the interconnections and suggests more profound questions to ask.

Some states have already set up review panels in their Social Services or Child Protection departments, but these have two major defects. First, they review only cases that are suspected of being child abuse; and, as this study has shown, a lot of children are killed under circumstances that do not meet the child abuse criteria. Second, even if the panel looks at all cases of child deaths, the review is limited to one state. A national clearinghouse that looks at all cases should be set up to collect the necessary information, which leads to the next two recommendations.

Improve Methods for Collecting and Determining Content for Data on Child Killings

In order to understand all of the variables that apply to child killings, better data need to be available. Newspapers, though useful for the kind of overview in this study, frequently lack necessary details. Court records of trials or police reports, moreover, are available to researchers only in limited situations. Just as national government organizations developed unified crime reports, there should be some instrument for collecting the information necessary to better understand the circumstances surrounding the killing of a child. National organizations for the protection of children, acting together, need to develop a checklist or form to gather information from state organizations, with the cooperation of federal, state, and local law enforcement agencies. A central body of data would allow researchers new avenues to explore. Much of this organizational infrastructure is already in place and only needs direction and coordination.

Reevaluate the Confidentiality Laws

One of the current barriers to research is the existence of confidentiality laws. Certainly, some level of protection for people who use social service agencies is necessary for their privacy, but legislators need to reevaluate the concept of confidentiality. At present, confidentiality laws deny legitimate researchers access to information that is essential to increasing an understanding of the problem. Confidentiality of records also must be modified to allow improved communication between agencies in cases where severe abuse has taken place.

At present, individual privacy is protected, resulting in ineffective action or no action at all, which can lead to the death of a child. Law enforcement personnel are handicapped, for example, when neighbors call in a complaint to the police, who have no way of knowing whether another complaint was made beforehand to social service agencies. If indeed a complaint was registered, police cannot know whether it was investigated. And similarly, if an agency receives a complaint, it may not know whether the local police or social services in another jurisdiction have received similar complaints. Just as police can now run a national check on an individual stopped for a traffic violation, so social service agencies or police departments should be able to determine whether someone whom they are investigating has been cited previously for a similar complaint.

Increase Collaboration between All Parties Involved in Social Services, Law, and Health

At present, police, judges, social workers, medical doctors, hospital personnel, teachers, school personnel, and psychologists or psychiatrists are all working to some extent independently, often from different frameworks—that is, goals and mandates of doctors, police, and social workers vary. The work group in Kentucky that investigated four child deaths revealed how often these different agendas conflicted with each other instead of working together. The classifications by police, case workers, and Vital Statistics personnel of a single case frequently differed. For a case worker, the death of a child might be filed as fatal child abuse due to neglect, but police might classify it as a form of homicide, and Vital Statistics personnel as an accident.

Collaboration would be greatly improved if the different agencies shared information about the children and families with whom they are interacting. In this instance, confidentiality laws are not the only problem. Police do not always inform social services, for example, if a child in a particular family is killed unless there are other children in the home. Another child may have died earlier in the same family, but if the two agencies cannot or will not share information, the knowledge will lie in separate files, sending no warning signals. Both law enforcement and social service personnel might proceed along different paths if they were aware of the whole situation.

Improve Counseling for Men, Women, and Children on How to Deal with Anger

Anger and rage in our society lead to a number of disruptive situations (road rage, for example). A common thread running through many of the cases in this study is anger. No organization teaches people in our society ways to deal effectively with their anger; or perhaps it is better to say that many organizations do so, but they do not agree. Religious groups, popular magazines, psychologists, psychiatrists, and advice columnists all offer different suggestions. Yet children have no approved way to express anger. Everything they might naturally do, such as yelling, hitting, and breaking things, is forbidden by caretakers, who usually fail to supply an acceptable substitute. Since such methods as "time-outs" do not necessarily affect the anger itself but only its immediate expression, children can grow up without learning any constructive ways of dealing with it. As adults they may "act out" their anger in ways that were denied them as children because they have no knowledge of alternatives, or because they rely on the examples set for them by other adults who interacted with them as they were growing up or copy behavior viewed on television. These models can lead to violent behavior against the people around them, with more serious consequences than those seen in cartoons or found in professional wrestling or other sports.

Impose Uniform and Stiffer Penalties on Those Who Prey on Children

At the present time there is enormous variation in the penalties for people who are convicted of killing children. Through plea bargaining, many child killers are sentenced for manslaughter or negligent homicide instead of murder. Child endangerment is often the charge for behavior that would have been murder or assault with a deadly weapon if the victim had been an adult. Both the laws and the punishments need to be more uniform from one jurisdiction to another, so that people in our mobile society can know what to expect in whatever part of the country they move to. Currently, behavior that leads to court-ordered psychiatric treatment in one state can result in a thirty-year prison sentence in another. This problem is not unique to the murderers of children, of course, but people who prey on defenseless children should receive greater punishment or more treatment, not less, than other perpetrators. Stiffer punishment is needed to send the message that mistreatment of children is intolerable. Increased treatment also is necessary to change abusers' behavior and attitudes so that when they are released from confinement, they will not brutalize children again.

Increase Gun Safety Education for Adults and Children

Only about one-fifth of the perpetrators in this study (21.8 percent) used rifles or handguns, but they killed a disproportionate share of victims (24.3 percent). None of the deaths that we counted was accidental in the sense that the gun simply fired when it was picked up or dropped. In at least two cases, young perpetrators made a considerable effort to obtain the rifle and to load it. There was a time, within the last hundred years, when every home had a rifle and young people were taught how to use it responsibly. Less than sixty years ago, children were also shown through movies and radio that violence was the last resort in a quarrel; the "good guys" never killed deliberately. Instead, only villains resorted to deadly force, and fist fights were more common than shootouts. Today, in contrast, sports, movies, television, and newspapers all depict violence as the solution in trivial situations. It is likely that the increasing deadly violence in the society is one consequence. As the descriptions of cases in this study demonstrate, some perpetrators killed for seemingly frivolous reasons: a 6 year old refused to give his father a dollar; a toddler would not stop dancing; a child called another a sissy. Any training in the use of guns should stress the occasions when it is appropriate to use a deadly weapon and when it is not. And when a gun is used to murder a child, the sentence should automatically be more severe.

Strengthen Laws to Protect Children When Parental and Child Rights Conflict

Children often have no one to speak for them when their rights conflict with those of their parents. Many states have a legal spokesperson for the child in abuse cases, a guardian *ad litem*, but courts do not always appoint the person who has the best interest of the child at heart and who can do the best job of protecting that interest. For example, in Kentucky, a judge appointed as the guardian *ad litem* the same individual who was the court-appointed lawyer for the defendant accused of abusing the child. Laws in all the states need to be reviewed and strengthened so that no child is left helpless when his parents are bent on exercising their rights.

Improve Education and Counseling on How to Cope with Children with Disabilities

Articles in the popular press, such as *Reader's Digest* and *Parade*, praise parents who care for children with developmental problems and often make the situation sound like a blessing for those parents fortunate enough to have a child with special needs. Unfortunately, not all parents are able to deal with a difficult situation as happily as those exceptional cases presented in the popular literature. People who suddenly have to take care of a disabled child often feel overwhelmed with the burden and responsibility. Although there are support groups, they may be difficult to access or not available in all parts of the country. There need to be more facilities in more places with easier access for people who have to raise a child with severe disabilities.

Increase Education about SIDS

Sudden infant death syndrome, or SIDS, has been used as an excuse by people who have killed a child, either accidently or on purpose. Presumed cases of

SIDS should always be autopsied by a medical examiner who is familiar with symptoms of both SIDS and smothering.

It has been found that legitimate incidents of SIDS can be reduced in two simple ways. First, simply putting babies to sleep on their backs instead of on their stomachs has cut the death rate from this disorder by about 30 percent. And second, reducing smoking by pregnant women and by adults around babies also appears to reduce the number of incidents. SIDS does not usually occur in children over 6 months of age.

Make Sure that Investigators and Service Providers Are Not the Same People

Case workers answering an abuse or neglect report are trying to help a child, but other family members may not think that the investigation is helping *them*. Investigators are attempting to determine whether the risk to the child is so high that he must be removed from the home. Removal of a child is realistically seen by the family as punishment. Less hostility and suspicion might be directed toward social service providers if they were not the same individuals as those who are investigating reports of abuse or neglect.

The police-like skills and training needed to investigate a report of child abuse are different from those required of service personnel, as are the personality characteristics. Consequently, even aside from the hostile reaction of a family under inspection, investigators should not also be service providers, and vice versa. More effective selection and training can be provided to both groups if the functions are clearly separated.

Summary

These recommendations are only a few that can be developed from the information found in this study. Consideration of them may give some hope that the violence against children can be reduced. The loss of innocents in our society is far too high. If this study helps in any way to save young lives, then it will have served its purpose.

Bibliography

Books and Articles

Alexander, Richard. *Darwinism and Human Affairs*. Seattle: University of Washington Press, 1979.

American Psychiatric Association. *Diagnostic and Statistical Manual of Mental Health*. Washington, DC: American Psychiatric Association, 1994.

Ammerman, R. T., and Hersen, M., eds. *Assessment of Family Violence: A Clinical and Legal Sourcebook*. New York: Wiley, 1992.

Anderson, Chris, and McGehee, Sharon. *Bodies of Evidence*. New York: Carol Publishing Group, 1991. A Lyle Stuart Book. [Female serial killer – husbands and an adult son]

Benedek, Elissa P., and Cornell, Dewey G., eds. *Juvenile Homicide*. Washington, DC: American Psychiatric Press, 1989.

Berrick, Jill Duerr, and Gilbert, Neil. *With the Best of Intentions*. New York: Guilford Press, 1991.

Bourget, Dominique, and Bradford, John M. W. "Homicidal Parents." *Canadian Journal of Psychiatry* 35, no. 3 (April 1990): 233–38.

Bradley, Bill. "Help America's Children." *Parade Magazine* (August 3, 1997): 4–6.

Cauffiel, Lowell. *Forever and Five Days*. New York: Zebra Books, 1992. [Female serial killers, nursing home residents]

Christoffel, Katherine K. "Homicide in Childhood: A Public Health Problem in Need of Attention." *American Journal of Public Health* 74, no. 1 (January 1984): 68–70.

Committee on Bioethics, American Academy of Pediatrics. "Religious Objections to Medical Care." Pediatrics 99, no. 2 (February 1997): 279–81.

Daly, Martin, and Wilson, Margo. "A Sociobiological Analysis of Human Infanticide." In *Infanticide*, edited by Glenn Hausfater and Sarah B. Hrdy, 487–502. New York: Aldine de Gruyter, 1984.

———. *Homicide*. New York: Aldine de Gruyter, 1988.

Dawkins, Richard. *The Selfish Gene*. New York: Oxford University Press, 1976.

Delambre, Jules W., and Wood, Murray. *Epidemiological Study of Abused and Neglect-Related Child Fatalities FY 1991–1995*. Frankfort: Kentucky Cabinet for Families and Children, 1997.

Dietz, Park Elliott. "Mass, Serial and Sensational Homicides." *Bulletin of the New York Academy of Medicine* 62, no. 5 (1986): 477–91.

Douglas, John, and Olshaker, Mark. *Mindhunter*. New York: Pocket Books, 1995.

———. *Journey into Darkness*. New York: Pocket Books, 1997.

Elias, Marilyn. "Pediatricians Condemn Laws on Faith Healing." *USA Today*, February 11, 1997.

Ewing, Charles P. *Kids Who Kill*. New York: Avon Books, 1990a.

———. *When Children Kill*. Lexington, MA: Lexington Books, 1990b.

Federal Register. Volume 62, Number 60. March 28, 1998. Washington, DC. Government Printing Office, 1998.

Firstman, Richard, and Talan, Jamie. *The Death of Innocents*. New York: Bantam Books, 1997.

Gelles, Richard J. *The Book of David*. New York: Basic Books, 1996.

Giannangelo, Stephen J. *The Psychopathology of Serial Murder*. Westport, CT: Praeger, 1996.

Hausfater, Glenn, and Hrdy, Sarah B., eds. *Infanticide: Comparative and Evolutionary Perspectives*. New York: Aldine de Gruyter, 1984.

Hickey, Eric W. *Serial Murderers and Their Victims*. Monterey, CA: Brooks-Cole/Wadsworth, 1991.

Holmes, Ronald M., and Holmes, Stephen T. "Understanding Mass Murder: A Starting Point." *Federal Probation* 56, no. 1 (March 1992): 53.

Jenkins, Philip. *Using Murder: The Social Construction of Serial Killers*. New York: Aldine de Gruyter, 1994.

Kahn, Ada P., and Fawcett, Jan. *Encyclopedia of Mental Health*. New York: Facts on File, 1993.

Kaplan, Joel, Papajohn, George, and Zorn, Eric. *Murder of Innocence: The Tragic Life and Final Rampage of Laurie Dann*. New York: Warner Books, 1990.

Kaplan, Sarah R. *Child Fatality Legislation in the United States*. Child Maltreatment Fatalities Project. Chicago: American Bar Association, 1991.

Kempe, C. Henry, et al. "The Battered Child Syndrome." *Journal of the American Medical Association* 181 (1962): 17–24.

King, Gary C. *Driven to Kill*. New York: Pinnacle Books, 1993.

Leyton, Elliott. *Hunting Humans*. New York: Pocket Books, 1988. First published as *Compulsive Killers*. New York: New York University Press, 1986.

Linedecker, Clifford, and Burt, William A. *Nurses Who Kill*. New York: Windsor, 1990.

Lundstrom, Marjie, and Sharpe, Rochelle. "Getting Away with Murder." *Public Welfare* 49 (Summer 1991): 18–29.

McCurdy, Karen, and Daro, Deborah. *Current Trends in Child Abuse Reporting and Fatalities: The Results of the 1992 Annual Fifty-State Survey*. Working Paper No. 808. Chicago: Committee for Prevention of Child Abuse, April 1993.

McIntyre, Tommy. *Wolf in Sheep's Clothing*. Detroit: Wayne State University Press, 1988.

Milner, Joel S. "Social Information Processing and Physical Child Abuse." *Clinical Psychology Review* 13 (1993): 275–94.

———. "Assessing Physical Child Abuse Risk: The Child Abuse Potential Inventory." *Clinical Psychology Review* 14, no. 6 (1994): 547–83.

Murphy, Jane M. "Psychiatric Labeling in Cross-Cultural Perspective." *Science* 191, no. 4231 (March 12, 1976): 1019–28.

National Foster Parent Association. *National Advocate*. Orlando, FL: National Foster Parent Association, 1994.

Newsom, Robert W., III, and Trotter, William R. *Deadly Kin*. New York: St. Martin's Press, 1988.

Policy Review Work Group. *Above and Beyond: Recommendations to the Secretary*. Frankfort, KY: Adult Protective Services and Child Protective Services, 1995.

Porter, J. R., and Russell, W. M. S., eds. *Animals in Folklore*. Cambridge, Eng.: D. S. Brewer; and Totowa, NJ: Rowman and Littlefield, 1978.

Richards, Cara E. "A Bum Rap." Unpublished Paper Presented at the 1995 Annual Meeting, Central States Anthropological Society, Indianapolis.

Richards, Cara E., and Weaver, Dorothy. "Newspapers as a Source of Data." *Proceedings of the Anthropologists and Sociologists of Kentucky*. Pikeville, KY, 1993.

Rule, Ann. *Small Sacrifices*. New York: Signet, 1988.

Russell, W. M. S., and Russell, Claire. "The Social Biology of Werewolves." In *Animals in Folklore*, edited by J. R. Porter and W. M. S. Russell, 143–82. Cambridge, Eng.: D. S. Brewer; and Totowa, NJ: Rowman and Littlefield, 1978.

Ryan, William B. *Infanticide: Its Law, Prevalence, Prevention and History*. London: Churchill, 1862.

Sears, Donald J. *To Kill Again: The Motivation and Development of Serial Murder*. Wilmington, DE: Scholarly Resources, 1991.

Shiflett, Dave. "America's Most Wanted Manhunter." *Reader's Digest* 150, no. 901 (May 1997): 50–55.

Sniffen, Michael J. "Killings by Male Teens Exploding." *Lexington Herald-Leader*, May 22, 1995.

U.S. Bureau of the Census. *Statistical Abstract of the United States: 1995* (115th edition). Washington, DC: Government Printing Office, 1995.

Webb, Eugene J., et al. *Unobtrusive Measures*. Chicago: Rand McNally & Co., 1966.

Cases

LCJ	*Louisville Courier-Journal*
LHL	*Lexington Herald-Leader*
NYT	*New York Times*
OWH	*Omaha World-Herald*

Case 2. Victim: Almeyda. Perpetrator: Almeyda. Sources: [1] *NYT* 1977 Je 26, 26:1; [2] S 6, 41:1; [3] S 16, 24:4; [4] S 20, 40:3; [5] N 24 II 2:2; [6] *NYT* 1979 Mr 23 II 3:1.

Case 4. Victims: Beaudoin, Santoro. Perpetrator: Acquin. Sources: [1] *NYT* 1977 Jl 23, 1:2; [2] Jl 23, 12:2; [3] Jl 24, 1:5; [4] Jl 24 IV 7:2; [5] Jl 25, 18:1; [6] Jl 26, 58:1; [7] Jl 27 IV 16:4; [8] Jl 27 II 2:3; [9] Jl 31 XXIII 4:2; [10] Ag 3 II 3:2; [11] S 8 IV 13:6; [12] *NYT* 1978 S 18 XXIII 16:3; [13] *NYT* 1979 Je 2.26:1; [14] Jl 17 II 2:3; [15] Jl 28, 10:3; [16] O 7, 34:1; [17] O 20, 25:6; [18] D 1, 24:6.

Case 9. Victims: DeCorleto. Perpetrator: DeCorleto. Sources: [1] *NYT* 1977 Ag 31 II 3:2; [2] S 1, 22:1.

Case 10. Victims: DePrima. Perpetrator: DePrima. Sources: [1] *NYT* 1977 O 16, 46:1; [2] O 18, 41:6; [3] O 19 II 23:4; [4] O 29, 51:3.

Case 21. Victims: Leach, Jackson, Jones. Perpetrators: Barrios, Garcia, Rodriguez. Sources: [1] *NYT* 1977 Mr 13, 1:1; [2] Mr 14, 33:6; [3] N 12, 34:6.

Case 23. Victim: Manwarren. Perpetrator: unknown. Source: *NYT* 1977 D 6, 31:5.

Case 40. Victim: Arroyo. Perpetrator: Ahmedoff. Sources: [1] *NYT* 1978 Jl 6, 15:1; [2] D 5 II 2:6.

Case 41. Victim: Cortez. Perpetrator: Cortez. Source: *NYT* 1978 N 28, 19:6.

Case 47. Victim: Leach. Perpetrator: Bundy. Sources: [1] *NYT* 1979 O 23, 16:6; [2] O 28, 64:1; [3] N 8, 16:6; [4] *NYT* 1980 Ja 19, 10:1; [5] F 8, 14:6; [6] F 10, 28:1; [7] F 11, 14:6; [8] F 13, 16:6; [9] Ag 24 VII 12; [10] *NYT* 1981 Jl 1, 15:1; [11] D 12, 53:6; [12] *NYT* 1985 My 10, 16:6; [13] *NYT* 1986 F 26 I 18:6; [14] F 27 I 19:1; [15] My 23 I 10:6.

Case 50. Victims: Nelson. Perpetrator: Nelson. Sources: [1] *NYT* 1978 Ja 8, 26:4; [2] Ja 9, 14:4; [3] Ja 12 II 9:2; [4] My 23, 16:6; [5] Je 14, 16:6.

Case 57. Victims: Trait. Perpetrator: Trait. Sources: [1] *NYT* 1979 D 21 II 2:6; [2] *Buffalo News* 1978 Jl 17, 1:1; [3] Jl 17, 1:5; [4] *Buffalo News* 1979 O 30, 33; [5] N 28, 41; [6] D 12, 22; [7] D 13, 28; [8] D 14, 25; [9] D 17, 17; [10] D 19, 39; [11] D 20, 41; [12] D 28, 1; [13] *Buffalo News* 1980 Ja 25, 25; [14] F 19, 35; [15] F 25, 1; [16] F 27, 16; [17] *Buffalo News* 1988 F 7 B 3; [18] F 24 no page given; [19] Je 15 D 11.

Case 58. Victim: Williams. Perpetrator: Williams. Source: *NYT* 1978 Jl 12, 16:3.

Case 63. Victims: Adams. Perpetrator: Adams. Source: *NYT* 1979 O 15 II 7:6.

Case 70. Victims: Cruz. Perpetrators: Cruz. Source: *NYT* 1979 Ja 15 II 3:2.

Case 78. Victim: Grudzinski. Perpetrator: Grudzinski. Sources: [1] *NYT* 1979 Mr 11, 1:4; [2] Mr 15 II 2:6.

Case 81. Victim: Harrison. Perpetrator: accident. Source: *NYT* 1979 Jl 30 II 2:5.

Case 87. Victim: Kratic. Perpetrator: juvenile. Source: *NYT* 1979 N 21 II 6:5.

Case 95. Victim: Williams. Perpetrators: Meachem, Herrera. Source: *NYT* 1979 O 8 II 3:1

Case 97. Victim: Adolphe. Perpetrator: juvenile. Source: *NYT* 1980 Ap 17 II 5:5.

Case 102. Victim: Bruen. Perpetrators: Bruen, Fisher. Sources: [1] *NYT* 1981 Ag 1, 28:1; [2] Ag 29, 26:1.

Case 104. Victims: Post. Perpetrator: Crump. Sources: [1] *NYT* 1980 S 21, 26:1; [2] S 23 II 12:4.

Case 106. Victim: Frazier. Perpetrator: Frazier. Source: *NYT* 1983 Je 7, 33:6.

Case 108. Victim: Garcia. Perpetrator: unknown. Source: *NYT* 1980 S 12 II 3:1

Case 109. Victims: Gilligan. Perpetrator: Wallace. Sources: [1] *NYT* 1980 Ja 16, 16:5; [2] *NYT* 1982 Ag 30, 10:6; [3] *LCJ* 1980 Mr 5 B 2:3.

Case 112. Victims: Johnson, Daniels, Coleman, Davis, Spring. Perpetrator: Falling. Sources: [1] *NYT* 1982 Jl 7, 10:6; [2] Jl 23, 8:6; [3] Jl 26, 12:1; [4] Ag 28, 6:6; [5] N 13, 8:6; [6] D 4, 8:1.

Case 118. Victims: Ortiz, Lopez, Reyes. Perpetrator: Pound. Sources: [1] *NYT* 1980 D 11 II 10:4; [2] D 12, 21:5.

Case 121. Victim: Saad. Perpetrator: Saad. Sources: [1] *NYT* 1980 Ja 2, 18:4; [2] Ja 5, 8:1.

Case 130. Victims: Ware. Perpetrator: Andrews. Sources: [1] *NYT* 1980 Ja 12, 7:2; [2] Ja 13, 26:5.

Case 136. Victim: Archibald. Perpetrator: Archibald. Source: *NYT* 1981 S 1 II 3:1.

Case 138. Victims: Bell. Perpetrator: Bell. Sources: [1] *NYT* 1981 Ag 22, 8:2; [2] *LCJ* 1982 Ap 2 B 4:1.

Case 139. Victims: Bloomfield, Evans. Perpetrators: juveniles. Source: *NYT* 1981 My 14 II 18:1.

Case 148. Victim: Fourthman. Perpetrators: Fourthman, Burchell. Sources: [1] *NYT* 1984 Ja 27, 10:6; [2] Ja 30, 8:6; [3] *NYT* 1985 Mr 1, 10:6.

Case 149. Victim: Frazier. Perpetrator: Frazier. Source: *NYT* 1981 O 14 II 3:6.

Case 150. Victims: Harmon, Harrison. Perpetrator: Buell. Sources: [1] *NYT* 1984 Ap 16, 19:1; [2] My 5, 8:6.

Case 156. Victim: McRoy. Perpetrator: McRoy. Source: *NYT* 1983 O 12 I 14:6.

Case 171. Victim: Walsh. Perpetrator: unknown. Sources: [1] NYT 1983 O 23 I 24:1; [2] O 27 I 24:6; [3] N 2 I 20:6; [4] *Reader's Digest* 150 (901) 1997 May: 50–55.

Case 174. Victims: Williams. Perpetrator: Williams. Source: *NYT* 1981 Ja 12, 14:6.

Case 175. Victim: Willis. Perpetrator: self. Source: *NYT* 1981 Ja 8 II 3:1.

Case 178. Victims: Banks, Mazzillo, Lyons. Perpetrator: Banks. Sources: [1] *NYT* 1982 S 26, 1:2; [2] S 27, 10:1; [3] S 28 II 5:1; [4] O 4 IV 11:1; [5] O 4 IV 12:1; [6] *NYT* 1983 Je 6 I 13:1; [7] Je 7 II 7:2; [8] Je 8 I 19:1; [9] Je 22 I 16:1; [10] Je 23 I 16:6; [11] *NYT* 1987 F 18 I 18:4.

Case 179. Victim: Castro. Perpetrator: unknown. Source: *NYT* 1982 F 14 I 28:6.

Case 187. Victims: Gaffney. Perpetrator: Haggart. Sources: [1] *NYT* 1982 F 18, 10:1; [2] F 19, 12:1; [3] O 9, 8:6; [4] O 24, 22:2.

Case 188. Victims: Galvez. Perpetrator: unknown. Sources: [1] *NYT* 1982 Ja 31, 33:1; [2] F 1 II 1:6.

Case 202. Victim: McClellan. Perpetrator: Turk. Sources: [1] *NYT* 1983 F 24 I 1:1; [2] F 25 I 10:3; [3] My 17 I 10:1; [4] My 29 I 28:1; [5] Jl 2 I 6:1; [6] O 13 I 16:6; [7] N 22 I 32:1; [8] *NYT* 1984 Ja 16 II 2:3; [9] Ja 20 II 7:1; [10] F 6, 15:1; [11] F 9, 20:6; [12] F 12, 25:1; [13] F 15, 12:6; [14] F 16, 18:1; [15] F 17, 16:6; [16] Mr 10, 6:6; [17] Ap 11, 23:1.

Case 205. Victim: Nicely. Perpetrator: Nicely, Bass. Sources: [1] *NYT* 1982 Jl 8 II 2:4; [2] Jl 28:II 2:6; [3] Jl 30 I 25:1; [4] Ag 5 II 2:6; [5] Ag 9 II 2:1; [6] Ag 10 II 2:5; [7] Ag 11 II 2:4; [8] S 2 II 1:1; [9] S 16 II 7:1; [10] S 23 II 2:1.

Case 206. Victim: O'Brien. Perpetrator: O'Brien. Source: *NYT* 1982 N 23 II 4:6.

Case 209. Victims: Paxton, Bates, Henry, Johnson. Perpetrator: Tuggle. Source: NYT 1984 Mr 23, 14:6.

Case 210. Victim: Paulson. Perpetrator: Karklins. Sources: [1] *NYT* 1982 Mr 14, 23:6; [2] Mr 15 II 6:4; [3] *NYT* 1983 F 26 I 7:6; [4] Mr 13 I 27:6.

Case 213. Victim: Sandor. Perpetrator: Sandor. Source: *NYT* 1982 S 4,25:6.

Case 216. Victims: Stuart. Perpetrator: Giambi. Sources: *NYT* 1982 Ap 19, II 2:6; [2] *NYT* 1984 Jl 21, 32:6.

Case 222. Victim: unnamed. Perpetrator: unknown. Source: *NYT* 1983 O 29 I 21:4.

Case 224. Victim: Arthur. Perpetrator: Hobson. Sources: [1] *NYT* 1983 Ap 9 I 27:6; [2] O 21 II 4:5.

Case 226. Victim: Carroll. Perpetrator: Carroll. Sources: [1] *NYT* 1983 Ap 23 I 12:1; [2] *LCJ* Ap 23 A 1:1; [3] Ap 25 B 5:2; [4] Ap 30 C 12:3; [5] Ap 26 B 6:4;

[6] Je 17 B 7:1 (Ky. ed.); [7] Ag 13 A 1:5; [8] Ag 21 B 16:2; [9] Ag 26 B 12:2. Ky. Death Certificate Vital Statistics Vol. 37, No. 18355.

Case 232. Victim: Davis. Perpetrator: Gormley. Source: *NYT* 1983 Ag 10 II 3:1.

Case 233. Victim: DeCasonova. Perpetrator: Gerlock. Sources: [1] *NYT* 1983 Mr 25 II 3:4; [2] Mr 26 I 25:1; [3] Mr 28 II 1:1; [4] Ap 15 II 2:6; [5] Ap 29 II 4:1; [6] Jl 3 I 21:6; [7] S 22 II 2:4; [8] S 23 II 2:4; [9] S 24 I 1:4; [10] S 24 I 26:1; [11] S 27 II 2:5; [12] S 28 II 2:5; [13] S 29 II 2:1; [14] S 30 II 2:4; [15] O 1 I 30:4; [16] O 4 II 2:1; [17] O 5 II 2:6; [18] O 6 II 2:3; [19] O 7 II 2:5; [20] O 8 I 25:1; [21] O 15 I 29:1; [22] *NYT* 1984 Ja 7, 26:1.

Case 238. Victim: Gonzales. Perpetrators: Lopez, Suarez, Cruz. Sources: [1] *NYT* 1983 My 23 II 6:1; [2] My 24 II 3:6; [3] My 30 I 24:2; [4] *NYT* 1984 F 2, 25:6.

Case 243. Victim: Johnson. Perpetrator: Johnson. Source: *NYT* 1983 D 27 I 14:6.

Case 249. Victim: Mason. Perpetrator: Sperl. Source: *NYT* 1983 S 6 I 18:5.

Case 250. Victim: McKay. Perpetrator: McKay. Sources: [1] *NYT* 1983 Je 30 IV 24:1; [2] Ag 4 II 24:6; [3] *NYT* 1985 F 15 II 16:1; [4] F 18, 14:1.

Case 254. Victim: Parks. Perpetrators: two juveniles. Sources: [1] *NYT* 1983 Ap 24, 16:2; [2] My 15, 14:6; [3] *NYT* 1986 Ap 11 I 14:5.

Case 260. Victims: Wright, Roldan, Andujar. Perpetrator: Wright. Sources: [1] *NYT* 1983 N 30 I 1:1; [2] D 1 II 1:1; [3] D 1 II 28:1; [4] D 14 II 20:1; [5] D 22 II 2:4; [6] *NYT* 1984 Ja 25 II 4:1; [7] F 5, 32:1; [8] F 22 II 2:1; [9] Ap 20 II 3:1.

Case 261. Victim: Yarbrough. Perpetrators: Yarbrough, Lewis Jr., Lewis Sr., McGee, Branson, Jones. Sources: [1] *NYT* 1983 Jl 9 I 5:5; [2] Jl 14 I 13:6; [3] Jl 15 I 6:6; [4] Ag I 16:1; [5] *NYT* 1984 Ja 13, 12:5; [6] S 13 I 6:6.

Case 264. Victims: Bermudez, Lopez, Perez. Perpetrator: Thomas. Sources: [1] *NYT* 1984 Ap 16, 1:1, II 5:1; [2] Ap 17, 1:1, II 3:2; [3] Ap 18 II 3:6; [4] Ap 21, 22:1; [5] My 27, 45:1; [6] Je 20, 1:1, IV 23:1; [7] Je 21, 1:2; [8] Je 27 II 6:4; [9] Jl 10 II 3:3; [10] O 25 II 1:6; [11] *NYT* 1985 Je 18 II 3:1; [12] Jl 9 II 3:1; [13] Jl 18 II 3:5; [14] Jl 19 II 3:5; [15] Jl 20 1:5; [16] Jl 20, 27:1; [17] S 11 II 3:5.

Case 271. Victims: Bonner, Gardner, Alexander. Perpetrators: Cox, Burns. Sources: [1] *NYT* 1984 S 1, 1:4; 6:4; [2] S 2, 33:1; [3] O 25, 24:3; [4] N 5 II 15:2; [5] N 8, 16:5.

Case 283. Victims: Dubs, O'Conner. Perpetrators: Lake, Ng. Sources: [1] *NYT* 1985 Je 10, 10:6; [2] Je 14, 12:4; [3] Je 15, 8:6; [4] Je 17, 15:5; [5] Je 19 II 7:2; [6]

Je 26, 17:4; [7] Jl 4, 15:1; [8] Jl 7, 15:1; [9] Jl 8, II 6:1; [10] Jl 9, 14:6; [11] Jl 9, II 1:6; [12] Jl 10, 13:2; [13] Jl 16, 8:6; [14] Jl 20, 6:6; [15] Ag 4, 17:1; [16] S 23, 17:1; [17] O 17, 16:6; [18] N 2, 32:2; [19] N 20, 25:1; [20] D 18, 23:1; [21] *NYT* 1991 F 12 A 18:1; [22] S 27 A 16:1.

Case 284. Victim: Lloyd. Perpetrator: Lloyd. Sources: [1] *NYT* 1984 Ag 7, 14:2; [2] Ag 19, 34:3.

Case 286. Victim: Morgan. Perpetrators: Morgan, two unidentified hired assassins. Sources: [1] *NYT* 1984 D 26, 21:1. [2] *Los Angeles Times* 1985 Ja 16, Metro ed., 1 (pt. 2):4; [3] D 25, Metro ed., 8 (pt. 2):3.

Case 290. Victims: Rendle. Perpetrator: Rendle. Source: *NYT* 1984 F 5, 21:1.

Case 293. Victims: Simmons, Davis. Perpetrator: Green. Sources: [1] *NYT* 1984 N 30 II 3:5, 1:2 (photo); [2] D 1, 26:6.

Case 297. Victims: Temple, Turks. Perpetrators: Coleman, Brown. Sources: [1] *NYT* 1984 Jl 9, 8:6; [2] Jl 12, 12:6; [3] Jl 17, 11:1; [4] Jl 18, 15:6; [5] Jl 21, 7:6; [6] Jl 23, 6:6; [7] N 27, 18:5; [8] *NYT* 1985 Ja 8, 10:6; [9] My 2, 16:6; [10] My 7, 18:6; [11] Je 9, 26:1; [12] *NYT* 1986 Ap 12 I 9:4; [13] Ap 13 I 28:5.

Case 301. Victim: Ayala. Perpetrators: Campbell, Maurice. Source: *NYT* 1985 Ag 17, 28:6. Not in sample analysis, innocent bystander.

Case 303. Victims: Pommerol, Briehl. Perpetrator: Briehl. Source: *NYT* 1985 Jl 17 II 2:1.

Case 305. Victim: Davis. Perpetrators: four juveniles. Source: *NYT* 1985 Ja 5, 5:1.

Case 307. Victims: Green. Perpetrator: Green. Source: *NYT* 1985 S 20 II 3:5.

Case 320. Victims: Urquhart. Perpetrator: Halsey. Sources: [1] *NYT* 1985 N 16, 30:5; [2] N 18 II 2:5; [3] N 19 II 2:3; [4] N 26 II 3:1.

Case 333. Victims: Gates, Brahm. Perpetrators: Gates, Rossney. Sources: [1] *NYT* 1986 D 15 II 8:3; [2] D 16 II 1:3, 18; [3] D 20 I 30:6; [4] *NYT* 1987 Ja 31 I 32:2; [5] O 7 II 1:2; [6] O 8 II 5:1; [7] O 13 II 1:2; [8] N 10 II 4:6.

Case 338. Victims: Howard, Jefferies. Perpetrator: Jefferies. Source: *NYT* 1986 My 2 II 4:2.

Case 339. Victims: Hull. Perpetrators: Hull, Dean. Sources: [1] *NYT* 1986 Mr 6 II 12:6; [2] Mr 7 I 12:2; [3] Mr 8 I 8:6.

Case 341. Victims: Leija. Perpetrator: Leija. Sources: [1] *NYT* 1986 Ap 20 I 24:6; [2] Ap 21 I 12:6; [3] *NYT* 1987 Je 19 IV 16:1.

Case 347. Victim: Shamoon. Perpetrator: Shamoon. Source: *NYT* 1987 N 16 II 1:2, 4:1.

Case 348. Victims: Sims. Perpetrator: Sims. Sources: [1] *NYT* 1989 My 2 I 14:5; [2] My 6 I 7:6; [3] My 9 I 29:1; [4] *NYT* 1990 Ja 31 A 18: 4.

Case 350. Victim: Spencer. Perpetrator: Stratford. Source: *NYT* 1986 Je 28 I 33:1.

Case 353. Victim: Washington. Perpetrator: Washington. Sources: [1] *NYT* 1986 Ag 5 I 10:6; [2] Ag 6 I 12:6; [3] *NYT* 1987 F 18 I 19:1.

Case 362. Victim: Bernstein. Perpetrator: Bernstein. Source: *NYT* 1987 My 14 I 28:1.

Case 363. Victim: Brenta. Perpetrator: Brenta. Source: *NYT* 1987 D 22 II 4:4.

Case 365. Victims: Buckner. Perpetrator: Schnick. Sources: [1] *NYT* 1987 S 26 I 49:1; [2] S 27 I 28:5; [3] S 29 I 21:1; [4] O 6 I 30:4; [5] O 7 I 1:2; [6] O 9 I 14:1; [7] O 10 I 64:5; [8] O 11 IV 4:5; [9] *NYT* 1988 Ap 16 I 7:4; [10] My 25 I 24:2.

Case 368. Victims: Dobben. Perpetrator: Dobben. Sources: [1] *NYT* 1987 N 29 I 37:1; [2] D 17 I 32:1; [3] *NYT* 1989 My 17 I 12:4; [4] My 24 I 14: 3.

Case 374. Victim: Jewell. Perpetrator: Jewell. Sources: [1] *NYT* 1987 Mr 15 I 33:6; [2] Mr 16 II 7:6.

Case 379. Victim: Mauro. Perpetrator: Mauro. Source: *NYT* 1987 My 5 II 5:3.

Case 381. Victims: McNulty, Simmons. Perpetrator: Simmons. Sources: [1] *NYT* 1987 D 29 I 12:4; [2] D 30 I 8:3; [3] D 31 I 8:1; [4] *NYT* 1988 Ja 1 I 32:1; [5] Mr 3 I 29:6; [6] Mr 4 I 19:2; [7] My 13 I 15:3; [8] *NYT* 1989 F 6 I 9:1; [9] F 11 I 6:6; [10] F 12 I 29:1; [11] Mr 16 II 11:2; [12] Mr 17 I 36:4; [13] *NYT* 1990 Je 26 A 21:1.

Case 384. Victim: Soto. Perpetrator: Berry. Sources: [1] *NYT* 1989 D 5 I 31:5; [2] D 11 I 16:5; [3] D 23 I 17:1; [4] *NYT* 1990 F 17 I 11:6.

Case 385. Victim: Steinberg. Perpetrator: Steinberg. Sources: [1] *NYT* 1987 N 3 II 1:5, 4:1; [38] D 17 II 5:5; [39] *NYT* 1988 Ja 20 II 1:6, B 5; [108] D 28 I 26:1; [109] *NYT* 1989 Ja 4 I 21:5; [148] O 13 II 2:6; [149] *NYT* 1990 Ap 29 I 39:5; [150] *NYT* 1991 Ag 9 B 3:1; [151] S 11 B 4:6; [152] *NYT* 1992 Ap 30 B 2:1; [153] Je 12 B 6:3. This case, a notorious one in New York City, has 153 entries in our files, from 1987 to 1992. Only the first and last articles from each year are entered here. Anyone interested in the complete citations may contact the publisher.

Case 386. Victim: Taloute. Perpetrator: Taloute. Source: *NYT* 1987 N 17 II 5:1.

Case 391. Victim: Upshur. Perpetrator: Reynolds. Source: *NYT* 1988 Ja 4 I 16:2.

Case 398. Victims: Brom. Perpetrator: Brom. Sources: [1] *NYT* 1988 F 20 I 50:1; [2] *NYT* 1989 O 16, I 14:1; [3] O 18 I 14:1.

Case 401. Victim: Butts. Perpetrator: Butts. Source: *NYT* 1988 O 2 I 37:6.

Case 402. Victim: Cortez. Perpetrators: Cortez, Lopez. Sources: [1] *NYT* 1988 D 16 II 1:5; [2] D 17 I 31:5; [3] D 18 I 54:5; [4] D 19 II 2:5; [5] D 20 I 1:1, B4:4; [6] D 21 I 1:4, B3:1; [7] D 22 I 1:1, B6:3; [8] D 22 II 6:3; [9] D 23 I 1:1, B4:2; [10] D 24 I 1:1, 46:1; [11] D 29 II 3:1; [12] *NYT* 1989 Ja 4 II 2:5; [13] Ja 7 I 31:6; [14] Ja 12 I 26:1; [15] Ja 19 I 1:3, B4:1; [16] Ja 21 I 29:2, 30:5; [17] Ja 30 I 16:1; [18] O 21 I 30:1; [19] N 10 II 3:6; [20] *NYT* 1990 F 3 I 30:1; [21] F 27 B 2:3; [22] F 3 I 30:1.

Case 403. Victim: Corwin. Perpetrator: Dann. Sources: [1] *NYT* 1989 N 10 I 24:1; [2] *NYT* 1991 D 9 B 1:4; [3] Kaplan et al., *Murder of Innocence*.

Case 418. Victim: Owens. Perpetrator: Hector. Sources: [1] *NYT* 1988 Je 25 I 31:1; [2] Je 26 I 23:1.

Case 419. Victim: Riggs. Perpetrator: Riggs. Source: *NYT* 1989 F 17 I 16:2.

Case 423. Victim: Swinton. Perpetrator: Norris. Source: *NYT* 1988 Ja 30 I 32:3.

Case 426. Victim: Abdul-Salaam. Perpetrator: Abdul-Salaam. Sources: [1] *NYT* 1989 O 6 II 3:4; [2] O 7 I 26:4.

Case 428. Victim: Caesar. Perpetrator: Betts. Sources: [1] *NYT* 1989 Ap 7 I 13:1; [2] *Ft. Lauderdale Sun Sentinal* 1989 Ap 6 A 1; [3] Ap 16 A 1; [4] Je 23 B 3.

Case 430. Victim: Buchanan. Perpetrator: Buchanan. Source: *NYT* 1989 O 28 I 30:5.

Case 432. Victim: Carr. Perpetrator: Kocher. Sources: [1] *NYT* 1989 Ag 26 I 6:1; [2] Ap 1 IV 19:1; [3] *NYT* 1992 S 3 A 16:4.

Case 435. Victim: Fuller. Perpetrator: unknown. Source: *NYT* 1989 Je 23 II 3:1.

Case 437. Victims: Harris. Perpetrator: Turner a.k.a. Kinge. Sources: [1] *NYT* 1989 D 25 I 36:1; [2] D 30 I 27:3, 28:4; [3] *NYT* 1990 F 8 B 2:1; [4] *NYT* 1992 O 8 B 20:5; [5] N 15 I 41:2; [6] N 17 B 6:1; [7] N 24 B 4:4; [8] D 17 B 13:1; [9] *NYT* 1993 D 6 B 6:1.

Case 439. Victims: James. Perpetrator: James. Source: *NYT* 1989 Jy 21 II 3:6.

Case 440. Victim: Johnson. Perpetrators: Smith, Grant. Source: *NYT* 1989 Mr 31 II 2:6.

Case 443. Victim: Jorgenson. Perpetrator: Acosta. Source: *NYT* 1989 N 27 II 2:4.

Case 450. Victims: Neer, Iseli. Perpetrator: Dodd. Sources: [1] *NYT* 1989 S 7 I 17:1; [2] *NYT* 1990 Ja 15 I 17:6; [3] *NYT* 1992 D 29 A 1:2, B 6:1; [4] *NYT* 1993 Ja 5 A 8:4; [5] Ja 5 A 15:1; [6] Ja 6 A 10:1; [7] Ja 10 I 23:1; [8] *Reader's Digest* 1993 Sept: 67–72; [9] *Seattle Times* 1994 Ja 5 A 1.

Case 457. Victims: Salcido, Richards. Perpetrator: Salcido. Sources: [1] *NYT* 1989 Ap 15 I 28:5; [2] Ap 16 I 22:3; [3] Ap 17 I 15:1; [4] Ap 18 I 16:1; [5] Ap 20 I 21:1; [6] Ap 21 I 15:4; [7] Ap 22 I 7:1; [8] Ap 23 I 31:5; [9] Ap 26 I 21:1; [10] My 7 I 31:5; [11] *NYT* 1990 S 31 A 23:1; [12] O 31 A 23:1; [13] N 17 I 9:3; [14] N 22 A 3:1; [15] D 18 B 16:1; [16] *NYT* 1991 F 13 A 18:1; [17] *Los Angeles Times* 1989 May 31 1:3; [18] Ag 15 1:1; [19] *Los Angeles Times* 1990 D 17 A 32.

Case 461. Victim: Short. Perpetrator: Peterson. Sources: [1] *NYT* 1989 Ag 13 XXIII 1:3, 9:1; [2] O 8 XXIII 17:1; [3] *NYT* 1990 Mr 31 I 28:1; [4] Jl 15 I 20:1; [5] *NYT* 1992 Jl 29 B 6:3.

Case 465. Victim: Tagliarinni. Perpetrator: unknown. Sources: [1] *NYT* 1989 Mr 20 II 1:5; [2] Dialog, *Philadelphia Inquirer* 1989 Mr 20 B 5.

Case 469. Victims: Goldmark. Perpetrator: Rice. Sources: [1] *NYT* 1986 Ja 8 I 15:1; [2] Ja 10 I 8:2; [3] F 2 I 22:6; [4] My 28 I 12:4; [5] Je 2 I 10:1; [6] Je 4 I 16:4; [7] Je 6 II 5:4; [8] Je 11 I 18:5; [9] Jl 22 I 20:1.

Case 473. Victims: Tinning. Perpetrator: Tinning. Sources: [1] *NYT* 1986 F 6 II 5:1; [2] F 8 I 1:2; [3] F 12 II 2:4; [4] *NYT* 1987 Je 28 I 42:4; [5] Jl 7 II 2:5; [6] Jl 16 II 2:1; [7] Jl 18 I 29:5, 30:1; [8] O 2 II 2:2.

Case 474. Victims: Etienne. Perpetrator: Etienne. Source: *NYT* 1988 Ap 22 II 3:6.

Case 478. Victim: Brown. Perpetrators: Boyden, Perritt. Source: *NYT* 1987 Jl 31, II 8:4.

Case 479. Victims: Pruit, Greene. Perpetrator: Greene. Sources: [1] *NYT* 1986 O 11 I 35:3; [2] *NYT* 1987 N 16 II 1:2.

Case 480. Victims: Green. Perpetrator: Green. Sources: [1] *NYT* 1986 Mr 4 II 1:1; [2] Mr 5 II 2:6; [3] *NYT* 1988 S 7 II 4:3; [4] S 15 II 8:4; [5] O 1 I 29:2.

Case 482. Victims: Almarez. Perpetrator: Almarez. Sources: [1] *NYT* 1980 Je 20 II 6:1; [2] Jeanie Donahoe, *OWH* Librarian, May 1992, personal conversation; exact date of source not given.

Case 486. Victim: Twitchell. Perpetrators: Twitchell. Sources: [1] *NYT* 1990 Jl 3 A 15:5; [2] Jl 5 A 12:11; [3] Jl 6 A 11:6; [4] Jl 7 I 8:5; [5] Jl 10 A 16:1; [6] Ag 6 A 1:2, 11:1; [7] Ag 6 A 11:4; [8] *LHL* 1993 Ag 12 A 8.

Case 494. Victims: Avery. Perpetrators: Lundgren. Sources: [1] *NYT* 1990 Ja 6 I 8:1; [2] Ja 8 A 15:1; [3] Ja 13 I 10:1; [4] S 1 I 20:5; [5] S 20 B 6:5; [6] S 22 I 24:5; [7] O 7 I 33:6.

Case 495. Victim: Perry. Perpetrator: Johnson. Sources: [1] *LCJ* 1978 Mr 27 B 1:4–5; [2] Mr 28 A 1:1; [3] Mr 29 A 1:2–5; [4] Ap 5 B 2:1–2; [5] *LCJ* 1979 Ag 14 A 6:1–2.

Case 496. Victim: Bush. Perpetrators: Bush, Mayes. Sources: [1] *LCJ* 1977 N 26 A 1:4, 6:5; [2] D 1 B 13:1–6; [3] D 2 A 1:1–6; [4] *LCJ* 1978 My 12 B 7:1–6.

Case 497. Victim: Barton. Perpetrator: Barton. Source: *LCJ* 1979 S 1 A 1:1.

Case 498. Victim: Johnson. Perpetrator: dog. Sources: [1] *LCJ* 1979 N 1 B 1:1–3; [2] D 13 B 1:1–2.

Case 515. Victim: Maglinger. Perpetrator: Maglinger. Sources: [1] *LCJ* 1982 Ap 1 B 12:3–4; [2] Ap 2 D 8:1–2; [3] Ap 2 B 4:1–3; [4] Ap 3 B 4:1–2; [5] Ap 21 B 4:3–4

Case 518. Victim: Hollis. Perpetrator: Hollis. Sources: [1] *LCJ* 1981 Jl 18 B 4:4–6; [2] Jl 19 A 1:1–2, 27:1–6; [3] Ag 20 A 1:2–4, 12:3; [4] S 3 A 1:1–2, 8:1; [5] S 3 A 8:2; [6] *LCJ* 1982 My 22 A 1:3–6; [7] *LCJ* 1983 Mr 31 A 1:4.

Case 520. Victim: Lloyd. Perpetrator: Lloyd. Sources: [1] *LCJ* 1981 N 24 B 1:6, 3:2; [2] *LCJ* 1982 Je 30 B 1:1–6, B 2:1; [3] Jl 1 A 1:1–2, A 16:4–6.

Case 522. Victim: Horton. Perpetrator: Horton. Sources: [1] *LCJ* 1982 Mr 15 B 1:5–6; [2] Mr 16 A 10:6; [3] Mr 13 A 1:1–6; [4] Mr 23 B 5:2; [5] Mr 30 B 3:3; [6] Je 30 B 4:1–4; [7] S 2 A 1:6, 12:1–4; [8] O 13 B 4:1–2.

Case 524. Victim: Bray. Perpetrator: no one. Source: *LCJ* 1982 Ag 20 B 4:1–2.

Case 526. Victim: Conner. Perpetrator: no one. Source: *LCJ* 1982 S 6 B 6:1.

Case 528. Victim: Hirschy. Perpetrators: Hirschy. Source: *LCJ* 1982 D 7 B 14:4 (early ed.) and B 7: 2–3 (Indiana ed.).

Case 544. Victims: McCord. Perpetrator: McCord. Sources: [1] *OWH* 1983 Ag 29. n.p. Mon. pm ed.; [2] Ag 29 n.p. Mon. am ed.; [3] O 26 n.p. Wed. pm ed.

Case 546. Victim: Cain. Perpetrator: no one. Source: *OWH* 1984 Mr 16 n.p. Sunrise ed.

Case 547. Victim: Hoffman. Perpetrator: LaChappell. Source: *OWH* 1985 Mr 28 n.p. Sunrise ed.

Case 556. Victim: Wells. Perpetrator: Wells. Source: *OWH* 1985 Mr 19 n.p. Iowa ed.

Case 564. Victim: Elliott. Perpetrators: Elliott. Source: *OWH* 1987 O 30 n.p. Iowa ed.

Case 569. Victim: Reints. Perpetrator: Reints. Source: *OWH* 1987 Mr 21 n.p. Iowa ed.

Case 570. Victim: Richmond. Perpetrators: Richmond. Source: *OWH* 1987 O 30 n.p. Iowa ed.

Case 574. Victim: Hillman. Perpetrator: Rice. Source: *OWH* 1989 D 9 pg. 62. Iowa ed

Case 604. Victim: Felton. Perpetrators: three unnamed. Source: *Chicago Tribune* 1993 Dialog File 632. Ja 3 pg. 1.

Case 608. Victim: Hernandez. Perpetrators: Travieso, Johnson. Sources: [1] *Chicago Tribune* 1992 Ag 3 pg. 3; [2] *Chicago Tribune* 1993 Ja 3 pg. 1.

Case 615. Victims: Amaya. Perpetrator: Amaya. Sources: [1] *NYT* 1990 My 31 B 1:2, 6:3; [2] Je 1 B 2:4.

Case 617. Victim: Brown. Perpetrators: Coley, Reid. Sources: [1] *NYT* 1990 Je 25 B 3:1; [2] Je 26 B 4:6; [3] Je 27 B 3:6; [4] Ag 26 I 1:5, 42:1.

Case 623. Victim: Fleming. Perpetrator: Maynor. Source: *NYT* 1990 O 24 B 3:6.

Case 629. Victim: Griffin. Perpetrator: Jimerson. Sources: [1] *NYT* 1990 F 28 A 25:6; [2] Mr 1 B 8:6.

Case 632. Victims: Jackson. Perpetrator: Jackson. Sources: [1] *NYT* 1990 N 3 I 8:2; [2] N 6 A 21:2; [3] *Memphis Commercial Appeal* 1990 N 6 A 1.

Case 638. Victims: Lumbrera. Perpetrator: Lumbrera. Sources: [1] *OWH* 1990 My 24 pg. 23 Sunrise ed.; [2] *NYT* 1990 O 6 I 24:6; [3] *Wichita Eagle* 1990 Dialog File 723 My 20 1 A; [4] *Wichita Eagle* Dialog File 723 Mike Berry byline, n.d., n.p.; [5] *Reader's Digest* 1992 Feb: 122–26.

Case 639. Victims: Miller. Perpetrator: Miller. Source: *NYT* 1991 F 12 B 7:2.

Case 640 Victim: Mann. Perpetrators: Mann, Chisham. Sources: [1] *NYT* 1990 Mr 6 B 6:5; [2] Mr 7 B 3:2; [3] Mr 8 B 4:5; [4] D 7 I 23:5.

Case 643. Victim: Paul. Perpetrator: Paul. Sources: [1] *NYT* 1990 Jl 18 D 20:1; [2] Jl 19 A 16:4.

Case 645. Victim: Radtke. Perpetrator: Radtke. Sources: [1] *NYT* 1990 Ag 11 I 29:6; [2] Ag 12 I 31:1; [3] *OWH* 1991 Ap 14 B 1 News Section.

Case 647. Victim: Riegler. Perpetrators: Riegler. Sources: [1] *NYT* 1990 N 13 B 1:5, B 9: 1; [2] N 14 B 1:2, B 2:3; [3] N 15 B 1:5, B 8; [4] N 16 B 4:5; [5] N 17 I 27:5; [6] N 28 B 4:1; [7] *NYT* 1991 Mr 10 I 31:1; [8] N 29 B 9:1; [9] *NYT*

1992 Ja 10 B 3:1; [10] F 10 A 1:1, B 10:1; [11] F 11 B 3:1; [12] F 13 A 26:1; [13] F 16 IV 9:1.

Case 648. Victim: Shipley. Perpetrators: Shipley. Sources: [1] *NYT* 1990 N 10 I 10:2; [2] *NYT* 1991 Ag 23 D 18:1; [3] O 13 I 26:1.

Case 654. Victims: Wohlers. Perpetrators: Zuliani. Source: *NYT* 1990 My 19 A 19:1.

Case 659. Victim: Ayers. Perpetrator: Kenyon. Source: *NYT* 1991 Mr 17 I 33:6.

Case 663. Victim: Clapton. Perpetrator: no one. Source: *NYT* 1991 Mr 21 B 3:3.

Case 665. Victims: Contreras. Perpetrator: Ward. Source: *NYT* 1991 Je 25 B 5:6.

Case 667. Victim: Diaz. Perpetrator: juvenile. Source: *NYT* 1991 Ag 25 B 2:5.

Case 677. Victim: Leute. Perpetrator: Leute. Source: *NYT* 1991 My 2 B 2:5.

Case 688. Victim: Russell. Perpetrator: Russell. Sources: [1] *NYT* 1991 Ap 25 I 38:1; [2] Ap 26 B2:5.

Case 690. Victim: Schnitzer. Perpetrator: Schnitzer. Sources: [1] *NYT* 1991 O 17 B 6:1; [2] D 25 I 37:1.

Case 705. Victim: Keller. Perpetrator: Keller. Source: *Chicago Tribune* 1993, Dialog File 632. Ja 3 pg. 1

Case 707. Victim: Maddox. Perpetrator: unidentified juvenile male. Source: *Chicago Tribune* 1993, Dialog File 632. Ja 3 pg. 1.

Case 715. Victim: Scott. Perpetrator: unidentified juvenile male. Source: *Chicago Tribune* 1993, Dialog File 632. Ja 3 pg. 1.

Case 723. Victim: Brendel. Perpetrator: Hightower. Source: *NYT* 1993 Ap 22 A 22.

Case 724. Victim: Harden. Perpetrator: Phillips. Source: *NYT* 1992 D 29 A 1:1.

Case 729. Victim: Miranda. Perpetrator: Miranda. Sources: [1] *NYT* 1992 O 10 I 27:5; [2] O 11 I 51:1.

Case 734. Victim: Fletcher. Perpetrators: Fletcher. Source: *NYT* 1992 Ap 26 I 30:1.

Case 745. Victims: Schatz, Lamb. Perpetrator: Schatz. Source: *NYT* 1992 Mr 22 I 16:1.

Case 746. Victims: Sharp, Bernard. Perpetrators: Millery, Ramos, Williams, Sealy. Sources: [1] *NYT* 1992 F 3 B 3:6; [2] F 4 A 1:3, B 23; [3] F 10 B 3:4; [4] *NYT* 1993 Ap 20 B 3:1.

Case 747. Victims: Seguin. Perpetrator: Seguin. Source: *NYT* 1993 F 7 I 25:1.

Case 748. Victim: Rodriguez. Perpetrator: Piquaad. Source: *NYT* 1992 Ja 12 I 25:1.

Case 756. Victim: Davis. Perpetrator: Livingston. Sources: [1] *Arizona Republic* 1993 N 19 A 1; [2] D 24 A 1; [3] D 31 B 1; [4] *Phoenix Gazette* 1993 D 24, A 1; [5] D 31 B 3.

Case 771. Victims: Wu. Perpetrator: Wu. Source: *NYT* 1993 Ja 23 A 25:5.

Case 774. Victim: Blackledge. Perpetrator: Poole. Sources: [1] *NYT* 1993 My 21 B 1:6, B 3; [2] My 22 I 21:1, 25; [3] My 23 I 29:5, 31; [4] My 24 B 1:2, B 5; [5] My 25 B 3:5; [6] My 26 B 3:3; [7] My 28 B 3:5; [8] My 31 I 25:5, 26; [9] Je 1 B 4:2; [10] Je 2 B 3:3; [11] *NYT* 1994 F 8 B 4:5; [12] Mr 5 I 27:3.

Case 775. Victims: Byers, Moore, Branch. Perpetrators: Misskeiley, Echols, Baldwin. Sources: [1] *NYT* 1993 Je 5 I 10:1; [2] Je 6 I 31:1; [3] *Atlanta Constitution* 1993 Dialog file 713 #7272151 S 18 A 3; [4] *New Orleans Times-Picayune* 1993 Dialog file 706 #7129016 My 9 A 3; [5] *New Orleans Times-Picayune* 1993 Dialog file 706 #7217157 Ag 5 A 16.

Case 777. Victim: Chez. Perpetrator: Pryce. Source: *NYT* 1992 N 12 B 3:1.

Case 778. Victim: Cook. Perpetrator: Cook. Source: *NYT* 1993 Ag 9 A 11:1.

Case 780. Victim: Emiliano. Perpetrators: Emiliano, Perez. Source: *NYT* 1993 O 27 B 6:1.

Case 781. Victim: Genao. Perpetrator: Jeffrey. Sources: [1] *NYT* 1993 My 7 B 4:1; [2] My 8 I 23:2; [3] My 8 I 26:1; [4] My 12 B 1:3; [5] My 13 B 6:5; [6] Ag 4 B 6:4.

Case 782. Victims: Getz, Javier. Perpetrator: Concepcion. Sources: [1] *NYT* 1993 My 4 A 1:1, B 3:1 [photos]; [2] My 5 B 3:1; [3] My 9 I 25:3 [photos only].

Case 783. Victim: Goodman. Perpetrator: Cooper. Sources: [1] *NYT* 1993 Jl 21 B 8:6; [2] Jl 22 B 7:1.

Case 784. Victim: Groom. Perpetrator: Groom. Source: *NYT* 1993 Ag 22 I 43:5.

Case 792. Victim: Mapp. Perpetrator: juvenile. Source: *NYT* 1993 Je 13 I 39:4.

Case 797. Victim: Murray. Perpetrator: Willis. Source: *NYT* 1993 Je 6 I 46:1.

Case 803. Victim: Robie. Perpetrator: Smith (juvenile). Sources: [1] *NYT* 1993 Ag 15 I 42:1; [2] Ag 22 I 33:2, 37; [3] S 3 B 5:1; [4] trial and sentencing in 1994. Trial in August, sentencing in November.

Case 805. Victim: Shook. Perpetrator: Shook. Source: *NYT* 1993 Jl 27 A 8:5.

Case 808. Victim: Smith. Perpetrator: Fuller. Source: *NYT* 1993 Jl 29 B 3:5.

Case 823. Victim: Farfolla. Perpetrator: Contreras. Source: *OWH* 1982 F 24 pg. 1 pm ed.

Case 827. Victim: Figuero. Perpetrators: Cardona, Gonzales-Mendoza. Sources: [1] *Miami Herald* 1990, Dialog File 702 D 12 B 2; [2] *Miami Herald* 1992, Dialog File #06517136 Mr 12 A 1.

Case 828. Victim: Epps. Perpetrator: Samaniego. Source: *Phoenix Gazette* 1986 Ja 30 A 17.

Case 832. Victim: Anderson. Perpetrator: Murray. Source: *NYT* 1992 S 9 A 1:2, B 2:1.

Case 834. Victims: Christopher. Perpetrator: Payne. Sources: [1] *NYT* 1991 Je 28 A 14:1; [2] Je 28 A 15:1.

Case 838. Victim: Ellwood. Perpetrator: Ellwood. Source: *NYT* 1991 Mr 21 B 6:2.

Case 854. Victim: Hunter. Perpetrator: Hunter. Source: *Reader's Digest* 1994 Feb: 87–92.

Case 855. Victim: Schmidt. Perpetrator: Patalsky. Source: *Reader's Digest* 1994 Feb: 87–92.

Case 856. Victim: Slone. Perpetrators: Terry, Slone. Source: *LHL* 1983 S 3 B 3.

Case 861. Victim: Daugherty. Perpetrator: Daugherty. Source: *Reader's Digest* 1994 Feb: 87–92.

Case 880. Victim: Poldevaart. Perpetrator: Stuhrenberg. Source: *OWH* 1991 Jl 23 pg. 9 News section.

Case 882. Victim: Gerdeman. Perpetrator: Buck. Sources: [1] *OWH* 1992 My 23 pg. 41 News section; [2] Je 9 pg. 16 News section.

Case 895. Victim: Newsome. Perpetrator: McNeely. Source: *LHL* 1992 S 24 B 1.

Case 898. Victim: Nethers. Perpetrator: Nethers. Source: *LHL* 1993 S 26 B 4.

Index